Understanding Challenging Behaviour in Inclusive Classrooms

Understanding Challenging Behaviour in Inclusive Classrooms

Colin Lever

**Longman
is an imprint of**

Harlow, England • London • New York • Boston • San Francisco • Toronto • Sydney • Singapore • Hong Kong
Tokyo • Seoul • Taipei • New Delhi • Cape Town • Madrid • Mexico City • Amsterdam • Munich • Paris • Milan

Pearson Education Limited
Edinburgh Gate
Harlow
Essex CM20 2JE
England

and Associated Companies throughout the world

Visit us on the World Wide Web at:
www.pearsoned.co.uk

First published 2011

ISBN: 978-1-4082-4827-0

British Library Cataloguing-in-Publication Data
A catalogue record for this book is available from the British Library.

Library of Congress Cataloging-in-Publication Data
A catalog record for this book is available from the Library of Congress.

10 9 8 7 6 5 4 3 2 1
15 14 13 12 11

Typeset in 10/12 Frutiger light by 35
Printed and bound in Great Britain by Henry Ling Ltd.,
at the Dorset Press, Dorchester, Dorset

Dedication

This book is dedicated to all disadvantaged children who are always seen but are rarely heard.

Contents

About the author

Colin Lever has spent all of his 34 years in education working in mainstream schools that have contained a high percentage of challenging children. As both a teacher and head of faculty he has been an advocate of a child-centred approach to teaching and learning, playing an active part in 'turning around' two failing schools, both of which were inclusive in their philosophy.

Following a secondment in 1988 he worked with a colleague from the Special Needs sector to set up an integration project that gave children with severe learning difficulties access to mainstream education. The project received national acclaim and established itself as one of the longest-running integration projects of its type at the time.

Colin has written extensively over the past 20 years for all Key Stages, principally in the areas of science and technology. He has written numerous articles for *Special Children* magazine as well as pieces for the national press.

At present Colin is employed as a behaviour 'specialist' in a mainstream school, working as part of an MAST (Multi-Agency Support Team) and SEBD (Social and Emotional Behaviour Disorders) team. He works with challenging children and advises colleagues and senior management on all aspects of behavioural management in order to facilitate inclusion.

Acknowledgements

It is impossible to acknowledge the contribution of each child highlighted in the case studies without naming names and by so doing running the risk of identifying specific people involved. So can I just take this opportunity to thank all those I have interviewed because without their input this text would lack the key ingredient that makes it different from other texts relating to behaviour in the classroom? Although this book is written as an aid to teachers, the message each child interviewed gives shouts out loud from the pages in the hope that the reader will listen and understand and for this reason I am truly grateful.

I must also thank colleagues both past and present, firstly those from my last school, with special mention of Jim Bleakley (my life-long mentor and role model), Ruth Ashworth, Andrew Hamelin and Richard Booth (a sad loss to the teaching profession), as well as those from my present place of employment, in particular my colleagues in the SEBD team and associates from the MAST team. Even though they may not have realised it, each has contributed either directly or indirectly to the construction of this book and without their contribution it would never have been written. May I give a special mention to the headteacher, Bob Fairhurst, who has stood by me, offered sage-like advice and supported me in the day-to-day delivery of my job?

Publisher's acknowledgements

We are grateful to the following for permission to reproduce copyright material:

Figures
Figure 9.2 adapted from *Emotional Intelligence in the Classroom: Creative Learning Strategies for 11 to 18 Year Olds* Crown House Publishing (Brearley, M. 2000); Figure 15.1 from *Drug use, drinking and smoking among young people in England in 2007*, National Centre for Social Research (Fuller, E. (Editor) 2008).

Tables
Table on page 137 adapted from *Society and the Adolescent Self-image*, Princeton University Press (Rosenberg, M. 1965).

Text
Boxes on page 270 and page 273 from *12 Outstanding Secondary Schools – Excelling against the odds*, Ofsted (2009), Crown Copyright material is reproduced with permission under the terms of the Click-Use Licence; Crown Copyright material is reproduced with the permission of the Controller, Office of Public Sector Information (OPSI).

Picture Credits
The publisher would like to thank the following for their kind permission to reproduce their photographs:

(Key: b-bottom; c-centre; l-left; r-right; t-top)

Alamy Images: © Blend Images 10, © Bubbles Photolibrary 165, © Catchlight Visual Services 57, © Celia Mannings 50, © Daniel Atkin 144, © David Hancock 70, © Emmeline Watkins 253, © Janine Wiedel Photolibrary 204, © Jeff Morgan 04 261, © Jennie Hart 119, © Jenny Matthews 136, © JPagetRFphotos 127, © Mary Evans Picture Library 88, © Mike Abrahams 63, © Paul Bradbury 30, © PhotoAlto 155, © Phototake Inc. 229; **Getty Images:** Martin Poole 212, Peter Dazeley 175 and 187; **Pearson Education Ltd:** Melinda Podor 104, MindStudio 18, Studio 8 43, 79, 268; **John Harris Report Digital:** 195

All other images © Pearson Education

In some instances we have been unable to trace the owners of copyright material, and we would appreciate any information that would enable us to do so.

Introduction

'Just over one in five pupils – 1.7 million school-age children in England – are identified as having special educational needs.'

(Ofsted, *The Special Educational Needs and Disability Review 2010*)

'However, we also recognise that as many as half of all pupils identified for School Action would not be identified as having special educational needs if schools focused on improving teaching and learning for all.'

(Ofsted, *The Special Educational Needs and Disability Review 2010*)

Rationale

You cannot effect a 'cure' if you don't know what is causing the problem. If you were ill and went to the doctor and he gave you medicine without first asking what the symptoms were, you would be (rightly) concerned. Likewise, if your car would not start and the mechanic told you it was only worth scrap without even trying to find out why it was not working, you would feel aggrieved. So why is it when it comes to dealing with challenging children many teachers and schools use sanctions or the threat of sanctions without even assessing the situation? Discipline is important, but control can be effected in more ways than just by using punitive sanctions.

In the present environment, where schools are judged (almost) entirely on their examination results, there is a temptation to 'offload' the awkward children who do not easily conform. There are a number of 'beacons of academic excellence' lauded by the great and good for having turned failure into success, and many a knighthood has been given to headteachers for their achievements. But if we scratch a little deeper we sometimes find that poor behaviour has not been 'cured' but has been surgically removed and left for another establishment to deal with. Such expediency has not resolved the problem and those schools that resort to such tactics under the banner of 'zero tolerance' are doing the education system as a whole a disservice and are not attending to the needs of the children they abort. How can any school not give a child who may have high-functioning autism or have been emotionally traumatised an equal opportunity to achieve their potential like all the rest? Surely it is worth going that extra mile to help these children before reaching for the exit button? If only such schools were a little more inclusive and worked with such 'difficult' children, they would find a depth of academic potential that would advance their desire for improved examination results.

> 'The achievement of disabled children and young people and those who had special educational needs was good or outstanding in less than half the providers visited.'
>
> (Ofsted, *The Special Educational Needs and Disability Review 2010*)

The one constant in any school is that all children want to achieve in their schooling. The variables that affect whether they are successful or not are the child's commitment and self-belief and the quality of the teaching and learning that they receive. **No child is unteachable**, although it is amazing the lengths that a child will go to in order to get their needs recognised. The key is to learn to recognise those needs and to have a curriculum that can accommodate them. This book aims to raise awareness of why children behave in the way they do, giving teachers in the classroom the tools they need to recognise patterns of behaviour and how to deal with a variety of challenging behaviours.

The language of discipline

The language of discipline is one that is close to every teacher's heart. Teachers speak hungrily of its possibilities. The older generation 'remember when . . .' and use maxims like 'if you spare the rod you will spoil the child'. There is a perception peddled by many texts relating to behaviour management that if you do this or try that the children will fall into line as if by magic. Oh that teaching was so easy! What other texts advise may sometimes work for the majority of children in the class, but when it comes to children who exhibit continually challenging behaviour the 'usual' strategies invariably do not work. This small minority seem resistant to 'discipline' and it is these children who account for most of the behavioural problems.

For some teachers (and politicians and the general public), good discipline is synonymous with the application of sanctions. The reality is the opposite. A teacher reliant on a sanction-based approach will soon find their classes mutinous, often led by the small minority. To ensure effective class discipline for the majority a teacher needs to make sure that the following are in place and then the job will become a lot easier:

● positive relationships between teacher and child
● differentiated work that is both challenging yet achievable
● 'active' as opposed to 'passive' learning techniques
● varying the stimulus (use of multiple intelligences)
● child-centred work that gives the child ownership of their learning

- development of 'thinking skills'
- creation of a 'can do' environment where a child is motivated to work
- commitment from the teacher
- high expectations of the child from the teacher.

Even with all these schemes in place the minority of 'difficult' children may still prove problematic. This is where other texts stop and this book continues, offering detailed strategies for how to deal with challenging behaviour on an individual level by looking at the needs of the individual. In order to meet the challenge, teachers need to know what it is they are dealing with. At this level of control the teacher has to be armed with an understanding of how the child is thinking and why they behave as they do. This minority are not just naughty children.

Not just naughty children

Challenging behaviour in the classroom is *the* bugbear for many teachers. From infants through to secondary school, children can (and do) disrupt all the good work put in place by the teacher. The stresses brought about by challenging behaviour have seen many teachers leave the profession, citing falling standards of discipline as the reason for going.

It was once thought that all poor behaviour occurred simply as a consequence of a child's premeditated actions and children were described as being 'naughty', with them disrupting the lesson 'just for the hell of it'. While this may be the case in some circumstances, the reality is that most challenging behaviour has its roots in something much more entrenched, and while good class management may quell some of the symptoms, it may do little to effect a change in behaviour of the persistent 'offender' in the long term.

Ofsted's *Special Educational Needs and Disability Review 2010* produced two key findings:

- 'Ensuring that schools do not identify pupils as having special educational needs when they simply need better teaching.'
- 'Improving teaching and pastoral support early on so that additional provision is not needed later.'

Teachers are on the front line when it comes to witnessing a child's disruptive behaviour and as such they are uniquely placed to raise concerns. To be able to do so in a professional and pragmatic manner requires the necessary skills and understanding in order to differentiate between misguided tomfoolery and deviant behaviour. For example, if a child continually disrupts a class and the teacher is able to say that the child is always fidgeting rather than just say that the child is a 'pest', it will help in the referral process and in designing work to alleviate issues that may arise.

'The consistency of the identification of special needs varied widely.'

(Ofsted, *The Special Educational Needs and Disability Review 2010*)

Disruptive behaviour that is persistent cannot be dismissed as childish antics. These sustained actions should raise concerns in the teacher's mind that all is not what it appears to be. Unlike adults, children often lack the capacity to communicate clearly what they are feeling and resort to other methods of expressing their inner concerns. (Continual) challenging behaviour is often a message that things are not right with the child and it is the teacher in the classroom who is the first to hear what is being said. If the teacher is skilled in recognising the signs, strategies can be put in place before negative behaviours become entrenched.

Consider the following statements and try to work out what it is the child is actually saying.

1. 'This work is s**t.'
2. 'F**k off and leave me alone.'
3. 'I don't care.'
4. 'S/he hates me.'
5. 'This is boring.'
6. 'I'm not doing this (work).'
7. 'I'm not going to (substitute any subject here).'
8. 'I hate you.'
9. 'I haven't got a pen (or other essential piece of equipment).'
10. 'I feel sick.'
11. 'Shut up.'
12. 'You can't make me (do this task).'

Translated, these statements might read as:

1. 'I am finding this work difficult.'
2. 'Please help me.'
3. 'I do care.'
4. 'S/he does not understand me.'
5. 'This work is too easy (or too hard).'
6. 'I'm frightened of failing and showing myself up in class.'
7. 'I find this subject difficult (or I am frightened of the class/teacher).'
8. 'I respect you because you have high expectations of me.'
9. 'I'm frightened of failure (I don't know how to start).'
10. 'I feel threatened and/or anxious (by the work/the teacher/children in the class).'
11. 'You are embarrassing me.'
12. 'I'm terrified of failing.'

Now you have had an introduction into the language of the challenging child you should be able to work out what this child is saying.

*'F**k off and leave me alone. I'm not going into that lesson, you can't make me. The work is s**t and it is boring. S/he hates me and I hate her/him. I don't care if I fall behind with my work, I haven't got a pen. Can I go home, I feel sick?'*

As a teacher as well as a writer, I have not set out to condone or excuse bad behaviour with this book. Whatever their personal circumstances, a child needs to learn to recognise the boundaries between what is acceptable and what is unacceptable. But to treat each child uniformly without understanding their individual needs may do more harm than good. For example, a child with autism may have to be corrected in a different way than a child with emotional difficulties. The skill is not so much in knowing how to sanction but rather in understanding the differences between the two and how to apply correction (if indeed correction is the best method of resolving the issue).

It is essential that they not only tackle the behaviour as it manifests itself but also deal with the issue in the context of the child's individual needs. For example, a child may disrupt a lesson because they cannot read the work given to them. The teacher cannot let their disruption pass without challenge, but in dealing with the issue they need to be aware of why the child is behaving in that manner and set about preventing a reoccurrence and search for a more lasting solution.

This book is about raising the awareness of classroom practitioners as to why children misbehave and offering ideas about how a teacher might put in place strategies to prevent challenging behaviour occurring in the first place. It also offers advice in respect of how they might deal with certain stereotypical behaviours.

To start this process the child needs to be given a voice. This can be done by asking one simple question:

'Why did you do (this)?'

If expressed in a non-threatening way the child is likely to respond, and it is that response that will lead the practitioner to a better understanding not only of what the child is thinking but also how they are thinking. Based on what they hear, a teacher is then better placed to decide on what course of action to take.

There are those in education who do not subscribe to labelling a child with one condition or another, but forewarned is forearmed and the recognition of specific traits and how to deal with them in situ is essential if inclusion in the classroom is to be successful. This book aims to give you, as a classroom practitioner, a clearer understanding of some of the more common conditions that influence children's behaviour in the classroom. The aim of the book is not to spawn a generation of quack psychologists, but rather to equip teachers so that they can put in place specific strategies that will target the individual needs of the child and effect a more inclusive, working atmosphere.

While ultimately it is your responsibility, as a teacher, to manage your classroom, it is important that you do not do so in isolation. Classroom management is a partnership between the teacher and the wider school policies and procedures laid out by the senior management team. One without the other is likely to lead to ineffective strategies within the classroom environment. The day-to-day issues that arise in the classroom are the responsibility of the individual teacher, but they take place within a broader, whole-school framework that should facilitate good teaching practice.

With this in mind the book is laid out in three broad sections:

- **Creating and maintaining an inclusive classroom.** This section explores key aspects of teaching and classroom management such as proactive planning, attention to detail in respect of what is taught, how it is delivered and the classroom environment in which teaching takes place.

- **Identifying and dealing with key social/emotional and cognitive aspects of inclusion.** This section focuses on the indicators that may be witnessed in an inclusive classroom and how teachers can facilitate inclusion as a consequence of their observations.

- **Whole-school management issues that affect the effectiveness of inclusion.** This section shows how broader school policies and procedures can affect what goes on within an inclusive classroom.

This book can be used in a number of ways, depending on your specific needs, including any of the following:

- as you plan and prepare for your lessons – the book can serve as a checklist, encouraging you to reflect on approaching planning from a number of different angles

- as a reference manual for you to use in the classroom – sitting on your desk so that as issues arise you can consult the text directly and find solutions to any problems you encounter

- as a tool to help you recognise specific patterns of behaviour – giving you the resources to put in place strategies to support every child in the classroom.

Each chapter contains a number of features designed to make the book more useful and accessible:

- **Tasks** have been designed to provoke reflection of personal and school working practices, challenging the status quo. Critical analysis allows us to review how robust our strategies are. Some tasks also aim to develop personal skills and improve knowledge and understanding by raising awareness.

- **Tips** are given as ideas and techniques to deal with specific situations and behaviours.

- **Information boxes** include essential background knowledge to encourage a better understanding of the reasons why behaviours occur as they do or the impact of actions upon a child's behaviour in the classroom.

- **Case studies** give the children a 'voice' because it is by stopping and listening to what they have to say that we, as teachers, can alter our perceptions and thereby put in place effective strategies that will facilitate inclusion.

For those new to the profession this text may initially seem to paint a bleak picture of teaching as it pulls no punches in terms of what some teachers have to face. There are those who ask, 'Why should we invest so many resources on so few children for such little return?' The question is a valid one and is answered by considering whether you see teaching as a vocation, a career or just a job. This small minority offer the greatest challenge to any teacher's skills, yet when they show progress the rewards are so much greater.

Colin Lever, 2011

Part

1

Creating and maintaining an inclusive classroom

Readability

Case study

Anita sits at the back of the class. The teacher introduces the lesson and invites children to read the first paragraph of the worksheet that he has prepared. Few hands are raised, so he asks a boy at the front to read. The boy starts enthusiastically but gets stuck on a word. The teacher says the word, the boy repeats it and then carries on. Again he stumbles over a word and is once corrected, gently, by the teacher. Three lines into the text he is struggling with all but the simplest words. Some children in the class giggle at his predicament so the teacher picks another child to carry on reading. Anita loses concentration and starts to whisper to her friend sitting next to her. At first the teacher does not notice her, but eventually, following a loud guffaw, Anita draws attention to herself.

'Will you carry on, from Steven?' the teacher requests, choosing direct action to quash Anita before she becomes too disruptive. Anita pretends to look for the place where Steven got to but she is lost.

'Can't find it,' comes the terse reply.

The girl sitting next to Anita shows her where to start reading from. Anita focuses on the text for a few seconds but says nothing.

Case study continued

'We are waiting, Anita,' the teacher prompts impatiently. There is a prolonged silence as Anita looks down at the sheet but refuses to comply. Tensions rise as the teacher, once more, tries to force Anita to read.

'The word is "because", surely you know that word.'

Anita feels threatened and embarrassed as all eyes in the class are upon her.

'I don't want to read,' she shouts defiantly.

'Anita, you could at least make an effort.' The teacher resorts to pleading in an attempt to get her to read.

'I'm not going to and you can't make me.' Anita openly challenges his authority. The situation ends in conflict, resulting in Anita being sent from the room and sanctioned. Closer inspection reveals that Anita has a reading age of 8.6 years and the piece of comprehension given to the class demands a reading age of 12 years.

'The world may be full of fourth-rate writers but it's also full of fourth-rate readers.'

(Stan Barstow, novelist)

Does it matter what a child reads?

Source: © Blend Images/Alamy

(!)

Do you know:

a) **The reading age of the children you teach?**

b) **The reading level of the text material you use with the children?**

Background

If a child is going to be able to access the curriculum they are going to have to be able to read the work that is placed before them. If their literacy skills are poor and they cannot do the work set, it is only a matter of time before problems will come to a head. Conversely, if a child can read, it improves their self-confidence and raises their self-esteem.

There are many reasons why a child may find it difficult to read. These include cognitive development (see p. 211), dyslexia (see p. 247), physical impairment, socio-economic background and EAL (English As a Second Language) (see p. 203). Literacy is a major issue in schools and it is the responsibility of all subject areas to support and develop literacy – it is not just the domain of 'English'.

England has dropped from 3rd to 19th in the International Reading league.

(*Daily Mail*, December 2007)

'20 per cent of 11 year olds in England have not mastered the literacy skills needed to achieve level 4 at Key Stage 2.

26 per cent of 14 year olds fail to reach the standard expected in English, with only 67 per cent of 14 year old boys achieving target level 5 at key stage 3.'

(*Sir Cyril Taylor, chairman of the SSAT (Specialist Schools and Academies Trust)*

What the statistics indicate is that some children in class will have difficulty reading text material put in front of them. This is likely to lead to numerous avoidance strategies, including disruptive behaviour, as they attempt to disguise their shortcomings.

Possible signs that a child is struggling to read written material

● A reluctance to offer to read in class.

● A refusal to read out loud when requested.

● Attempting to read but struggling with the text.

● Disruptive and/or diversionary tactics when a reading task is introduced.

Children are adept at finding ways of avoiding tasks that they find 'threatening'. This can be anything from blatant confrontation and disruption to more subtle methods such as not opening the book at the right page or losing the worksheet. They may pretend to lose concentration (thereby not knowing where they are up to if asked to read in the hope that the teacher will not force them to read and move on to somebody else). The strategies are endless and it is not always easy for the teacher to recognise these as avoidance strategies because the child is 'nervous' of reading in case they appear 'stupid' in front of their peers and therefore leave themselves open to ridicule. The last thing a child is going to admit to (at least in public) is that they cannot read what is in front of them.

The first step in addressing these shortcomings and tackling the problem of illiteracy is to make sure that all written work presented to the class is 'readable' by all. By doing so the teacher knows that all (most of) the children in the class can access the material presented to them. This is done by checking all material for its 'readability'.

Readability is the process whereby the text is matched to the reader. It involves looking at:

- legibility of the writing
- typeface
- layout of the work
- reading age of the text
- sentence structure
- general interest
- reading conditions (illumination).

Most children prefer lower case print,

not joined up writing that is more difficult to read

10–12 point type is best for fluent readers with a slightly larger type for those with literacy problems.
Other things to consider are:

- Line length (7–12 words)
- Space between lines.

A reading age of a text shows the top age limit of a piece of prose. For example, if the words have a reading age of 12 years this means that an average 12 year old will be at the limit of their comprehension of the text. If this fact is applied to a mixed-ability class, it is likely that the reading age of the class will span a wide spectrum either side of their average chronological age.

Children prefer to read at a level below their actual reading age, so when creating a worksheet it is pertinent to construct a text that has a reading age a couple of years below the chronological age of the class. This also applies when choosing textbooks for children.

There are a number of formulae that can be used to calculate the reading age of a body of text. A couple are shown below. You may like to check out the others highlighted in the box.

Information

FOG formula

1. Select a sample of 100 words.
2. Calculate the average sentence length (**L**) (no. words/no. sentences).
3. Count the number of words with 3 or more syllables (**N**).
4. Now work out the equation **[(L + N) × 0.4] + 5**.

SMOG formula

1. Select 10 consecutive sentences.
2. Count the number of words with 3 or more syllables (**N**).
3. Times N by 3 **(N × 3)**.
4. Find the **square root** of this number.
5. **Add 8**.
6. **/(N × 3) + 8**.

Some other readability tests

- Fry Readability Graph.
- Flesch–Kincaid Formula.
- Powers–Sumner–Kearl Formula.

Information

Newspaper reading ages

The Sun: below 14 years
Daily Express: under 16 years
The Guardian: over 17 years

Source: NIACE (The National Institute of Adult Continuing Education)

Task

Try one of the formulae out on:

a) A worksheet that you have written.

b) A textbook that you use in class.

- Does the material match the chronological age of the children who use it?
- Does the material match their reading ages?
- Do you know the reading age of every child you teach?

Fluent readers (those with a reading age of 12 years or more) should be able to cope with most written material given to them in school. Those with a low reading age will require reading material that is specially chosen or prepared. It is a skill to actually construct written material to match a certain reading age range. When doing so make sure that:

- sentences are short in length
- most words contain no more than 2 syllables (the more words in a sentence that contain 3 or more syllables will increase the reading age of the material)
- when introducing new words, the sentence is packed with simple, familiar words
- key words are written on the board or displayed on the wall.

TOP TIP!

Sentence structure

Short sentences are easy to read.

Longer sentences with polysyllabic words of a complexity typical of a more discerning clientele are much more difficult to read.

Good readers may find text too simplistic so it is useful to differentiate reading material to try to take account of a wide range of ability. While it is important not to alienate the struggling reader, it is just as important not to let the more able child become disaffected. The balance can be addressed by placing harder words (those with multi-syllables) in a text surrounded by words that are familiar and easier to read.

Task

Read the piece of text taken from a GCSE Resistant Materials textbook.

'Continuous heating of timber or plastic (depending on the intensity of the heat) may cause the material to char or blister and eventually to be set alight.'

- Highlight the words with 3 or more syllables.
- Simplify the text to make it easier for a child to read.

Try rewriting one of your own worksheets to make it suitable for a child with a reading age of:

a) 10 years   b) 7 years.

Possible answer to previous task

Heating timber and plastic can cause problems. (7 words)
The material may char or blister. (6 words)
It may even set alight if the heat is too strong. (11 words)

Note:

This restructuring uses only 1 word with more than 3 syllables.
The sentences do not go beyond 12 words.
Nothing is lost in translation.

In conclusion

'If you want to work on the core problem, it's early school literacy.'

(J. Barksdale, former CEO of Netscape)

If a child cannot read a question then it follows that they cannot answer the question (unless it is read out loud to them). So fundamental is literacy in the education of a child that not to be able to read will haunt them throughout their school life and beyond. They may excel at sports, be adept when working with their hands, verbally they may prove to be innately able, but such potential is ultimately doomed to failure because modern-day society demands that a person is able to read. The stigma of being 'illiterate' eats away at a child's self-esteem, leading them along the path of deviance and possible truancy. No matter what subject a teacher teaches, their first commitment should be to develop literacy skills in the children they teach. This may be something as simple as single words on a board placed in the context of a practical activity. There is no subject that should be exempt from this commitment.

It is important not to forget that we read for enjoyment as well as to learn. If the reading material is dry then it is harder for the reader to become interested in the text, unless they have a leaning in the direction that work is about. Try reading a telephone directory or a dictionary. The layout of this book is designed with text boxes, icons and activities in an attempt to stimulate the reader. Does the layout make the text easier to read and/or more stimulating?

To encourage children to read they need motivation that helps to build self-confidence. In a subject teacher's literacy plan they should include the opportunity for children to read any written material. Even items such as comics and magazines play a key role in promoting and supporting literacy.

Further reading

www.literacytrust.org.uk

www.timetabler.com

Differentiation

Case study

Explain the equation below:

$$\text{I}h \, d/dt \, \underset{\rightarrow}{\Psi}(x,t) = H\underset{\rightarrow}{\Psi}(x,t)$$

'Can't do it.'
'Why not?'
'Too hard.'
'Oh come on, it's not that difficult.'
'Don't know what to do!'
'Well, I'm not going to spoon feed you, you have to stand on your own two feet some time.'
'Don't understand.'
'Well, you wouldn't, would you, because you never listen in class, you're always too busy talking.'
'Boring!'

Case study continued

Do you recognise the scenario being played out?
Would the reader be any wiser if they were told it is Shroedinger's wave equation?

Independent learning is a high-order skill

Source: © Pearson Education Ltd/MindStudio

Background

If as the reader you cannot complete the task, why can you not do so? You could (and probably have) made a fist at trying to work out what some of the symbols mean, but that's as far as you are likely to get without more help unless you have a degree in Science.

The same excuses are peddled by children, some of whom are prone to exhibiting challenging behaviour. The teacher may consider the source of the complaints and dismiss them as avoidance tactics, but how can they be certain that the child is trying to avoid the work and cannot actually do what has been presented to them?

The traditional style of teaching is to impart information to children and expect them to learn what is being taught. Any children who cannot grasp the information are filtered out and put down into the class below. (I know this because I was one of those children, dropping down four sets in Maths until I found my 'level'. The scars remain with me to this day!) Can there be anything more demotivating to a child than to have failure reinforced in this way? This method of teaching allied itself to the IQ perception of education, whereby it is deemed some children will never attain the dizzy heights of academia (and will be destined to a life of physical labour). This narrow approach to education is exclusive, allowing only the most able access to certain aspects of learning.

The converse of such a top-down, subject-centred approach, where children are filtered out on the basis of what they cannot do, is, of course, a bottom-up approach where the emphasis is on providing work that the children can do, a stepping-stone approach whereby a child progresses upwards through the educational strata, acquiring skills and knowledge as they progress. This is a wider, inclusive approach to teaching and learning and is underpinned by the process of differentiation. Differentiation is very much a child-centred methodology because it takes into account each child's individual educational needs.

Differentiation can mean increasing the complexity and demand of the work required.

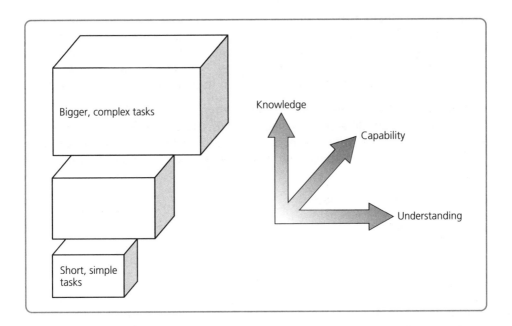

Possible signs that work is not differentiated properly

Signs that work in class is not differentiating across the ability range include:

- a group of children who cannot access the work set (too hard)
- a group of children who find the work too easy (finish the work quickly)
- children who begin to get frustrated/angry at the work set and/or lose concentration.

In any given class there are likely to be children with a range of educational needs, diagnosed or otherwise. They may be on the autistic spectrum, be dyslexic or have other specific learning difficulties. If a teacher uses a 'one cap fits all' approach then it is likely that some in the class will not be able to attempt the work because they do not have the necessary 'thinking skills' to tackle the questions. To get around this, some teachers pitch their teaching somewhere in the middle of the assumed ability range. The problem with this approach is that those of a lower ability will still not be able to do the work and those of a higher ability will find the work too easy. This may lead to disruptive behaviour from within either or both groups of children. Even in a class that is set according to ability there is likely to be a range of capabilities. Learning is not a linear process and children can (and do) access higher thinking skills.

There are perceptions that differentiation involves vast numbers of individual work-sheets and the horrors of all the time that they will take to prepare. This is indeed one possibility, but there are other methods that are as effective and that are a lot less time consuming.

At its simplest, differentiation can be a matter of outcome. There are those in education who think this is a bit of a 'cop out', but there are times when it does have merit. Ultimately all work set is a matter of outcome because children will always offer up a variety of answers and possibilities. Here differentiation by outcome differs in the fact that the task set is engineered to produce a range of answers.

Differentiation by outcome means that children are set the same task and the end product will be different. The technique is useful in the Creative Arts and Technology where the starting point is the same for all but it is what they produce that differentiates between them. They may choose to work in ceramics, textiles, oils or pastels.

Differentiation by outcome tasks:

- fixed-time exercise
- open-ended work
- heuristic (discovery)
- independent learning.

Look at these two 'self-portraits' painted by children. How have they been differentiated by outcome? (Possible answers include attention to detail, accuracy of drawing, interpretation.)

In most cases differentiation is about setting a variety of tasks. These may be linear, graded tasks that increase in difficulty and complexity as they get harder or they may be tasks that take different routes in order to end up at the same point.

What is key to all methods of differentiation is where the children start from. It is easiest to begin at the point of assuming zero knowledge. Starting from here allows the teacher to assess where each child is in terms of comprehension and/or pre-existing knowledge; it also serves as a useful reinforcement for the children, allowing them the opportunity to recall work done previously.

Ways to begin differentiation assuming zero knowledge include:

● quiz
● short recall test
● discussion
● leading questions.

TOP TIP!

When introducing a new word or concept, ask the children what they think the key word or phrase means. For example:

'Can anybody tell me what a force is?'

Grading work in order of increasing difficulty is a common method of differentiating work for children. This may take the guise of:

● you **must** complete questions 1–3
● you **should** be able to finish questions 4 and 5
● you **could** actually get up to question 10.

Such a simplistic strategy does not differentiate in respect of ability if the questions themselves are not graded.

- Questions 1–3 must be **easy**.
- questions 4 and 5 will be **harder**.
- questions 6–10 will be the most **difficult**.

TOP TIP!

A differentiated stepping stone for modern and foreign languages:

- Use simple words.
- Construct short sentences in the present tense.
- Construct larger sentences containing linking words and phrases.
- Construct paragraphs using more than one tense.

Task

1) Try creating a graduated scale of learning for a subject of your choice.
2) Study the National Curriculum criteria for a subject. Do they follow a logical and differentiated progression? If not, alter them so that they do.

A Piagetian approach to differentiation is based on the principle of conceptual 'readiness' and then developing 'thinking skills' to facilitate cognitive development (this is dealt with in more detail in Chapter 20). At face value the principle is that a child cannot progress from one level to another until they have successfully mastered the one below. This perception has been challenged by other educationists, but the message Piagetian thinking brings to the table in respect of differentiation is that each stage in the process should be appropriate to a child's cognitive capability at that time.

Piagetian stages of development

- **Sensorimotor** (0–2 years). Children gain an understanding of the world through sensory experience.
- **Preoperational** (2–7 years). Children learn to represent objects by using words and drawings. They are curious and gain lots of knowledge, but their reasoning skills are flawed.
- **Concrete** (7–12 years). Children are able to sequence objects and recognise logical relationships. They are able to classify groups and can manipulate basic mathematical equations.
- **Formal operations** (12–adult). Adolescents and adults can think abstractly, draw conclusions and reason logically. They can apply information to new situations.

> **Task**
>
> Study these 3 maths questions. Notice the change in cognitive demand of each.
>
> **Piaget level 2A**   2 oranges cost 4p, 1 orange will cost?
> **Piaget level 2B**   2 sweets cost 5p, 6 sweets will cost?
> **Piaget level 3A**   2kg cost 12p and 3kg cost 15p, which is the best buy?
>
> **Answers**
>
> 4/2 = 2p A simple division involving 1 stage
> 5/2 × 6 = 15p Solution involves 2 stages
> 12/2 = 6p per kg 15/3= 5p per kg Solution involves 3 stages.

The significance of grading work in this way is that all children can access the work and they will each find their own level at which they can achieve. For the most able the early work is useful as reinforcement material, and the less able will achieve, albeit at a lower level, and they have the chance of tackling more challenging work at a higher level. If teaching and learning are on a continuum then all children should have the opportunity to progress to the summit.

> **(!)**
>
> **Do you know what factors limit or restrict their progress?**

However, even this model can be too simplistic because frustrations may set in if a child reaches their limit and cannot progress. If the jumps between the levels are too high, negating access for some children, then the motivation of a challenge that is difficult but achievable turns into a demotivating stress that hinders progress and may lead to behavioural problems as frustration eats away at the child's self-confidence. It is not an easy balance to get right.

> **(!)**
>
> **Do you recognise when a challenge becomes a stress?**
>
> (Answer: when a child lacks the skills to complete the task and gets frustrated.)

This is where guidance and support in the form of further differentiated material can help them make the necessary inroads into a higher level of thinking. The role of the work moves from heavily guided, teacher-led, structured work at the start to open-ended, independent work later on. Throwing children into an open-ended task without the necessary skills, especially if they have been used to a lot of teacher support, can be a recipe for creating challenging behaviour as frustration and boredom set in very quickly, unless of course the task set is not a demanding one. For example, you may ask children to build the tallest tower that they can as an unstructured, open-ended activity that is easy to complete. At a more demanding level you may ask them to build a structure that uses the principle of triangulation of forces.

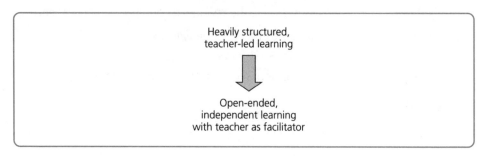

Examples of support to aid development using differentiation:

● Writing frames
● Prompt sheets
● Handouts
● Mind maps
● Leading questions.

Bloom's Taxonomy is a classification model that presets thinking skills as a developmental process. As with Piagetian classification, Bloom's Taxonomy suggests a bottom-up approach whereby children cannot progress to a higher level until they have mastered the one before.

Knowledge. Tasks include *describe, label, select, recall.*

Comprehension. Tasks include *explain, clarify, reword.*

Application. Tasks include *construct, role play, solve.*

Analysis. Tasks include *compare, test, extrapolate.*

Synthesis. Tasks include *modify, assemble, rearrange.*

Evaluation. Tasks include *review, justify, assess, debate.*

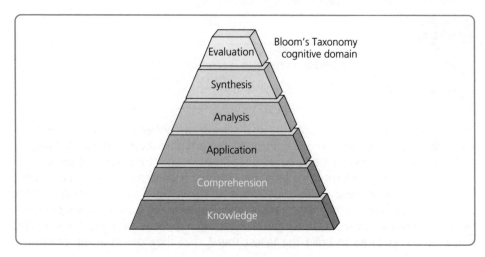

However, advocates of Bloom's Taxonomy break the classification into two distinct areas and suggest that work targeted at all levels of ability should include both:

Mastery tasks (tasks that allow children to succeed, e.g. knowledge, comprehension, application)

Developmental tasks (understanding type of tasks, e.g. analysis, synthesis, evaluation).

Task

- Compare Bloom's cognitive domains with the National Curriculum in a subject or an examination syllabus.
- Use the classification model to construct a scheme of work of your choice.

Using this approach to differentiation means that children visit more cognitively challenging work early on in their development but it is presented in a way that allows them to succeed and build experience so that they move on to more demanding work at a later date. Rather than a stepping-stone picture of learning this approach can be viewed more as a spiral, constantly returning to specific skills but in an ever more challenging situation.

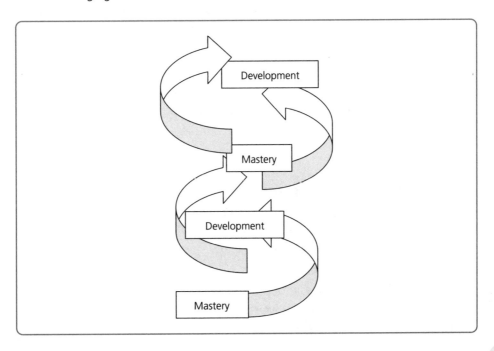

Task

Example:

a) Label the diagram of the volcano

b) Compare it with the one in the book

c) Identify the parts that you have missed

d) Fill in the missing parts.

Categorise each of the questions above using Bloom's Taxonomy.

Try setting out an exercise like this on a topic for the children you teach.

(Answer: a) knowledge, b) application, c) analysis, d) application)

Within this type of differentiation, strategies from teacher-led, guided work to more independent learning can be incorporated so that a child can begin to access levels above their original capability.

If the methodologies mentioned are pieced together, a differentiated approach by process emerges.

	Level of difficulty	Piagetian type	Bloom's Taxonomy	Structure and teacher involvement
Must	Easy	Pre-operational	Mastery	Closed, teacher-led
Should	Hard	Concrete	Mastery	
Could	Harder	Formal operations	Development	Open-ended, independent

The concept of multiple intelligence is dealt with in Chapter 20, which looks at cognitive ability, but this approach to teaching and learning is another tool by which a teacher can differentiate work for a class. The categories are shown in the box and they can be allied to Bloom's Taxonomy or Piagetian principles, or can be used on their own to provide differentiation by task.

Multiple intelligences

- Verbal–linguistic (written or spoken words)
- Logical–mathematical (numbers, reasoning, logic)
- Visual–spatial (artistic, spatial awareness)
- Bodily–kinaesthetic (movement, physicality)
- Musical (rhythm, music, hearing)
- Interpersonal (extrovert, likes group work)
- Intrapersonal (self-reflective, introvert)
- Naturalist (sensitive to the natural environment)

(!)

Think of a different exercise for each of the 'intelligences' to deliver the topic of 'friends'.

In conclusion

Differentiation occurs in all subjects, from Physical Education to Art, and can also be a consideration when dealing with aspects of challenging behaviour. Bloom's Taxonomy is not limited just to the 'cognitive domain' as exemplified earlier, it also has two other domains:

- **cognitive domain** categorises knowledge structures
- **psycho-motor domain** categorises physical and motor skills
- **affective domain** categorises feelings and emotions.

As with the cognitive domain these other two domains can be used as a basis for differentiating material for children.

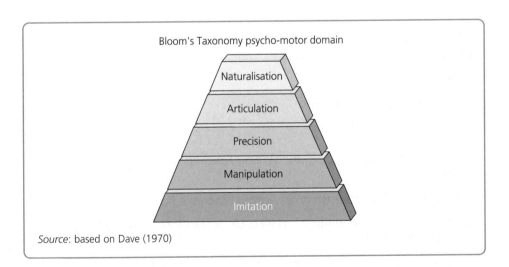

Bloom's Taxonomy psycho-motor domain

Naturalisation
Articulation
Precision
Manipulation
Imitation

Source: based on Dave (1970)

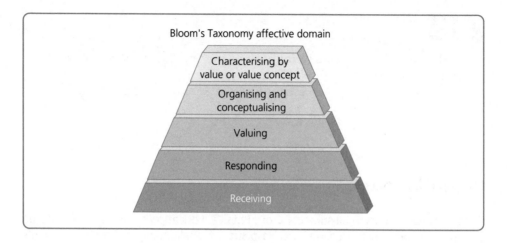

Differentiation provides the teacher with a variety of techniques so that all children can access the curriculum and thereby facilitate cognitive development. How differentiation becomes manifest is down to the priorities imposed on the teacher by the National Curriculum. It is fair to say that National Curriculum levels have improved over time in terms of their progressively increasing (cognitive) demand, but there are still places where the leap from one level to the next requires the class teacher to be adept at creating the necessary differentiated material to help children make the step up.

Further reading

www.icelp.org

www.learningandteaching.info

www.businessballs.com

Dave, R.H. (1970) *Developing and Writing Educational Objectives*, Educational Innovators Press.

Dodge, J. (2005) *Differentiation in Action*, Scholastic Publications.

McNamara, S. and Moreton, G. (1997) *Understanding Differentiation*, David Fulton Publishers.

O'Brien, T. and Guiney, D. (2001) *Differentiation in Teaching and Learning*, Continuum Books.

Petty, G. (2004) *Teaching Today*, Nelson Thornes.

Chapter 3

Active learning

Case study

The teacher attempts to make herself heard over the din of children shouting expletives at each other and passing comment about what they are going to do that evening. She yells at the top of her voice, momentarily silencing the throng.

'If you're not going to listen then you leave me no choice but to hand out the textbooks and let you copy out the page.'

Satisfied that there was no immediate crisis, the class return to their conversations. Frustrated and close to tears, the teacher stops trying to get their attention and makes for a pile of textbooks. She quietly makes her way around the desks handing out both textbooks and exercise books, totally ignored by the class as they continue their conversations until she returns to the sanctuary of her own desk, piled up with papers as if she had built a wall around her to protect herself from the hordes. Without shouting, she puts the page number on the board. Casually, one by one the class open up their textbook at the correct page and begin to copy what is written, still chatting away but this time without shouting across the room. There is a semblance of order as most of the children go about their usual routine.

Case study continued

'I hate French,' one girl says loud enough for the teacher to hear.
'I don't understand any of it,' her friend concurs.
'What's the point of learning this stuff anyway, we're never going to use it. I mean, who ever goes to France?'
'I've been once for a day, with my dad, to fill up the car with booze.'
'Did you have to speak any French?'
'No, they all speak English.'
'French is boring, all we do is copy from a book, draw stupid pictures or sit and listen to some old fart speaking on a tape.'
'I hate her, she's always shouting, she can't even control the class.'
'If she asks me to speak in French I'll tell her where to go.'

A person who is truly passive is incapable of learning

Source: © Paul Bradbury/Alamy

Possible signs that classwork is not active

If a teacher's lesson is not engaging, it is likely that the children will be:

- unsettled
- unruly
- bored.

(!)

Do you know how to make the passive active?

Suppose you ask the children to watch an educational DVD. How can you get them to interact with the material being viewed?

It is a simple cause and effect situation that if a child is actively engaged in the learning process then it is unlikely that they are misbehaving. While motivation is the driving force that delivers engagement in a lesson, it is the work that is presented to the class that 'primes the pump'. The work in class must serve to stimulate as well as to educate. There are those in teaching who bleat something along the lines of 'we are not here to entertain', but the brutal truth is that if the work a teacher presents to a class is dull and boring then the children will, eventually, become increasingly restless and discipline issues are likely to emerge.

Have you ever played the old party game 'Pass the orange'? The idea is that you have two rows of people and they have to pass an orange from one end of the row to the other using only their chins; they are not allowed to use their hands at all. A similar game can be carried out using a balloon between the legs.

Apply this to a lesson:

- Place children in groups of five or more.
- Give a sequencing task (spelling a word, putting a sentence in the correct order in French, identifying the parts of the alimentary canal in Science) with the components jumbled up.
- The group has to create the correct sequence, get in line and then pass the orange front to back.

(!)

Do you think that this is entertainment or education?

It is a constant challenge for teachers to seek out novel ways of gaining and maintaining a child's attention in class. As long as the work is balanced in favour of 'active' learning, the odds will be in the teacher's favour. Even the most mundane of tasks can be given an active makeover.

The following tasks could be construed as 'active', they vary the stimulus in a lesson, but do children learn much by doing them?

- colouring in a picture
- cutting and pasting a worksheet
- copying from a book
- watching a DVD.

> **(!)**
>
> **How might each activity be made more purposeful?**
>
> (Answer: colouring is a useful way of highlighting and annotating; cut and paste can be used to organise a jumbled-up sequence of pictures, words or phrases; copying from a book can be made active by asking children to précis the text; watching a DVD can be made active by taking notes of what is on screen, possibly using a previously prepared worksheet.)

Consider the task of reading a piece of text. How might it be made more active?

- Read the text and underline the key words.
- Read the text and summarise what you have read in no more than 50 words.
- Who can read the text and condense it into the fewest number of words so that it still makes sense?

'What we have to learn to do we learn by doing.'

(Aristotle)

In the 1970s the Nuffield Foundation produced a range of educational materials to stimulate the learning process in Science by bringing a series of investigative practical tasks to the lessons. Much of the science taught previously was by book, teacher demonstration or practical work that followed a rigid recipe approach. The underlying philosophy of Nuffield was a heuristic one. Heuristic learning is learning by discovery, finding the answers for yourself.

Examples of heuristic learning

- Observing and recording
- Think about
- Analysing
- Deducing
- Dissemination
- Role play (puppetry).

When asking children to work heuristically get them to use De Bono's CAF (consider all factors) and PMI (pluses, minuses, interesting). For example:

- Write down everything you can about a chair.
- Try to get more than 10 items.
- Now list each item as a plus, a minus or interesting (the last item encourages children to explore ideas outside of the plus–minus framework).
- Change some aspects of the chair.

Role play

This involves putting yourself in someone else's shoes.

- As a teacher, write down how you would feel being a child in your class copying out of a book every lesson.
- As a child, how would you feel being a teacher in a class where the children will not sit and listen?

Learning heuristically is about learning by/from experience. Trial and error play a large part in this educational 'experience'. Clearly, using such heuristic learning all the time would be fraught with logistical problems, not least actually getting through a syllabus as well as the chaos such an unstructured approach would bring to the classroom. However, it would resolve any issues of differentiation as the outcome each child brought to the conclusion would be proof of their capability, allowing each child to work at their own pace and make sense of the challenge using their own 'multiple intelligences' and preferred learning style.

> **TOP TIP!**
>
> Combine components from the list of multiple intelligences with De Bono's CAF process to create a variety of 'active learning' tasks.

Using multiple intelligences with CAF on the passive task of copying notes from a book

- **Verbal–linguistic (written or spoken words).** Read what you have written, explain it to a partner.
- **Logical–mathematical (numbers, reasoning, logic).** Bullet point the work in order of importance.
- **Visual–spatial (artistic, spatial awareness).** Represent what you have written as a picture, storyboard.
- **Bodily–kinaesthetic (movement, physicality).** Use puppetry or role play to explain what you have written.
- **Musical (rhythm, music, hearing).** Write a jingle to remind yourself of what you have written.
- **Interpersonal (extrovert, likes group work).** As a group, produce a talk about what you have written.
- **Intrapersonal (self-reflective, introvert).** Think about the key aspects of what you have written.
- **Naturalist (sensitive to the natural environment).** Relate what you have written to climate control.

A less open-ended approach is to focus on preferred learning styles using VAK (Visual, Auditory, Kinaesthetic) and linking them to the creation of active learning tasks.

Visual . . . look at, watch, write down what you see
Auditory . . . listen to, take note of what is said about
Kinaesthetic . . . touch, act out, pretend

'If you have difficulty solving a problem, draw a picture.'

(George Pólya, Hungarian Mathematician, 1887–1985)

Visual learners (29 per cent) enjoy presenting work through pictures, story-boards, graphs, etc.
Auditory learners (34 per cent) enjoy the spoken word, discussions and such like.
Kinaesthetic learners (37 per cent) enjoy touch, movement, role play.

(!)

Do you know what your preferred learning style is?

(!)

Which of the children you teach have a preferred learning style that is V, A or K?

Children are naturally inquisitive. They will explore by physically examining an object and/or by asking questions. This is where active learning begins. Passive learning ignores a child's natural instincts whereas active learning stimulates them. If a class has had their natural inquisitiveness drummed out of them due to a perceived need for strict discipline in lessons, getting them 'fired up' once more can be difficult. Many will seek reassurance that an answer or action is right or wrong, but given time most children will shake off the mantle and set about learning actively with enthusiasm.

There are fewer exhilarating circumstances in teaching than seeing a child taking over their own learning and running with an idea, driving a lesson. Their enthusiasm is infectious as empowerment kicks in. The key is to ask the right questions to get the children motivated. This is the essence of problem solving. Problem solving gives heurism a context and direction.

Developing a questioning approach

● Why (does this do that?) [criticise]
● What if (something else was to occur?) [extrapolation]
● Where (might the information be seen as odd?) [cognitive conflict]
● When (would another person think differently?) [interpretation]
● How (does the object work?) [analysis]

It is important to use questioning that probes understanding and requires thinking, not just recall. This in itself can be construed as active learning – whereas to an observer the children are all sitting and listening to the teacher, it is what the teacher is asking of the children that is key.

Socratic questions are questions that help to develop thinking skills in children. They can be grouped as follows:

1) Questions that seek clarification (Explain why . . . , What do you mean by . . . ?, Give me an example of . . .).

2) Questions that probe reasons and evidence (Why do you think that . . . ?, How do we know that . . . ?).

3) Questions that explore alternative views (Can you put it another way?, What would somebody who disagreed with you say?).

4) Questions that test implications and consequences (What can we work out from what you have said?, What would be the consequences of . . . ?).

5) Questions about the question/discussion (Who can summarise so far?, Are we any closer to answering the question?).

Source: Robert Fisher Brunel University.

TOP TIP!

If asking children a question, allow at least 10 seconds before looking for an answer.

Time yourself in class to find out how long, on average, you give a child before you demand an answer.

TOP TIP!

When designing a programme of work for a class, ask yourself this question: What do you want the children to learn and why do you want them to learn it? (Critical skills)

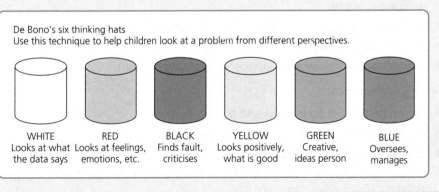

De Bono's six thinking hats
Use this technique to help children look at a problem from different perspectives.

WHITE	RED	BLACK	YELLOW	GREEN	BLUE
Looks at what the data says	Looks at feelings, emotions, etc.	Finds fault, criticises	Looks positively, what is good	Creative, ideas person	Oversees, manages

If the activity is carefully structured, the teacher can manipulate the children's thinking while allowing them to maintain (some) ownership of what they are actually doing. Critical skills is one method of engineering a balance between a truly open-ended challenge and a teacher-led piece of work. In critical skills the teacher is described as a facilitator of children's learning rather than an instructor. For a teacher new to the critical skills approach it can be a daunting task to let go of the reins and allow the children to take a more active role in their own learning. Noise levels invariably rise and there is likely to be a lot of activity and energy generated as the children set about the task. However, a closer look at the children in action is likely to reveal that they are, in fact, on task and the cacophony is the result of productive work.

With classes that are particularly unruly, the transition from a heavily structured, teacher-led approach to a student-centred, open-ended affair can sometimes become a free for all. As with all aspects of classroom work, children have to be schooled in developing the skills needed to work independently, and so critical skill challenges might be introduced gradually, maybe for a short time within a lesson, building to once a half term and then more frequently as suits the needs of the curriculum.

While such an approach is not truly heuristic, it is a much more pragmatic way of educating, empowering the children to have ownership of their own learning. Using this method, the children work within a framework constructed by the teacher yet are still allowed to explore and discover while reducing many of the blind alleys that bring with them frustration and confusion.

Critical skills learning is a much more formalised method of providing active learning. It describes itself as an 'education by design' programme and like all truly active learning approaches it puts the child firmly in the driving seat of managing their own education. Its aim is to turn the curriculum into a challenge, making the passive active.

Students have to act for themselves to solve a problem

(Critical Skills, 1997)

Critical skills asks the child to engage with the challenge by:

- actively solving meaningful tasks
- taking ownership of their own learning
- reflecting on what they are learning and doing
- working in teams
- exhibiting their learning (showing knowledge and understanding)
- applying quality criteria to their learning
- understanding that work is interconnected (application).

Teachers are asked to:

- design (what is to be learned and how)
- mediate, coach, support the learning process
- provide a forum for feedback
- ensure the classroom culture, curriculum and assessment are guided by specific targets.

Task

a) Identify how the critical skills programme is active.

b) How is the role of the teacher different than in passive teaching?

(Answer: Critical skills involves children performing different roles, working as teams to produce an outcome that is delivered to the whole class. There is likely to be movement around the room, lots of discussion between students, possibly role play and giving a talk to the rest of the class. The teacher's role is usually described as being one of facilitator rather than instructor.)

A critical skills lesson may take the format of:

- starting with a challenge or problem
- the children working in teams (picked by the teacher)
- the children being given objectives to help them to focus on the challenge
- the children exploring the challenge (within the constraints of certain resources)
- the children being encouraged to reflect on what they are doing/learning at key stages
- the children presenting their work to the rest of the class
- the children evaluating their own and other children's work.

It is a natural progression that if a child is to take charge of their own learning they should also have a hand in assessing the work they have undertaken. Children constantly seek reassurance that what they are doing is correct or not, and as teachers we usually give them verbal feedback immediately, a response that acts as a guide and as a confidence-booster. It is of little value for a child to learn in a vacuum without recourse to assessment, qualitative or otherwise.

Assessment for learning takes this idea one stage further:

- learning objectives are shared at the outset
- targets are set (by negotiation if the work is to be truly active)
- children assess their own (self-assessment) and others' (peer assessment) work using agreed criteria.

Targets set should be:

Specific
Measurable
Achievable
Realistic
Time bound

Assessment for learning develops key skills such as evaluation and analysis as well as metacognition at all levels of ability and in so doing provides a fuller framework for the active learning process.

Task

- Where are the links between critical skills and A4L (Assessment for Learning)?
- Compare the format of critical skills and A4L with Bloom's Taxonomy.
- Where are the links?
- Do they give the child the opportunity to access higher levels of thinking skills?

(Answer: both styles are active and involve peer assessment. Yes, they do give access to higher levels of thinking. NB: it is important to maintain rigour in all aspects of teaching.)

While seeking to create lessons that are essentially active, a full hour of high-octane excitement and activity is likely to leave even the most resilient teacher in need of a break. Multiply this by five and by the end of the day the 'active' teacher is going to feel exhausted. Full-on, active lessons can also lead to student antipathy, where activity becomes the norm and tedium sets in. To keep the lessons fresh and interesting the stimulus should be varied both from lesson to lesson and within the lesson. Allied to breaking up a lesson is the need to pace the lesson so that it is not too laboured or too rushed. Achieving such a balance is not easy.

There are a number of ways to break up a lesson, if that is what is needed (there are occasions when a single activity can easily engage students for a full hour without any need for dividing up the lesson). One of the most common ways is to use a starter activity, followed by the main bulk of the lesson and finally a plenary.

Starter: a short 5-minute activity to introduce or recap work done last lesson, possibly of a brain gym type. This activity may also serve the purpose of settling the children down as they enter. It should require minimal instruction, being self-explanatory in nature.

Main: this is where the bulk of the lesson material is delivered. In an hour-long lesson this will take up somewhere between 45 and 50 minutes. This section of the lesson may also be broken up into chunks in order to provide variety. Each chunk might:
- use a different stimulus (VAK)
- be cognitively more demanding
- be differentiated.

Alternatively, the main part of the lesson may have:
- **pit-stops** where children are encouraged to reflect on the work completed so far
- **mini-breaks** where the children are encouraged to relax in order to refresh, possibly using brain gym activities.

Plenary: this may be teacher led, where the teacher brings together what has been achieved or covered in the lesson. It may again involve brain gym activities or high-order thinking skills such as evaluation, analysis, discussion, etc. The plenary should be no more than 10 minutes in length.

When designing a lesson with many subsections it is important that the flow of the work is not compromised, otherwise it becomes 'bitty'. Every time the teacher has to stop is a moment when the chances of disruption and challenge increase. With a difficult class it is useful to keep teacher talk and instruction to a minimum.

'If the teacher is working harder than the children then the balance of the lesson is wrong.'

Task

Consider the following lesson.

Starter: Little teacher input

Introduction to main: 5-minute teacher talk

Each pit-stop: 5-minute teacher talk

Plenary: 5-minute teacher talk

Debate the effectiveness of the lesson design above in terms of:

a) Class control

b) Effective teaching.

Compare it with a teacher-led lesson where the teacher lectures for the bulk of the lesson.

(Answer: in the lesson above the teacher is acting more as a facilitator, stopping only to ensure children are on task and are clear what it is they are supposedt to be doing at each stage. As long as the instructions are simple and clear, possibly on the board to remind them, the teacher can work around the room. Too much stop and start will create possible points of conflict.)

When engaged in a passive activity that requires them to learn (compare active reading as opposed to reading just for pleasure), most people can really concentrate for about 30 minutes at a time before needing a break. The ability to remain focused on task is dependent on age, ability, interest, motivation and delivery. Hence a young child who is not interested in what is being said and has learning difficulties is less likely to concentrate on a topic than an able, motivated child being taught by an enthusiastic teacher. Breaking up a lesson helps to maintain a challenging child's focus throughout without pandering to their whims, while also helping to develop the motivated child.

In conclusion

Earlier in the chapter the perception that active teaching is tantamount to 'entertainment' was dismissed, principally because those who subscribe to this view do so because they lack commitment to their teaching. However, a cautionary note should be given in that if a teacher chooses to operate this style of teaching, they must not lose sight of the academic rigour required. A teacher can be all too easily seduced by an active lesson which the children have enjoyed, but when the dust settles (literally!) and the question 'how much have they learned?' is asked, the lesson is found wanting. This is what the detractors latch on to. However, it is *not* the case that you can have only one or the other – the most successful teachers combine active teaching with high academic achievement and that is what all teachers should aim for.

There is no doubt that active teaching demands much more of the class teacher than a passive approach to teaching and learning, and this is why some teachers opt for the easy life because to sustain an active philosophy in the classroom lesson after lesson, day after day, requires stamina and can result in exhaustion if the teacher is not careful. However, the rewards speak for themselves in terms of increased motivation (on the part of both teacher and children), improved academic performance and significant job satisfaction. There is 'no gain without pain' and it is with this approach that the best teachers stand head and shoulders above the rest. Teachers should not be frightened by the demands of active teaching but rather should embrace it and find a level of delivery that suits their abilities. If not every lesson, then perhaps one in two lessons might be active or even one a day until resilience has been acquired.

Further reading

www.criticalskills.co.uk

www.open.ac.uk

www.teachingthinking.net

www.assessmentforlearning.edu.au

www.nationalstrategies.standards.dcsf.gov.uk

Fisher, R. (2005) *Teaching Children to Think*, Nelson Thomes.

Fisher, R. (2005) *Teaching Children to Learn*, Nelson Thomes.

Nash, R. (2008) *The Active Classroom*, Corwin Press.

Chapter 4

Classroom logistics

Case study

The bell rings for the end of break, the class pile in off the corridor and into the classroom. There is a free for all as the children vie for the best seats. If it was a theatre or a cinema they would make for the front but, being a school class-room, the place they aim for is furthest away from the teacher, the back of the room. If there is no seating plan in place, it is likely that a gang of students will sit in close proximity, with their ring leader holding court in their midst, his or her closest associates nearest to hand and those who aspire to be part of the peer group around the edges.

There is strength in numbers and from this hornet's nest comes a continuous barrage that persistently challenges the authority of the teacher. It might be overt disobedience or something more subtle such as silly noises or constant chatter. Whatever the symptom, the cause is the gaggle of children all in one place.

Possible signs that the classroom logistics are not correct

The signs that a teacher has not got the classroom logistics right include:

- noisy class, talking across the room, turning around, etc.
- class disrespecting the contents of the room
- evidence of graffiti
- children catching themselves on snags.

The creation of a seating plan utilises a divide-and-rule approach to the problem. Its success is subject to the number of 'challenging children' in the group. If the ratio is greater than around 1:10, the success of any seating plan will be compromised. It goes without saying that the more challenging children there are in a class, the harder it is to keep them apart and spread them about the room.

It could be argued that if the work in class was engaging and interesting, there would be no need for a seating plan, but if a teacher is proactive and arranges a class with behaviour (and other criteria, such as ability) in mind, any possible problems are likely to be nipped in the bud.

Possible criteria for seating plan arrangements

- Behaviour (well behaved next to challenging)
- Ability (less able next to more able)
- Ethnic, cultural, creed (preventing like-minded groups forming)

Seating plans are an effective tool in reducing class noise associated with chatter, but they are no panacea. Challenging children, if sat apart, may shout across a room or make contact via missiles and/or texting under the table, thereby continuing to undermine the teacher's authority. It is important to think carefully when arranging children in a class. Once in place the class will settle eventually, but trying to impose a seating plan part way into the school year is fraught with problems as children will become resentful.

Working in tandem with a seating plan is the arrangement of the children's desks in the classroom. If they are fixed to the floor, there is little a teacher can do to move them, but if they are not, altering the position of the desks along with a seating plan may help in settling down a class and/or creating an environment that is conducive to learning.

Task

Carry out a PMI (plus/minus/interesting) on each of the seating arrangements below. Apply each to classes that you teach:

- Boy/girl, boy/girl alternate arrangement, possibly in alphabetical order
- Placed in friendship pairs to split up gangs but allow them the comfort of having one friend close by
- No seating plan.

A good seating plan enhances peer support

Source: Pearson Education Ltd/Studio 8

Traditional row arrangement

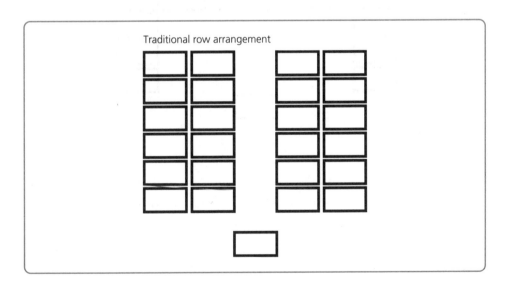

Horizontal row arrangement

Horseshoe arrangement

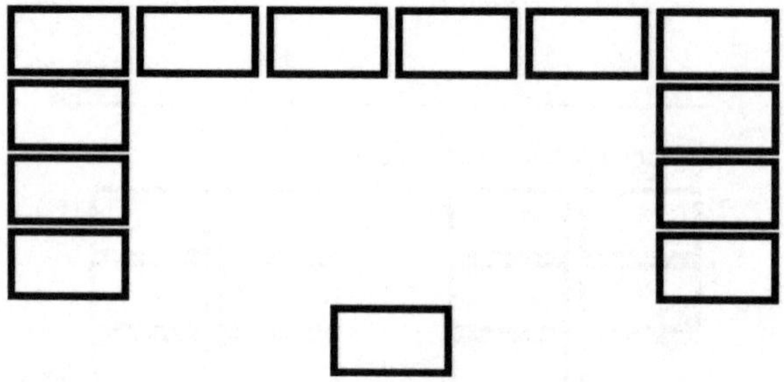

(!)

Which desk arrangement do you have in your classroom?

What problems do you have with the arrangement?

Have you ever tried a different desk arrangement? If so, how did it compare?

(Answer: children facing each other are prone to chat and lose concentration; the class is likely to be noisier than children sitting in traditional rows. The downside of working in rows is that group work is difficult.)

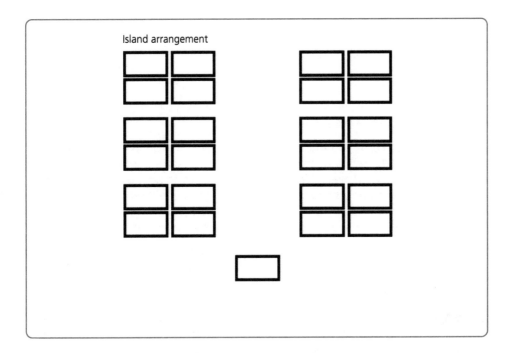

Island arrangement

What type of desk arrangement a teacher decides upon depends on its intended function. Traditional rows with everybody facing forward, combined with a seating plan, tend to reduce chat among students. An island arrangement is useful for group work, but the noise level is likely to go up as communication between children is easier. An active lesson might involve altering desk arrangements to suit the activity.

It is important to evaluate each desk arrangement in respect of:

- health and safety (requires that all 'corridors' should be at least 1 metre wide)
- the teacher's access to all children
- critical skills and other practical work.

Group work is part and parcel of modern-day teaching, but like seating plans, the structure of a group can be crucial to the success or failure of a task. Group dynamics play a large part in the smooth running of such activities. Critical skills approaches suggest job roles such as facilitator, scribe, designer, etc., but research has shown that a group size larger than three is likely to result in one or more children being marginalised.

Getting children to work together can be challenge in itself. As with a seating plan, if the children are given free rein friends will tend to gravitate to each other. It is also likely that the vulnerable in the class will be ostracised, further reinforcing negative emotions. It is important therefore that the teacher proactively engineers the make-up of groups.

When organising children into groups it is useful to consider the following, choosing only one from each category to make up the group (of three):

- more able/less able
- Boy/girl
- SEN/non-SEN
- even cultural split.

There is likely to be initial resistance but with time a class will get used to such strategies and will begin to embrace them.

If a room is cluttered by too much furniture, movement around the room is going to be compromised. The more space there is to move around in, the less potential there is for disruption. Some children will invariably seek to get up out of their chairs for legitimate reasons or otherwise – endeavouring to keep 'bums on seats' can be a constant source of irritation and potential conflict. For this reason a teacher must decide on whether reasonable movement around the room is allowed or not.

Most traffic is linked to seeking out basic equipment – pens, pencils, rulers, etc. A resource area where these are kept along with basic rules of engagement will help to establish a routine that will alleviate possible flash points.

(!)

Should children provide their own equipment?

Some children are barely able to bring themselves to school. Should they be sanctioned for not bringing their own basic equipment?

If a teacher supplies the basics, are they pandering to the children?

If a teacher has to move from one classroom to another, a small, portable toolbox filled with essentials is a must:

- pens
- pencils
- rulers
- coloured pencils
- pencil sharpeners
- erasers
- paper.

Sometimes little attention is paid to the walls in a classroom, particularly in secondary school. There has been an improvement, but some displays remain static for months and are little better than wallpaper, their interest fading as fast as the colour in the sugar paper they are mounted on. Putting children's work on the walls personalises the room and gives the children an association with their environment, as well as having the kudos of their work displayed for all to see. However, even this type of display is passive and its interest transitory. With a little creativity, wall displays can become active and even interactive. This will draw attention to them and give them a longer shelf life.

TOP TIP!

Consider breaking a wall display into different sections:

- children's work
- key words and phrases
- puzzles (brain gym)
- interactive (touch and move)
- iconic pictures and quotes

Why is the sky blue? (Answer: refraction of light.)

abcdefghijklm

What is the hidden science word? (Answer: aTOm.)

By having different sections and changing them frequently, what children see will constantly alter. There are many striking posters with thought-provoking quotes on sale. Customised posters can be made by searching through supplement magazines and adding your own thought-provoking statements. Having key words and phrases is another way of making displays interactive.

In conclusion

The layout of a classroom is something many teachers take for granted, yet its influence on behaviour can be profound, if somewhat subtle. Children with autism may be affected by a flickering light, other children may be claustrophobic. Those with ADHD may be easily distracted by goings-on outside the classroom or by children sitting next to them inside the classroom. There is also the perception given by an untidy teacher's desk, shelves cluttered with papers and faded children's work on display – it sets an example that the teacher does not really care about the children and the effort they are expected to bring to the lesson. It is often only when things start to go awry that some teachers act, but by then it may be too late. It is important to be proactive and look carefully at classroom logistics as part of any planning and preparation.

Further reading

www.theteachersguide.com

www.behaviour4learning.ac.uk

Baines, E., Blatchford, P. *et al.* (2008) *Promoting Effective Group Work in the Primary Classroom*, Routledge.

A solution-focused approach to dealing with challenging behaviour in class

Case study

'Hamed is a good for nothing, lazy, pain in the neck! He's an inveterate bully, he's always winding children up, calling them names and being horrid. He's usually late to class and disrupts proceedings just as they are getting started. Yes, he's bright, but his concentration is so poor he never finishes anything he starts. He won't do as he is told and if challenged it invariably ends in an argument. He is such a distraction to the others it is a blessing when he is off sick, which is hardly ever. I think it is wrong that he is allowed to represent the school at football and rugby. He should be banned from these activities unless he learns how to behave in lessons.'

Task

Study the dialogue. Identify the words that are used to describe the boy's behaviour.

Always is a long time to exhibit one type of behaviour (although if you are on the receiving end it feels never-ending!).

(!)

Do you teach a child like this? If so, carry out a check to find out:

● when s/he is misbehaving
● for how long
● what s/he is doing for the rest of the time.

How do you teach the unteachable?

Source: © Celia Mannings/Alamy

Just where does a teacher start with teaching the seemingly unteachable? Chances are that they have tried every sanction there is, plus bribery, to get the child to comply. Children like Hamed will have been removed from class frequently, spent time in a 'sin bin'. Detentions were given up on a while back because he never turned up; besides, he had accumulated so many that there were not enough hours in the day to accommodate them. Children like Hamed are just too challenging for the mainstream, so it is easier to refer them to a 'special school', one that would better suit their 'special needs'.

It is the perception that creates the reality because the truth is that challenging children do not misbehave all the time – even they have to pause for rest. If a teacher can find out what it is that keeps the child's attention, even if only for a short while, maybe this can be useful in getting the child to settle down to work in class.

Possible signs that a teacher is not solution focused

A teacher who is not solution focused is likely to:

- recognise poor behaviour in preference to what a child does well
- resort to sanction-based solutions as the only outcome
- seek reasons for challenging behaviour (looking back)
- make excuses for challenging behaviour.

A solution-focused approach recognises the problem but seeks a solution by finding what a child can do, what their strengths are, and then building on these. Children do get abused, they have traumas in their life that shape their behaviour. Teachers cannot change history, but they can affect the future and this is the driving force behind a solution-focused approach.

> 'A small change in any aspect of a problem or even a failed solution can initiate a solution.'
>
> *(Solution focused)*

Our (unspoken) expectation is that challenging children should go from 'zero to hero' in an instant. If the teacher's expectations are too prohibitive, change is unlikely to occur because it does not meet the level of expectation set. A way around this is to construct a scale by which progress can be measured. At one end zero marks the behaviour at its worst and at the other end ten marks the behaviour at its best. Scaling is used a lot in therapy to gauge opinion.

worst										best
0	1	2	3	4	5	6	7	8	9	10

(!)

Use scaling (scoring 1 to 10) to assess:

● how badly behaved a naughty class is that you teach

● how often in a lesson a child actually misbehaves

● what would be a reasonable level that you would tolerate either

● how you might reduce the level of disruption by just one scale point.

When trying to educate challenging children it is all too easy to blame them for their behaviour. We see clearly what they are not doing, that they are not behaving as we would like them to. It is rare that a child misbehaves 'just for the hell of it'. The underlying causes can be anything:

● abuse at home

● negligence

● special educational needs (dyslexia, autism, etc.)

● low self-esteem.

One viewpoint is that the child needs 'therapy' to discover what is the cause of the problem. However, such a search can take years to find the root cause and then, once it is 'discovered', finding the best strategy to effect a remedy, if indeed there is one, can also take years. Meanwhile, the child continues to disrupt and slip down the educational ladder. A solution-focused approach tackles the problem in a different way. It focuses on the behaviour as the problem and not the child. By taking this view the child is no longer demonised. They may have had years of being told they are 'good for nothing' and so they begin to believe they are indeed bad and thus behave as expected.

Task

Ask a challenging child to draw a circle to represent themselves. Now ask them to shade in the amount they think they are bad.

You draw the same circle and fill in what you see. Discuss.

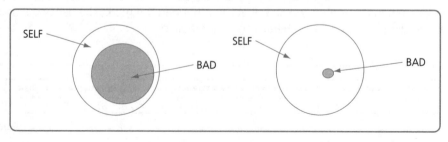

'The problem is the problem not the child'

(Solution focused)

The problem is the child's (in)ability to:

- concentrate
- maintain self-control
- stop fidgeting
- be non-confrontational.

The problem is not the child

By honing in on the problem, the issue is depersonalised while at the same time externalising the problem in the child's eyes and so it can be dealt with in a functional and unemotive manner. Separating the behaviour from the child allows the child to begin to remove the label they have carried around with them.

The solution to the problem is:

- how to solve the problem
- how to educate the child to deal with the problem.

'There are an infinite number of ways, both positive and negative, to solve a problem.'

(Solution focused)

Task

A child in class chatters to her friends constantly. Think of 3 positive ways and 3 negative ways to stop her from disturbing others.

(Answer: positive ways might include acknowledgement when she is quiet, a reward for being quiet, teacher talks to her instead, engaging work that overrides her need to talk. Negative ways might include shouting, detention, being sent out of class.)

There can be an element of trial and error in trying to find a solution, but using De Bono techniques such as CAF, PMI and 'six thinking hats' should help to narrow down the search, especially when efforts are focused on dealing with the 'behaviour' in isolation. However, the solution is likely to lie closer to home.

In the case study, Hamed would appear to be quite a challenge in the lesson, but he is not without skills. He is good at sport, he is intelligent, and it is these innate qualities that a solution-focused approach endeavours to tap into in order to facilitate change. It is likely that a child like Hamed wants to behave and fit in with the rest but lacks the commitment to change his habits, perhaps because he has been knocked back so often or because it is difficult to shake off entrenched behaviours which give him the attention he craves.

There will be occasions when the child:

● settles down to work
● is compliant
● is calm
● is polite.

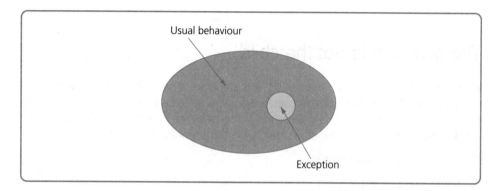

It is a case of the teacher recognising when such desired behaviours occur and noticing why and/or how the correct response has been elicited. It may be the activity, the way a request has been couched, the level of challenge posed by the work set. Teachers' responses are hard-wired to react to the misbehaviours, so it is a skill that has to be nurtured. Once a possible solution emerges it is a case of trying it again to see whether the desired response is repeated.

'If it works, do more of it; if it does not work, try something else.'

(Solution focused)

(!)

Consider the situation where a child gets a detention every time she does not do her homework, yet she persists in not doing any homework.

a) Is the sanction effective?

b) What might the teacher do to resolve the problem?

(Answer: a) No! It does not solve the problem of the child not doing homework. b) Identify the problem. Is it that she does not understand what to do? Is it that there is nowhere at home that is conducive for doing homework? Once the problem has been identified, a solution can be elicited, for example make the work more accessible, set time after school.)

When searching for 'what works' it may help to try things from the opposite perspective. As a teacher you will be aware of what a challenging child 'cannot do', but:

- Are you as aware of what they *can* do?
- How do you acknowledge when a child is being good?

'Catch them being good.'

(Solution focused)

When working with children, the usual teacher response ratio is 1 positive : 2 negatives. The ideal ratio is 4 positives : 1 negative.

(!)

Do you know what your response ratio is? Make a note of it in your next lesson.

Antecedent	Behaviour	Consequence
Reprimanded	Abusive	Sanction
Congratulated	Compliant	Reward

It is learned behaviour on the part of teachers to look out for trouble within a classroom setting, and so it may be the case that the teacher has to learn to recognise good behaviour and be sincere in acknowledging it. Here are some examples:

'Thank you for not interrupting, I really appreciate that.'

'I have just realised that you have stayed in your seat for 5 minutes. Have a house point.'

'I have noticed that you have tried really hard today, have a sweet.'

'Thanks for making the effort not to shout out.'

'Well done, you managed to write a whole sentence.'

(!)

Do you have a stock of tried-and-tested 'catch them being good' phrases?

If we recognise and reward children when they are being 'good', they are more likely to repeat that behaviour, especially those who have a propensity for attention seeking.

Solution focused is as much a philosophy as it is a psychology of working. Its principles apply to all aspects within a school and as such they are as relevant to the teacher in the classroom as they are to senior management. A solution-focused approach recognises that there are issues, but rather than dwelling on them it seeks to find a solution to the issues without looking outside the immediate environment (that is usually the person).

'Children have unique ways of solving problems.'

(Solution focused)

'Children have the necessary resources to make change possible.'

(Solution focused)

A child may be adept at sport or drama, activities that require high levels of concentration, determination and self-discipline, yet when asked to sit quietly and get on with a task in the classroom these same skills are absent. Children, especially, do not transfer skills easily from one situation to another, but a solution-focused teacher would work with a child to enable them to transfer their skills from the sports field or the stage and utilise them in a classroom environment. Working with a child and pointing out what they are already doing, albeit in a different environment, will raise their awareness that they do indeed have the skills needed to deal with their 'problem'.

Activity	Skills used	Virtues
Goalkeeper	Concentration	Commitment
	Agility	Bravery
	Coordination	Determination
	Anticipation	

(!)

- **Choose an activity that you enjoy.**
- **List the skills used.**
- **List the virtues involved.**
- **Reflect on how they might be utilised in your teaching.**

If change is going to occur, the child is going to have to cooperate. As a teacher you may lecture the child, point out the errors of their ways and how it will affect their future. The child nods and agrees to be better in the future, they may even sign a contract to that effect and promise you faithfully that it will never happen again. No sooner have they stepped out of the door than they are back to their old tricks.

'No sign-up, no change.'

(Solution focused)

Catch them being good

Source: © Catchlight Visual Services/Alamy

A child was a persistent truant, so the teacher promised him a large bag of sweets if he came into school. The next day he arrived in school, stayed the day and received his reward. The next day he truanted.

!

What techniques do you use to try to get a child to conform?

- Bribery?
- Threat of sanctions?
- Actual sanctions?
- Emotional blackmail?

Do these techniques work?

Case study

Sam's story

Sam was an angry young boy. His mother was desperate to get him to behave in school, but despite all her pleading he still kept getting into trouble. In class he was always talking and joking with his friends. When challenged he was adept at twisting arguments to his advantage and when that did not work he would resort to aggressive or personal verbal attacks on the teacher. None of the usual sanctions worked. It appeared as if he was totally out of control. Suspensions started to mount and he was referred for therapy to try to curb his anger, but even this had little effect on his actions. He stalked the school with a permanent frown, to the point that teachers approached him with caution. Being a bright lad he was as angry at himself for his lack of self-control as he was at others for their perceived persistent targeting of him. He ended the school year feeling frustrated and anxious.

The start of a new academic year saw little of what had gone before – Sam had literally 'turned over a new leaf'. When asked what had caused the change, he revealed that he had 'taken up martial arts and one of the guys in the class had been like me at school and had been expelled. It made me stop and take a good look at myself and I decided that I did not want that to happen. I now sit in class and watch others messing around and see how childish they are behaving.'

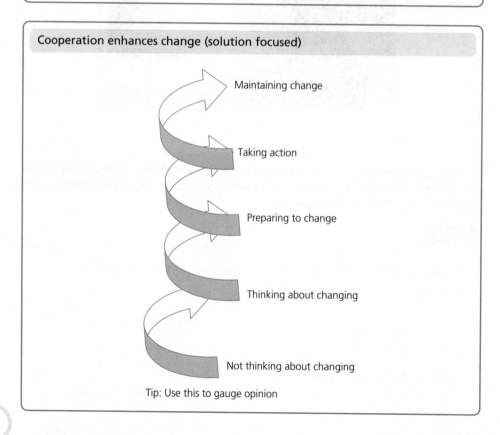

Cooperation enhances change (solution focused)

Maintaining change

Taking action

Preparing to change

Thinking about changing

Not thinking about changing

Tip: Use this to gauge opinion

For some children the threat of sanctions is enough to elicit cooperation, but with many challenging children sanctions have little effect. For a long-term, permanent change in challenging behaviour, what is 'on offer' has to be better than what is happening at present. The teacher has to find a way to create the 'want' in a child. This is why difficult children with a troubled home life tend to come to school every day despite constantly getting into trouble. School offers them a safe haven, warmth, attention (albeit negative attention) and a place where they feel valued. Likewise, children who truant find comfort in the friends they hang around with out-side of school instead of coming to school.

Finding a solution to the problem may not be easy, but unless the child is included in the process, the chances are that they will not sign up to change. Invariably (but not always) it is the child who has to make the changes. A change in circumstances may instigate a change in a child's attitude (perhaps a parent leaves or returns to the family home, or bullying ceases), but if a change is not imminent, other strategies have to come into play.

'One foot in the pain and one in the possibility.'

(Solution focused)

It is important to hear a child's story about what is troubling them, without ques-tioning the rights and wrongs of their perceptions (in the first instance, at least). This is the 'pain' part. Having listened to what they have to say the teacher can then look forward to a time when things will be better. This offers the child hope and with hope comes motivation.

TOP TIP!

'I can see that it has been a difficult time for you. Do you remember how you felt when you did well in that test last week? Think how you will feel if you produce a top piece of work now.'

'I understand that you are angry, but if you can stay in control then you will be free to go and play football at break.'

(!)

Do you use any similar phrases? Try to construct your own pain and possibility phrases.

Acknowledging a child's distress creates an empathy that goes a long way towards enhancing cooperation and without being expedient the disadvantage can be turned to an advantage.

It is easy to resort to threats of sanctions when children do not cooperate, but with children who are hard-wired to react negatively in order to defend themselves from a perceived threat, offering them choices with a positive outcome gives them the oppor-tunity to feel that they are still in control and offers them a way out without losing face.

A child may be trouble on a daily, possibly even hourly, basis. Chances are that they are tired of always being in the spotlight and receiving persistent negative attention. In a one-to-one meeting it is useful to remind them of their dilemma but then get them to paint a different picture of how things could be and/or how they would like things to be.

'A focus on future possibilities enhances change.'

(Solution focused)

'The possibilities are endless.'

(Solution focused)

TOP TIP!

'If you continue working as hard as this your grades will go through the roof!'

'If you come into school more often, you will not fall behind with your work and so you will not get into trouble as much.'

'What do you think will happen if you continue to work well?'

In conclusion

To some, a solution-focused approach would appear to be a collection of clichés that is common sense to many. This brief chapter does not really do the solution-focused process justice, even though many of the elements are present. Some schools, even whole authorities, have picked up the solution-focused baton and used it as an ethos to underpin education policy. When it is taken up as a whole-school approach, the effects can be quite dramatic. A solution-focused approach can help dictate not only how teachers deal with children but also how teachers interact with each other and members of the public. The possibilities are indeed endless.

This approach is commonly used by experts in special needs, but its value to the teacher in the classroom should not be lost. Many teachers who experience discipline issues in class have problems building positive relationships with their charges, resulting in tensions between teacher and child(ren). If teachers utilise many of the solution-focused 'mantras', they will soon build up a positive working relationship.

Further reading

www.sycol.org

George, E., Iveson, C. and Ratner, H. (1999) *Problem to Solution*, BT Press.

Rhodes, J. and Ajmal, Y. (1995) *Solution Focused Thinking in Schools*, BT Press.

Chapter 6

Intervention strategies

Case study

The class are in the room; some are on mobile phones, a few are listening, singing and dancing to music on their iPods. Two children chase each other around the room, another couple are wrestling right in front of the teacher. The noise is so loud that the teacher can't hear himself think. All he wants to do is scream 'Shut up!' But then he has tried this so many times before they have learned to ignore him.

'If he shouts at me like that I'm going to ignore him, aren't I? It's rude, I mean all he has to do is ask politely and we will stop and listen.'

So the teacher stands in front of the class in silence, arms folded, waiting impatiently for them to take the hint that he wants to start the lesson. There are a few cursory glances in his direction, followed by knowing grins as they return to what they were doing, perhaps a little more animated to show who is or, more precisely, who is not in control.

'If only I had a whistle,' the teacher thinks, searching desperately for a way in which he can gain the upper hand. In exasperation, fearing the lesson may never begin, he yells: 'If you don't shut up now, you'll all stay in at break!'

Case study continued

There is a lull as the class weigh up the threat. The teacher, seizing his opportunity, starts the lesson. 'Right then, go and get your books.' He has barely started to speak as the class move, en masse, to where the books are kept and the noise level rises to what it was previously.

'Sssh, class.' His voice has a pleading quality. 'While you are up, get yourself a textbook.' His request is lost as exercise books are tossed here and there, to the amusement of the majority. 'Ssssh, sssh,' he says even louder, sounding like an old steam engine coming into the railway station.

The teacher cuts a lonely figure as he is ignored, intimidated by what confronts him. What does he have to do to get control of the class so that he can begin teaching? He has spent hours preparing the lesson, it was going to be active and exciting. It had been carefully differentiated to suit all needs in the class. They know the seating plan and seemed to be, more or less, where they should be. It wasn't as if he was late to the lesson – he was there before the bell had even sounded.

Possible signs

A teacher not adept at intervening in classroom situations is likely to:

- experience lessons that are noisy and unruly
- end up in face-to-face arguments with children
- have to say sssh all the time to get quiet.

The teacher might try the following strategies:

- use a small brass bell, ring it gently to gain the class's attention
- count down from 5 to 1
- raise a hand in the air, silently, until the children take notice.

One of these strategies may provide the solution, but what if none of them works?

The answer lies in getting to the children before they have gathered as a large group. It may be that the class have to line up before they enter or that they arrive in dribs and drabs. Whatever the situation, the teacher should be at the door as gatekeeper, welcoming them in, perhaps dealing with uniform issues to avoid confrontation in the room. On the board or on the desk is a settling activity. They are told what to do as they come in, quietly. Everything must be in place – the work, the writing equipment, the books – nothing should be left to chance. The settling activity should:

- be simple and easy to understand
- involve no conversation
- make the children think
- be easy to complete.

How do I stop them?

Source: © Mike Abrahams/Alamy

Types of settling activities

- Wordsearch
- Crossword
- Brain gym
- Quiz or mini-test

As the class settle, the register can be done. The class may not be completely silent, but the noise level should be low enough to start the main part of the lesson. If the lesson is active and interesting, there is every chance that the class will settle and be compliant. If the noise level rises, these settling strategies indicated earlier can be brought back into the equation. The key to reducing noise in a class and maintaining a level of decorum is in being proactive and establishing routines and simple rules that the children become familiar with.

The class teacher must decide:

- what level of noise they think is acceptable for any given activity
- whether it is worth struggling with a particular class to get them to meet the teacher's expectations (complete silence may be an unrealistic expectation).

This is not meant to be a cop-out, but if the teacher is looking for a highly challenging class to sit in silence for long periods of time, they may become disillusioned very quickly. By the same token, if the teacher does not impose a certain level of crowd control on a class, their ability to keep them in check will be severely compromised. The balance required must be a pragmatic one based on priorities.

63

(!)

Does the class need to be in silence for this activity?

What level of noise is acceptable for the given activity?

Task

Scale the following from 0 to 10 (where 0 means silence and 10 is very noisy) to show the level of noise that you would expect for:

- a short test
- an important exam
- critical skills group work
- working from a textbook
- creative writing.

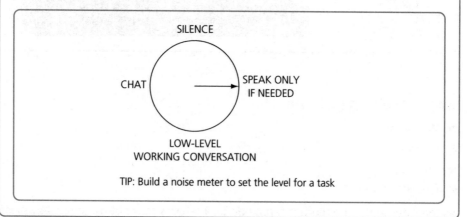

TIP: Build a noise meter to set the level for a task

(!)

Music or no music?

Where do you stand on the issue of allowing children to listen to music in the classroom?

FOR

Anecdotal evidence shows that children will settle to passive work if they are allowed to listen to music.

AGAINST

If children are listening to music they may use it as a tool to undermine the teacher's authority in class.

Disruptions spoil the flow of a lesson – they cause the teacher to stop what they are trying to do and focus their attention on the interruption. Disruption also interferes with the concentration of the rest of the class – it is hard to focus on classwork if somebody is being silly or is challenging the teacher. The aim is to deal with disruption without it affecting the flow of a lesson. But the child may be intent on being:

- confrontational
- attention seeking
- disruptive.

So how does the teacher balance having to deal with the interruption without having to stop midstream?

When an incident occurs, the teacher is faced with a choice. How they react is likely to determine what will happen next. The focus is as much on the teacher as it is on the child.

The teacher could ignore the disruption, but this might undermine their authority.

OR

The teacher could challenge the child, but an argument might ensue and make the disruption worse.

The solution lies in:

- the timing of the teacher's intervention
- the context in which they intervene
- the degree of self-control exhibited by the teacher.

'You can deliver the message in a large package, loud and in front of everyone, or in a small package, quietly and unobtrusively, one to one; the message is the same.'

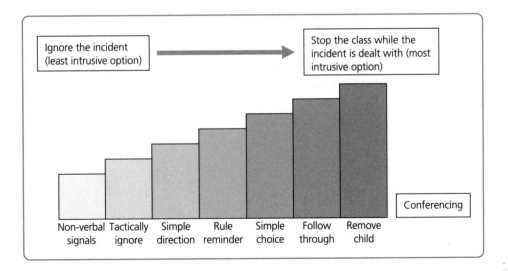

Ignore the incident (least intrusive option)

Stop the class while the incident is dealt with (most intrusive option)

Conferencing

Non-verbal signals | Tactically ignore | Simple direction | Rule reminder | Simple choice | Follow through | Remove child

The aim is to keep to the lighter areas and avoid the darker ones. Use the lighter ones more often and the darker ones less often.

- The teacher chooses the time to challenge the child.
- The teacher chooses the context that the challenge will take.

Timing and context of the intervention	Examples
Non-verbal commands and messages	Eye contact, raised eyebrows, pointing, simulation (e.g. finger to mouth to indicate stop talking or stand next to child)
Tactical ignoring	The choice may be not to react immediately. But the intention is to deal with the issue **Timing:** The teacher might react once everybody has settled (or at the end of the lesson if the issue is not of immediate concern) **Context:** Outside the classroom, at the teacher's desk
Simple direction	A clear verbal instruction, delivered politely: 'Please get on with your work'
Rule reminder	'This is your first warning, please stop talking and settle down to your work'
Choice	'Take time out. If you come back in and settle you will be allowed to remain, if you do not you will be asked to leave for the rest of the lesson'
Follow through	'I am sorry that you have chosen not to settle, you must now leave the room' (it is essential that you have a contingency plan. Empty threats will be exploited)
Conferencing	Usually a detention whereby the first part – the reasons for the child's removal from class – are explained in order to provide closure

This puts the teacher back in control. Deciding on the best course of action if a child transgresses is usually a decision which is taken quickly – there is an urgency to get on with the lesson as well as an underlying feeling that the child has to be dealt with straight away. Experience brings with it the skills to know:

- when to react
- how to react
- to what degree.

TOP TIP!

Giving the child a choice is another method of retaining control while allowing the child to think that they have not lost control. A confrontational approach says to the child, 'the teacher wants to control me', and for many reasons the child may rail against losing control (for example, a child with low self-esteem, a child who has suffered abuse, an autistic child). By offering a choice, the child has options.

- It is important to offer choices in a matter-of-fact, low-key manner so that no threat is implied.
- Also, allow them a short space of time to consider 'the offer'.

For example:

'If you do the work asked you can join in with class when we have puzzle time; if you do not, then you will have to work on your own. I'll come back in a minute so that you can have time to think about it.'

'If you take off the coat you can come in the room and be with your friends; if you do not, you will have to go and sit outside the headteacher's office. I'll leave you a moment so that you can decide.'

This technique is not a cop-out; it fits in with the change in today's society where parents now tend to ask their children what they want rather than telling them what they can have. This technique uses the key skills of diffusion, deflection and to an extent confusion. If the child chooses not to opt in then they have chosen the 'sanction'. If they do not comply after agreeing to do so, the teacher follows through with the sanction. They have made the choice, they must stick to it.

It is important that the level of intervention matches the transgression. It would be unfair to suspend a child for chewing in class and it would be unwise to ignore a child who is physically assaulting another child. Like changing gears in a car, the idea is to move through the intervention strategies one by one until the teacher reaches the appropriate one to match what is before them. As a teacher gains experience they may pay scant attention to the earlier ones in favour of the latter choices, but they will consider them all the same.

Task

Evaluate the following situation.

A child is 5 minutes late to class. The teacher raises his eyebrows at the child's tardiness but allows her to sit and get on with her work. At the end of the lesson as the class are leaving he calls her over and speaks to her about the issue.

- Is the intervention appropriate?
- How has the teacher dictated the timing and context?
- What might have happened if the teacher had chosen to chastise the child as she entered the room late?

(Answer: yes, it is important to highlight when a child has transgressed. The teacher has chosen to speak with the child at the end of the lesson. They might have chosen a time within the lesson if it was appropriate. If the child is admonished at the start then the beginning would have been stalled and may have caused disruption to the whole lesson, making the rest of the class unsettled.)

Task

Study the following challenging situations and decide what strategies you would choose to deal with each of them.

1. A child is 5 minutes late to class.
2. A child is 20 minutes late to class.
3. A child is wearing earrings (non-uniform).
4. A child is texting on his mobile phone.
5. A class won't settle down.
6. A child is rude to the teacher.
7. A child refuses to follow an instruction.
8. A child uses threatening behaviour towards another child.

(Answers: 1) Non-verbal signal or rule reminder. 2) Follow up. 3) Simple choice, 'Please remove or they will be confiscated'. 4) Simple choice, 'Please put it away or it will be confiscated'. 5) Simple choice then follow through. 6) Simple choice to apologise or follow through. 7) Simple choice then follow through. 8) Follow through then conferencing.)

How a teacher speaks to a child is as important as the timing and context. If the teacher reacts in a calm and self-controlled manner, it is more likely to effect a positive outcome. If the teacher reacts aggressively or angrily, the situation may become more inflamed and end up in conflict. If the teacher reacts negatively and loses their self-control, this may justify, in the child's eyes, a retaliatory response as they seek to defend themselves. In psychology terms it is described as mirroring – the child will mirror the emotion displayed by the teacher. It can also occur the other way – the teacher can get sucked into reacting aggressively when faced with an angry child. It is about the teacher keeping their self-control even in the most challenging of situations.

Rather than confront, the teacher can elect to:

- diffuse
- deflect
- confuse.

Even in the face of a determined attempt to provoke it is important that the teacher maintains their composure. Some children are adept at knowing which buttons to press to get a reaction from a teacher.

(!)

What gets you hot under the collar?

On a scale of 1 to 10, how do the following annoy you?

- **Children talking across you when you try to give an instruction.**
- **A child spitting.**
- **A child laughing at you as you speak to them.**
- **A child using the 'F' word at you.**
- **A child being late to class.**
- **A child tapping on a desk while you are speaking.**

It is important to bear in mind that any personal attack or affront by a child towards the teacher is designed to get a reaction. By not 'taking the bait' the teacher disarms the child and forces them to rethink their strategy.

'I'll manage my behaviour, please manage yours.'

'I am showing you respect by not shouting so please show me the same respect.'

What's your reaction?

Source: © David Hancock/Alamy

Case study

The teacher was of the old school. He believed that children should be seen and not heard and that, within the school boundaries, his word was law and he should be respected because of his status as a senior teacher. If a child was transgressing he would bellow at the top of his voice, whether they were 100 metres away or standing next to him. Amie was a truculent 15 year old seeking to turn any situation to her advantage. She would be late to class on purpose and sit with her coat on – it usually got her the attention she craved so that she could then hold court. If a teacher did not 'play ball' she would sometimes choose to raise the stakes. When Amie and the teacher met, which they did every day as she was in one of his classes, it would invariably end up in conflict.

'He's easily wound up,' she commented. 'He thinks he is scary because he shouts but he doesn't frighten me. He can't touch me – if he tried I'd get him done.'

'So why don't you just sit quietly and get on with your work?'

'He doesn't respect me so why should I respect him? I don't want to be in his class so I wind him up until he loses his temper and throws me out. You know when he gets angry he goes bright red in the face and spits, it's funny,' she mocks.

'Do you do that every lesson?'

'Not every lesson but most days. It works every time, he hasn't even twigged he's so stupid.'

If a child is proving difficult it is important that the teacher maintains control of the situation using assertiveness rather than aggression. Assertiveness is a method of conveying authority without causing rancour. The assertive teacher does not demand respect by way of their perceived position but rather commands respect in the way that they conduct themselves. The assertive teacher speaks confidently, decisively and with assurance.

(!)

Compare and contrast the following:

'Please be quiet.' Said meekly.
'Be quiet!' Expressed loudly and aggressively.
'John, I need you to stop talking.' Spoken assertively.

The key features of being assertive are:

- body language (facing people, open body, no arms folded, not too close, non-threatening)
- voice tone (calm, audible but not too loud)
- eye contact (direct without staring)
- relaxed stance (calm and in control of self, no indecision or anger)
- gestures (open-handed, avoid pointing, non-threatening).

(!)

How would you feel if a colleague:

- glared at you?
- pointed threateningly at you?
- shouted at you?

How do you think a child would feel if you did the same to them?

In an already difficult situation such aggressive gestures may spark conflict between teacher and child, making a bad situation a whole lot worse. In truth, it is difficult to act assertively; it is very much a case of 'being rather than doing'. Assertiveness comes from the self-confidence of a teacher who is in control of their emotions. It is a persona that comes naturally to some people, but nevertheless it is skill that can be nurtured.

There are occasions when no matter how the teacher tries to control the situation the child is unable or unwillingly to comply. In this event the teacher should have a well-rehearsed exit strategy designed to remove the child without causing too much disruption. It is essential that the child knows that they are fast approaching the point of no return. This is easiest to achieve by giving the child a final choice: 'Sian, this is your final warning, either settle down to your work or you will be asked to leave the room.'

Examples of exit locations

- Outside the room to cool down (5-minute maximum).
- Sin bin room.
- Other teacher's classroom.
- Outside the headteacher's office.

(!)

Does your school have a place where a child can be sent?

If the child transgresses, send them out – do not give them any more chances because to do so puts them in control of the situation and undermines the teacher's authority. Schools should have their own agreed procedures for sending children out of a lesson for disciplinary reasons. If your school does not, this is an issue that needs to be tackled because leaving a child in a class who has exhausted all a teacher's strategies to get them to behave will convey to the child, and others, that they can push the boundaries as far they like and there will be no comeback.

Removing a child from a lesson can be very stressful for both teacher and child alike. It is a potential flashpoint whereby the child may let loose a stream of verbal abuse at the teacher as they realise that they are no longer in control or because they are frustrated at their lack of self-discipline. When dealing with the situation it is important that the teacher recognises this in any report that they write and does not focus just on a child's outburst as they were leaving the room. Loss of self-discipline cannot be condoned, but such outbursts should be judged in context.

Conversely, a child may get angry and seek to leave the room. If this occurs the teacher should step aside and let them leave. Some anger-management advice (see Chapter 11) encourages children to walk away from possible conflicts, so standing in a doorway blocking a child's path is likely to lead to a serious situation, possibly a physical assault on the teacher.

When faced with a child who is intent on leaving, a teacher may feel that their authority has been compromised, but it is more a case of timing and context. Once the child has left and cooled down they can then be summoned and the situation dealt with at a later time, preferably the same day.

If a child refuses to leave the room then again the school should have a set procedure to deal with this event (another whole-school policy issue). In this event a school policy system might take the shape of:

a. Class teacher sends another child to bring support.
b. If the child causing the problem still refuses to move, the teacher moves the rest of the class out and into another room, leaving the child with the staff member called out.
c. Eventually the child will be persuaded to leave and the class can return.
d. If the child still refuses to move, they will have to be removed forcibly.
e. The child can then be dealt with when they have calmed down.

This seems a long-winded way of removing a student, but in these days of litigation it is important that such procedures and policies are in place to protect both the teacher and the child.

In terms of using force to remove a child:

Information

10. section 93 of the Education and Inspections Act 2006 enables staff to use such force as is reasonable in the circumstances to prevent a child from doing, or continuing to do, any of the following:

a. Committing any offence (or, for a pupil under the age of criminal responsibility, what would be an offence for an older pupil);
b. Causing personal injury to, or damage to the property of, any person (including the person himself); or
c. Prejudicing the maintenance of good order and discipline at the school or among any pupils receiving education at the school, whether during a teaching session or otherwise.

The Act goes on to say:

13. There is no definition of when it is reasonable to use force. That will always depend on the precise circumstances of individual cases. To be judged lawful, the force used would need to be in proportion to the consequences it is intended to prevent. The degree of force used should be the minimum needed to achieve the desired result. Use of force could not be justified to prevent trivial misbehaviour.

While a teacher may be protected in law, laying hands on a child, especially an irate child, means that the teacher runs the serious risk of being physically assaulted and so it should be used only as a last resort. It would be helpful for a number of key staff in a school to be properly trained in physical intervention techniques to reduce the risk to staff and children if force is required.

At the time of writing there are concerns that some children are seeking to accuse teachers of assault in order to manipulate situations in class to their own advantage. Grabbing hold of a child without knowing how to do so without causing harm to the child may result in legal action against the teacher.

In conclusion

It is rare that a teacher will find themselves in a challenging situation that they have not played a part in creating. The class teacher should be aware that what they bring to the classroom will influence how an individual or class group are likely to react. If a teacher is poorly organised, if the work is repeatedly unstimulating, if the teacher is terse, aggressive and/or overtly sarcastic or patronising, then disaffection and conflict are going to ensue. If a teacher is respectful of the children, they are more than likely to reciprocate. If a teacher produces lessons that are interesting and motivating, the children will look forward to the lessons and are less likely to misbehave as a result. Children are not stupid – they know if a teacher is giving of their best. Even a teacher new to a school is usually given time to show what they can do. However, such windows of opportunity can be fleeting and if the teacher fails to impress, they become fair game. It is that elusive 'empathy' built on mutual respect that gives some teachers what appears to be magical powers to control the 'seething masses' or individuals hell-bent on causing mayhem. In times of extreme tension the experienced teacher rarely jumps in without assessing the situation and seeking to resolve the issues in a step-by-step process: separate the warring factions, allow them to calm down and then deal with the situation without rancour.

Further reading

www.teachernet.org

www.janebluestein.com

www.education.com

Rogers, B. (2006) *Classroom Behaviour*, Sage Publications.

Rogers, B. (2006) *Cracking the Hard Class*, Sage Publications.

Chapter 7

Building and maintaining positive relationships with children in the classroom

Case study

Consider the following teacher.

While he enjoys a relaxing coffee in the staffroom, waxing lyrical about how he believes in zero tolerance in the classroom, the children stand outside in the rain even though the bell for the end of break sounded minutes ago. He laughs and jokes with other teachers as he saunters towards his room. He chastises, curses and berates the children who get in his way even though he is late and by now they should be seated and working. Those children who are outspoken are given lines or a detention before the books are handed out. The lesson is heavily teacher-led; he talks for ages, relating anecdotes from his past in between the work he is relaying to them. A good 20 minutes have passed and they have still not put pen to paper. The children start to lose concentration – many had done so within the first 5 minutes. Eventually he tells them to open their books and get on with copying the paragraphs and completing the questions.

Case study continued

One child questions his teaching and so he takes affront at her criticism. He insists that the child stands up as he points to the whole class that the child is a troublemaker and will probably end up in prison or on the dole if he continues to be so badly behaved. He then puts her initials on the board. The child takes exception to the insult and an argument ensues. The teacher sends the child out but she refuses to go. Support is called for and the child is removed, blamed for causing a disruption and sanctioned. In the child's eyes she has done nothing wrong, it was the teacher who insulted her and started the furore, but nobody is prepared to listen to her side of the story.

The situation leaves her feeling angry and frustrated at the injustice. The next lesson she arrives at his room and seeks confrontation so that she does not have to stay in the room because she is worried that she might do something violent. The teacher uses her confrontational attitude to reinforce what he has already pointed out: that she is a good-for-nothing layabout who will achieve little in life. She is removed; he goes back to his lesson assured in the knowledge that she will now be put in another class and will no longer be his problem.

Case study

Compare the above teacher with the one below.

The teacher is in the classroom before the children arrive, books are out on the desk and there is a starting activity on the board. As each child comes in they are greeted with a smile and she shares in some banter with one or two. She does the register as the class settle to the well-rehearsed routine. Any non-uniform issues are dealt with as she passes by, tugging gently at coats and lifting scarves, all the time smiling, with the odd raised eyebrow or nod.

The children comply without complaint. Any expletives are dealt with, with a swift 'no thank you' or 'leave it in the playground'. The culprits apologise and carry on working. If a child repeats the offence she steps over to them and has a quiet word in their ear, warning them of future consequences but also remarking positively on their work.

The starter activity is marked in situ, rewards are given and she moves on to the main part of the lesson. She takes no longer than 5 minutes explaining what has to be done and the instructions are on the board as reference. The work is active and engaging, provoking much thought and interaction between the teacher and individual children. The work is presented as a challenge. 'You should be able to do the first part but it does get harder as you progress. I will give you 10 minutes to try the first part and then we will stop before we move on to the harder work.' As the deadline approaches she encourages them to finish. She then asks questions and takes answers from the class. The next piece of work is introduced. With those children who are struggling or are reluctant to start, she spends time rephrasing questions, encouraging and supporting.

The persistent offender is reminded of what is acceptable in the lesson and given a clear choice: they can fit in and try to get a reward for their effort, or they can carry on and risk getting a sanction. They choose to carry on being disruptive and so she sends them out of the room. As the sanction is given, she does so non-judgementally. 'Let's hope that you settle better next lesson; you have so much to offer.'

(!)

What are the similarities in the two case studies? How does each teacher differ in their approach? Which one is likely to have most empathy with children in their class? How is that empathy likely to manifest itself in respect of behaviour in the classroom?

(Answers: no similarities! One talks about what should be done in class but is not child centred and is reactive; the other is child centred and is working with and for the children and is proactive. The children are more likely to want to be in the child-centred teacher's class and will be more willing to comply.)

Background

It is a generally held perception among those not involved in education that to be a teacher all you have to do is prepare a few notes, stand in front of a class of children and transfer the information to the children, all of whom sit attentively (oh, that the job was as easy as that!). What many people fail to realise (including some teachers) is that the personality the teacher brings to the classroom can have a major impact on whether they will be successful as a teacher or not. Whether a teacher is a strict disciplinarian or a laid-back libertarian, the teacher's ability to empathise with a class or with individuals within a class is going to influence the discipline of that teacher.

Empathy is not about surrendering to a child's plaintive pleas – teachers who do 'give in' are deemed a 'soft touch' and are likely to be ruthlessly exploited; they command little respect in the eyes of children. Likewise, the teacher who is too harsh and unforgiving also commands little respect and their unbending nature will, ultimately, lead to their undoing.

Children are no different to adults, they are drawn to those teachers who have good interpersonal skills as much as they are put off by those teachers with whom they do not have empathy. Teaching is as much about personality as it is about being organised or being academically skilled, and there are those in teaching for whom the profession is not suited. It is for each teacher to examine their own performance and be honest in their assessment – if they are not up to the job it would be better for them and for the children in their charge if they sought alternative employment.

Building positive relationships with children is key to effecting good classroom management. Get it right and the children will be eating out of your hand; get it wrong and a lesson is likely to unravel before your very eyes. Repairing damaged relationships is a struggle.

The difference between a competent teacher and a struggling teacher has much to do with their commitment to the job in terms of planning and organisation; the difference between a successful teacher and a competent teacher has more to do with empathy, even though they share a commitment to the job. As with assertiveness, empathy is an innate quality, but there are skills and techniques that a teacher can acquire in order to become more empathic.

Possible signs of a lack of positive relationships in the class

If a teacher is not able to build positive working relationships with the children in the class then the children are likely to:

- be openly rude to the teacher
- disrespect, ignore the teacher
- target the teacher with disparaging remarks
- blame the teacher when things go awry.

A thumbnail survey was carried out in 2010 asking 46 15–16 year olds what attributes they thought a good teacher exhibited and what attributes a bad teacher exhibited. The findings are summarised below.

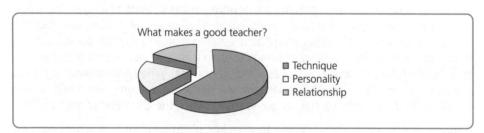

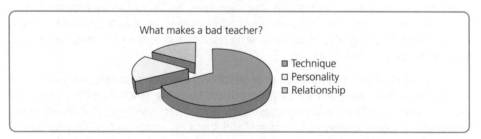

The two charts show that children view teaching technique as significant in defining whether a teacher is good or bad. Some of their comments are as follows:

A good teacher is someone who can put their point across well without making it confusing.

A good teacher does not use their authority to bully students.

A good teacher makes you think and varies the work.

A good teacher makes a lesson fun even when you are learning.

A bad teacher does not stay on task, is a pushover and cannot control a class.

A bad teacher gives you too much copying down.

Good teachers make you think.

Although both charts show technique as the most significant indicator of whether children view a teacher as good or bad, the comments indicate that many techniques are associated with relationship issues. For example, a fun lesson puts children at ease; some bad teachers are seen as 'pushovers'.

Personality and relationship issues combined account for around 40 per cent of how the children viewed teachers as good or bad. The comments below indicate some of the detail behind their observations:

A bad teacher is someone who gets frustrated with a student even when they have tried.

Bad teachers have no sense of humour.

Good teachers don't talk down to us.

A good teacher is someone who is easy to talk to and generally happy.

Good teachers are helpful, kind and understanding.

'Smile'

Source: © Pearson Education Ltd/Studio 8

(!)

The table shows some key words used by the children in the survey. Tick the ones that apply to you when you are in front of a class.

Good teachers	Bad teachers
Happy	Too strict
Fun	Moody
Interesting	Moan
Fair	Talk too much
Listen	Shout
Understand	Blame
Help	Harsh
Relaxed	Get irritated
Enjoyable	Get frustrated

Task

So how do you shape up? How good are your interpersonal skills in the classroom? Try the questionnaire below and see how you fare.

Answer the following questions:

1) If children enter the room making a lot of noise, do you?
   a. Shout at them to be quiet
   b. Threaten them with a sanction if they don't be quiet
   c. Stay calm and patient
2) If a child arrives in tears, do you?
   a. Ignore them
   b. Tell them to sort themselves out
   c. Take them to one side and find out why they are crying
   d. Take them to one side, find out why they are crying and try to sort out the matter
3) If a child is struggling with their work and starting to misbehave, do you?
   a. Ignore them
   b. Tell them to sort it out themselves, you have already told them how to do the work
   c. Try to help them

4) If a child is struggling with their work, do you?

    a. Accept that they are not bright enough to answer it correctly

    b. Bully them into trying to do the work

    c. Encourage them to have a go

5) If a child gets an answer wrong, do you?

    a. Make an example of them (you should know that, we only did it last lesson)

    b. Tell them tersely that they are wrong ('wrong answer') and move on

    c. Soften the blow ('good try but that's not quite what I was after')

6) How often do you raise your voice to chastise children when they are not behaving?

    a. Never   b. Rarely   c. About half and half   d. A lot

7) If a child is misbehaving, do you?

    a. Blame the child (it's always you, you should know better, you are always being naughty)

    b. Ignore them

    c. Deal with the behaviour without blaming ('John, swearing is not acceptable in class')

8) If a child is misbehaving, do you?

    a. Tear a strip off them

    b. Point out what they are doing wrong and present them with a choice

    c. Ignore them

9) If a child is misbehaving, do you?

    a. Shame them in front of the class (name on board, stand them up, bring them to the front)

    b. Ignore them

    c. Go over to them and have words with them quietly

10) When you mark a child's work, do you?

    a. Mark all the corrections in red and add critical comments (not good enough, could do better)

    b. Just give a mark out of 10 (or the equivalent)

    c. Emphasise what they have done well but suggest improvements (2* and a wish)

11) When you mark a child's work, do you?

    a. Mark it quickly and return it to them

    b. Mark it when you can

    c. Rarely mark work

12) If a child gets an 'F' grade, do you?

    a. Just tell them how it is

    b. Offer suggestions as to how they might improve the work

    c. Give them support so that they can improve the work

    d. Tell them their work is not up to standard

13) When it's break time, do you?

    a. Dash to the staffroom, you need some peace and quiet
    b. Stay in your classroom on your own
    c. Sit with the children

14) Do children in school?

    a. Seek you out when they have a problem
    b. Rarely share their worries with you

15) Do you?

    a. Laugh with children   b. Laugh at children
    c. Not believe in fraternising with children

16) Are children?

    a. Usually respectful and polite to you   b. Often rude to you
    c. Never noticed

Work out your score using the information below. How do you shape up?

1) c, 1.	9) c, 1.
2) c, 1, d, 2.	10) c, 1.
3) c, 1.	11) a, 1.
4) c, 1.	12) b, 1, c, 2.
5) c, 1.	13) c, 2.
6) a, 2, b, 1.	14) a, 2.
7) c, 1.	15) a, 1.
8) b, 1.	16) a, 2.

Score 0–5: Perhaps you are in the wrong career? Are you doing the job just for the money or for the holidays?

Score 6–12: You would be better off in the private sector. The stress of teaching in your present school may get the better of you eventually.

Score 13–19: Your empathy with children is good in parts, but have a look at where you might improve.

Score 20–22: You are the teaching equivalent of Florence Nightingale – you must have the patience of a saint! For you, teaching is truly a vocation. Good luck to you – but watch those stress levels.

More thorough studies have shown that, particularly in one-to-one situations, technique is not as critical as interpersonal skills when it comes to influencing the way people think and subsequently act. One-to-one situations are occasions when a teacher's mettle comes under the closest scrutiny from a child.

Task

Study the pie chart, which shows the influence on a child's behaviour in respect of whether they are likely to take any notice of a teacher. How much influence is brought about by

a) how a teacher acts

b) how a teacher empathises?

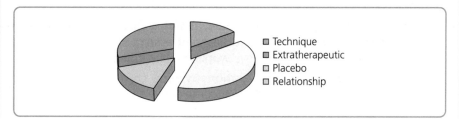

□ Technique
□ Extratherapeutic
□ Placebo
□ Relationship

Answers:

- Technique (shouts/counsels/interviews, etc.) (15 per cent)
- Extratherapeutic (skills not relevant to the problem, e.g. personality) (40 per cent)
- Placebo (what the child expects of/brings to the interaction) (15 per cent)
- Relationship (whether the child likes the teacher or not) (30 per cent).

Carl Rogers, an eminent American psychologist, identified three core conditions that need to be brought to a relationship if it is to be a positive one. The conditions are:

1. **Acceptance** of what a child is feeling at any moment in time, being non-judgemental.
2. **Congruence**, being genuine, being yourself.
3. **Empathy**, sensing accurately the feelings of the children, active listening.

- Compare Rogers's core conditions with those of Lambert.
- Compare these with the children's perceptions of what makes a good teacher.
- What are the common factors?
- How do you measure up against the criteria?

Your personality is something that you are born with and something that develops over time. Your ability to develop relationships is linked to your personality, but it is possible to improve your interpersonal skills, at least within a classroom setting. It is not a case of offering treats and rewards in an attempt to curry favour, although such acts may help in the short term.

The observations made by the children give an indication of what they value in a teacher, and technique in terms of basic classroom management is a significant factor.

- **Children like structure and routine** and generally speaking there is indirect correlation between these and age and ability. The younger the class and the less able the child, the more they rely on structure and routine.
- **Well-planned and well-organised lessons** and classrooms make a child feel at ease, 'at home'. They take comfort from knowing what they can and cannot do within a classroom environment.
- **They respect a teacher with good classroom control**, one who is assertive, firm but fair. Again there is comfort in knowing that you are being looked after, particularly for those children who are most vulnerable.
- **Having good listening skills, eye contact, allowing children to air their views and being there for them when they need assistance** (either academically or emotionally) all help foster positive working relationships.
- **Being able to depersonalise situations** when a child is being challenging, focusing on the issue and being non-judgemental, is a powerful tool.

Rather

'The challenge you have is to try to improve your concentration'

than

'You are such a time waster!'

On the flip side, personalising situations when children are achieving helps to improve confidence and raise self-esteem. Children are keenly aware that they are often challenged when they do something wrong but are rarely praised when they do something right. Catching them being good is another skill that will engender a positive working relationship.

Rather

'Your work today has been brilliant!'

than

'Your grade is a C' (spoken clinically).

Children warm to teachers:

- who are approachable
- in whom they can confide
- who understand their needs
- who are non-judgemental in their interactions with the child.

There is a myth that to be 'professional' a teacher must not engage at an emotional level with a child. Comparisons are made with other 'professionals': doctors, lawyers, social workers, police officers. However, the difference between these other professions and teaching is one of time spent in the company of the clients that they serve. Teachers spend a large proportion of their time over a day, a week, a year with the children they teach. It is nigh on impossible to work in an emotional vacuum and so relationships, either positive or negative, develop. There is nothing sinister in this, it is a natural consequence of human beings being in close proximity and interacting over a period of time. If a child chooses to bare their soul to a teacher or arrives at the lesson in floods of tears, it is difficult for a teacher and possibly damaging to the child to ignore the child's emotions.

Where a relationship becomes unhealthy is when barriers are crossed and the teacher and/or child become too familiar. There is what is described as maintaining a 'professional distance', but this does not mean a teacher should not have empathy with the children they teach because it is often as a result of this empathy that mutual respect, understanding and trust build. Without such empathy the ability of a teacher to control a class is compromised. Nevertheless, a professional distance is essential in order that a child does not become too dependent on a teacher or attached emotionally. Smiling, listening to a child's worries and being sensitive to their needs creates a heightened emotional state, but learning to maintain a distance is essential.

TOP TIP!

How to maintain a professional distance

Physically:

a. Avoid any physical contact.

b. Keep a desk between you and the child.

c. Do not remain alone with a door closed (door open, CCTV, etc.).

Emotionally:

a. Do not reveal personal information about yourself.

b. Do not express feelings towards a child (avoid expressions such as like, care, love, hate, dislike)

In conclusion

There are those who say teaching is not a popularity contest, but I defy any teacher to succeed in the profession in an emotional vacuum. It is human nature to like and to want to be liked. It is also natural to respond negatively to something or to someone who is disliked especially at a young age when a child is not in control of their emotions and/or is unable to disguise their true feelings. Successful teaching, and with it behaviour control, has its foundations in mutual respect. Children will put their trust in a teacher who is empathic but who retains a professional dignity. Children will externalise this by committing to work set and modifying their behaviour accordingly. A respectful teacher places a belief in a child's capability to surmount obstacles that lie in their path. If doubts set in from either side then trust is compromised and disagreements start to appear. If respect and trust break down completely then quality teaching and learning will not take place.

'The poor teacher struggles
The mediocre teacher tells
The good teacher explains
The superior teacher engages
The great teacher inspires.'

(Adapted from a quote by William Arthur Ward)

(!)

Which teacher are you? Which one do you aspire to be?

Further reading

Dix, P. (2007) *Taking Care of Behaviour*, Pearson.

Hook, P. and Vass, A. (2004) *Behaviour Management Pocketbook*, Teachers Pocketbooks.

Lemov, D. (2010) *Teach Like a Champion*, Jossey-Bass.

Cowley, S. (2009) *Teaching Skills for Dummies*, John Wiley & Sons.

Rewards and sanctions

Case study

Claudia's story

'What's the point of stupid rules? I mean, how is wearing jewellery going to hurt someone? He picks on me, I know he does. There were loads of others with rings and earrings on and he says to me, "Give me your bracelet, jewellery is banned in school. You can get it back at the end of the week from the office." So I told him he wasn't having the bracelet. I said, "Give it to me or else." Who does he think he is, coming over all hard? So I said go for it! There was no way he was getting the bracelet, it was my Gran's. She died last year and I swore I would keep it on at all times. He said if I didn't give it to him I would get a detention. I said I wouldn't come – besides I had detentions every night already anyway. He started to get angry and put me in an internal suspension until I handed over the bracelet. I said fine but I was not giving it to him. I stayed most of the day and then got fed up and skipped lunch so they suspended me. Big deal! Now I get to hang out with my mates around the shops. If he had just asked me to take it off I would have.'

(!)

What is the purpose of a sanction?

● **to correct unacceptable behaviour**
● **to reinforce a teacher's authority**
● **to establish boundaries, school rules.**

Background

Historically, punitive sanctions often involved something physical – anything from a 'clip around the ear' to caning. In today's society such actions would be described as a physical assault and now seem almost barbaric, yet corporal punishment was banned in state schools in the UK only in 1986. There are those who still hanker for the 'good old days' and say 'it did us no harm'. But did it? The application of sanctions causes stress and distress to both teacher and student.

'Correction does much but encouragement does much more.'

(Goethe)

Physical punishment was part of school life until 1986 in the UK

Source: Mary Evans Picture Library/Alamy

As with corporal punishment, the psychology of sanctions is to effect control by creating an atmosphere of fear. A child learns 'the hard way' that if they transgress they will be punished. The technique is typically behaviourist. With the demise of corporal punishment, other punitive sanctions have come to the fore:

- lines
- detentions
- external suspensions
- loss of privileges.

These sanctions seem tame compared with corporal punishment and it is moot to question their effectiveness in maintaining order in the classroom.

(!)

Do you know the sanctions used in your school?

a) How effective are they in preventing errant behaviour (scale 1 to 10)?

b) How might they be improved?

If a teacher is going to resort to sanctions, it stands to reason that the sanction should act as a deterrent, otherwise it is valueless and may even prove to be counterproductive as sanctions are not conducive to building positive relationships. If a teacher threatens sanctions they must make sure:

- the sanction is enforceable (you cannot issue an after-school detention if children have to catch a school bus home in the evening)
- they are prepared to impose the sanction (children will soon twig whether a teacher 'means what they say' or is a 'soft touch')
- that the sanction is fair (the punishment fits the crime).

Task

Study the comments below.

'If you don't behave I will ban you from using the computer for a whole year.'

'If the person who threw the paper plane does not own up, the whole class will be kept behind.'

- Are they enforceable?
- Are they fair?
- How might they be changed to make them fair and enforceable?

(Answer: they are neither fair nor enforceable. Asking a child to log off for a short time (5–30 minutes) is enforceable. The paper aeroplane issue is a little more problematic. It may be easier to acknowledge the incident and warn against a repeat. The teacher can then keep a wary eye for another projectile. This should allow the teacher to narrow down where it came from. Then likely suspects can be targeted – being mindful that people are usually innocent until proven guilty.)

It would be naive to think that a teacher could get through the year without issuing a sanction, but an overreliance on sanctions in the classroom will lead to resentment as teacher–student relationships break down. If a teacher is too reliant on sanctions, the children may become:

- resentful of the teacher
- defensive and sullen when corrected
- uncooperative when asked to carry out tasks
- prone to mirror the teacher's strident approach.

If sanctions are used:

- they should be delivered immediately (within 24/48 hours, otherwise the child may forget why they are being sanctioned)
- the reason for the sanction should be explained to the child
- once completed the slate should be wiped clean.

Challenging children can collect sanctions like confetti, to the point where there are not enough hours in the school day to accommodate them. This stacking-up effect calls into question the effectiveness of sanctions, particularly with very challenging children. If a teacher issues a sanction, it is important that the sanction has a deterrent effect, therefore it must be onerous enough to reduce the risk of the child reoffending. There is no clear-cut strategy in respect of what will work and what will not, it is a case of trial and error – what works with one child may not work with another and what works in one school may have little effect in a different school. What is common to all is that if the sanction is ineffective it will not have the desired effect. Sanctions that are merely an inconvenience rarely work.

TOP TIP!

Give them useful/productive work to carry out within the time allocated.

Engage in restorative approaches.

Use some of the allotted time to discuss future behaviours.

Avoid:

- writing lines
- copying from a textbook
- sitting them in front of a computer playing games.

Many schools have tariffs, with each misdemeanour carrying a fixed penalty. The advantage of having a tariff is that the child knows exactly what will happen if they carry out a certain action, so everything is fair and equitable. The downside of tariffs is that not all misdemeanours are as cut and dried as they might appear to be.

(!)

Consider a child who uses foul language:

- directly at a teacher
- within earshot of the teacher but targeted at another child
- as a first offence when they have been severely provoked by another child.

Should they all receive the same sanction?

What words constitute 'foul' language?

a) List all the swear words children might use.

b) List them from most offensive to least offensive.

c) How do you decide which ones carry the heaviest sanction?

(Comment: it is perhaps more pertinent to challenge the intent rather than the content of an abusive word/statement. Children may hear 'foul' language at home and copy; sometimes they may not be aware that they are saying something that others find offensive. Such incidents can be tackled by challenging and educating. Where children are verbally abusive to peers and/or staff, it is the intent to cause hurt that is the issue and that needs to be tackled at a more serious level.)

In the criminal justice system a judge is able to work within a tariff range. Life can mean anything from 10 years to 30 years or more. A tariff range allows for flexibility and may also give the teacher some leeway in getting the child to 'put right' what they have done wrong.

TOP TIP!

(This requires the teacher to be confident and assertive.)

Give a child a sanction for a certain misdemeanour.

Tell them that the sanction will be reduced (be unspecific) if they achieve certain (be specific) targets between now and the end of the lesson.

This builds an element of choice in the child's mind and allows them to 'work off' their 'sanction', turning a negative situation into a positive. At the end of the lesson, if they have redeemed themselves they can be congratulated for turning things around.

(Be careful not to get embroiled in a debate with the child about what they have and have not achieved.)

If a child is given a fixed tariff and there is no flexibility, they may decide that they have nothing to lose and so will continue to disrupt. Establishing that there will be a sanction but that they can influence its severity by complying gives them an element of control (this can also be viewed as a type of restorative approach), but the control is skewed towards positive actions rather than further negative responses.

NB: It is important to note that the sanction actually delivered should act as a deterrent. It is also important to note that the teacher does not fall into the trap of getting drawn into tit-for-tat negotiations where the child wrests control from the teacher (e.g. 'I will do the work as long as you let me off the detention').

Trying to impose a sanction may result in an escalation of conflict as the child seeks to maintain control of a situation and so the teacher is tempted to raise the stakes.

Case study

'You have a 15-minute detention.'
'I'm not doing that.'
'Then you will get a 30-minute detention.'
'I'm still not doing it.'
'Make it an hour.'
'There's no way I'm doing an hour.'
'Then you will get 2 hours.'
'This is pathetic, a 2-hour detention for being 5 minutes late to a lesson.'

> 'Whipping and abuse are like laudanum. You have to double the dose as the sensibilities decline.'
>
> (*Harriet Beecher Stowe*, Uncle Tom's Cabin)

Where does the teacher go next? A formal suspension? Expulsion? The teacher is impelled to follow the agreed policies and procedures or else their authority will be undermined. Chances are that the child's refusal to comply is carried out in front of their peers so they are unlikely to want to lose face. It is the teacher who is made to look the fool by raising the stakes to a point where the sanction becomes unenforceable.

So how does the teacher stop the situation getting out of hand?

'You have a 15-minute detention. If you refuse to comply then the matter will be taken further.'
'How?' asked truculently.
'You will have to wait and see. It's your choice.'

The child has had the initiative taken from them. This gives the teacher and the child time to reflect and reduces conflict escalation. The argument is finished at least until the time comes to carry out the sanction. If they don't comply then make sure the next step is in place. This may require support from other, senior, staff.

Ultimately sanctions do not work. In the days of corporal punishment, there was always a hard core of children who wore their weals as a badge of honour. Many children who are externally suspended will happily just sit at home and play games all day. The disaffected child may even seek confrontation at school so that they are suspended, legitimising their absence from school. These sanctions turn out to be not much of a deterrent and so their effectiveness is compromised.

Many situations can be resolved by a child simply apologising for their misdemeanour, but getting a child to issue an apology and mean it is not as easy as it would first appear. For a child to apologise they must:

● meet with their victim face to face
● admit to those present that they were at fault
● recognise that they must take responsibility for their actions.

'Sorry seems to be the hardest word.'

(Elton John)

Giving an apology is one aspect of a process known as restorative action. Restorative action in a school environment is a process whereby a child is made accountable for their misdemeanour by trying to put right what they have done wrong. A bully may be sat down with his victim or an abusive child may be placed with the teacher they have sworn at. The essential prerequisite of restorative justice is that both parties agree to meet; there should be no coercion to get either side to comply. The fact that it is voluntary makes restorative justice all the more powerful in terms of effecting a positive outcome. Restorative action:

● is not sanction based
● is voluntary on the part of offender and victim.

Restorative action allows the victim to:

● play an active part in ensuring that justice has been done
● gain an understanding of why they were targeted
● question the offender
● explain to the offender how their actions have affected them
● receive an apology and/or reparation.

Restorative action allows the offender to:

● make amends for their wrong doing
● recognise that they are responsible for their actions (they cannot shift the blame)
● gain increased awareness of the effect of their actions on the victim
● have a chance to reflect on and/or modify their behaviour.

Restorative action can be carried out via a third party who coordinates the meeting. If either finds it impossible to come face to face, a third party can convey their comments, sentiments or feelings to the other.

TOP TIP!

Chairing a restorative action meeting:

a) Explain why the meeting is taking place (non-judgemental).

b) Find out what actually took place (facts from both sides, no arguments).

Ask the victim:

a) If they would like to say something about how they felt during/after the offence and how it has affected them.

b) If they would like to ask the offender any questions.

Ask the offender:

a) To explain why they did what they did.

b) How they think their action has affected the victim.

c) What they feel about how their action has affected the victim.

d) How they might put right what they have done wrong.

Ask the victim if they will accept the offender's offer of reparation.

'No sign up No change'

(Solution focused)

Students will behave only if they want to behave. Rewards and sanctions are the strategies teachers use to create the 'want'. Technically this would be described as creating the motivation for behaving. While sanctions and the threat of sanctions work for some, for others they have little impact. For some children sanctions are a way of life both at home and in school. A dysfunctional family background may mean that they are screamed and yelled at constantly, or physically hit, so giving them a school detention may not even register on their radar.

The most successful teachers are not reliant on sanctions, while the least effective teachers tend to rely heavily on them. It is possible to maintain control by being proactive (detailed planning to create an environment that is conducive to good behaviour) and this includes the effective use of rewards.

(!)

Do you prefer to be chastised every time you make an error or to be acknowledged every time you do something well? Children are no different. Recognising good behaviour, work that is well done, or even that a child has made an effort helps to create a positive working atmosphere.

Task

List the rewards that your school gives to the children.

Do all the children value them?

Carry out a PMI on the system. Suggest improvements to the rewards system.

Many schools have a graduated reward system. However, some children rarely get beyond the odd credit throughout a school year. It is sometimes the case that those who get most rewards are at both ends of the behavioural spectrum. The challenging child may be festooned with plaudits to the consternation of others who rarely get recognised.

'If you are naughty you get rewarded for being good, if you are always good you get nothing.'

(14-year-old girl)

Recognising and rewarding good behaviour at every occurrence is nigh on impossible and such a volume of rewards would, most likely, devalue the whole reward system. For many children a simple 'well done' is recognition enough, or perhaps a non-verbal sign such as a 'thumbs up' or a 'wink'. For children who receive little positive reinforcement in their lives, basic recognition can have a massive impact, especially if the action is sincere. Actions such as this and the tip below are crucial first steps for many children: they help build self-confidence.

TOP TIP!

Bullet points

- Every time a child gives a correct answer, say well done (or excellent or fantastic or brilliant).
- Every time a child gives a correct answer, also give them a bullet point.
- Every time a child gets a bullet point they log it at the back of their book.
- 10 bullet points (set your own threshold) mean they get a bigger reward.

This simple system rewards potentially everybody.

Giving bullet points is non-discriminatory.

It can be engineered so that the teacher can target any single child in the class.

Bullet points can be fast and furious, given during a quick-fire question/ answer session around the room.

Bullet points can be used to target key issues with a class (sitting quietly, hands up, etc.).

It is open to cheating, but it is good to trust the children to be honest (if in doubt get them to record the date).

It maintains a positive atmosphere in the classroom.

It gives them immediate positive feedback.

'Catch them being good.'

(Solution focused)

Rewards can also have a negative effect on behaviour. For example, an overindulgence of rewards can result in children:

- demanding a reward every time they do something good and reacting badly if there is no reward offered
- being dismissive of a reward if they do not feel its value matches their effort
- being unmotivated by the 'carrot' that is being proffered.

It is important that rewards have an intrinsic value to the children. If they are too difficult to access or if they are doled out too often they may lose that intrinsic value. (NB: Although the bullet point tip above appears to fit this criterion, it is the fact that it leads to a less frequent, larger award that helps it to maintain credibility.) What works for a child of a young age may not work for older children. It is essential, therefore, to get the balance right.

There is a temptation to use rewards as bribes and while this may help in the short term (to get you to the end of the lesson without any more disruption), it is unlikely to work as a long-term strategy. Rewards operate at their best when they have to be earneds; unlike sanctions it is moot to have tariffs so that children have targets to aim for and are rewarded when they achieve agreed benchmarks.

Challenging children may appear averse to receiving awards, fearing a loss of face among their peers or just not knowing how to 'deal' with positive feedback. So they may refuse a reward rather than have the embarrassment of being made a public spectacle, albeit for the right reasons. In this situation a non-verbal recognition or a quiet acknowledgement should suffice.

'I feel numb and sick when someone says well done.'

(13-year-old girl)

Celebrating success can manifest itself in many ways. Teachers may place exemplary work on the wall or the successful may be congratulated publicly, in class or in a school assembly. Often an element of competition is injected into the proceedings to further reinforce positive behaviours. This may be an inter-class or inter-house competition, with the winners being the group that accumulates the most points. This is exemplified by tally charts on a classroom notice board. In the desire to promote good behaviour a teacher may unwittingly provide a disincentive to those children who generally don't succeed at anything and with the challenging child reinforce stereotypes.

Name	1	2	3	4	5	6	7	8	Total
John	★	★	★	★	★	★	★	★	8
Ameera	★	★	★	★	★	★	★		7
José	★								1

Consider the child who scores the least on a tally chart. The motivated, the conscientious, the gregarious race ahead, leaving behind the introvert, the reluctant worker and the insecure. Their self-esteem, already low, is further undermined, proving statistically their worthlessness: the evidence is writ large on the wall.

(!)

- How might José be affected by the chart?
- How might José be helped to deal with his apparent lack of progress?

It would appear that José 'must try harder!'.

- But what if he is already trying his best?
- Perhaps he has special educational needs that are preventing his progress.
- Maybe he does not know what to do to make progress.
- It is important that the teacher is sensitive to situations like these and gives the child the necessary tools to help them make progress and to be able to compete with their peers.

(Answer: José may see himself as failing in comparison with other children in the class. To help raise his self-esteem the teacher might add some bias to boost José's standing to the chart, but this bias might be construed as unfair by others in the class. A subtle way to effect bias may be to award 'credits' for a wide range of achievements, not just academic ones.)

There are those who believe that competition is healthy and there are others who do not subscribe to competition in any form because they believe that to fail is damaging to a child's self-esteem.

For competition to be healthy it must compare like with like and/or ensure a level playing field (the same is true for school league tables!). If children are disadvantaged in any way and are then compared openly with their peers, their performance is going to be compromised. To get around this the principle of 'value added' is useful. This means looking at progress on an individual level and encouraging personal endeavour rather than competing openly with peers.

(!)

Value added

A child scores 2/10 when the rest get 7/10 or better.

- Is it fair to highlight the child's 'failure'?
- What if they are dyslexic and could not read the questions properly?
- What if the child scores 4/10 on the next test while the rest score more or less the same?

TOP TIP!

Emphasising the positive

A child scores 2/10 in a test.

'Well done, you got on the scoreboard. What are you going to aim for next?'

The child then gets 4/10.

'Well done, you got double the mark you got last time.'

The next time the child scores 3/10.

'Well done, you did better than the first time and you only dropped 1 point! What are you going to try to get in the next test?'

This is another example of using scaling to alter perceptions and facilitate motivation.

In conclusion

Teachers who are not confident in their teaching ability tend to hide behind sanctions, using them frequently in an attempt to maintain class control. Such an approach is doomed to failure as children at first resent the apparent intolerance on the part of the teacher and then realise that the teacher is 'lacking'. Once this point has been reached persistent conflict is likely to ensue as the children openly defy the teacher, despite the threat of sanctions. The teacher in turn becomes increasingly strident as their 'authority' is constantly challenged. They presume that the threat of sanctions will instil 'fear' into the child and so they will comply. This method of control has a name: bullying.

Should sanctions rely on a fear factor or should they (can they?) merely act as a regulator to temper excesses without recourse to scare tactics? Would they work if they were merely a consequence of poor choice? There are situations where a child will knowingly 'take what is coming to them' rather than conform. Once the sanction has been completed, the slate is wiped clean, but the child will show no remorse.

Teachers may feel they must choose between the carrot or the stick in order to keep 'unruly' children in check. In truth, there is a third way that is under the teacher's very nose and is often missed or at the very least undervalued. For many children achievement and the sense of satisfaction that it brings is often reward enough. Look at the face of a child who gets top marks in a test, or reads the first line of a page for the very first time. Do they need anything 'extra'? If children are rewarded with a little 'carrot' when they do well, they may come to expect a little something 'extra' every time they do well, and if it is not forthcoming their success becomes tinged with disappointment. Likewise, having to deal with failure is an important life skill and is acceptable as long as it does not undermine self-confidence. It can be the driving force to try harder next time. In a supportive classroom atmosphere where children are encouraged and enthused, there is likely to be little need to resort to any form of sanction.

Further reading

www.transformingconflict.org

www.teachernet.gov.uk

www.nationalstrategies.standards.dcsf.gov

Cowley, S. (2001) *Getting the Buggers to Behave*, Continuum Books.

Rogers, B. (1994) *The Language of Discipline*, Northcete House Publishers.

Part

2

Identifying and dealing with key social/emotional and cognitive aspects of inclusion

Chapter

9

Social and emotional aspects of behaviour

Case study

Mariella's story

'I feel like my mum's living her life through me. I can't be best friends with someone I've known since I moved because our mums fell out. I'm an ungrateful shit that doesn't want to be pushed and pulled into place. Nobody gives me a chance and every time I make up a different way of me dying a hero. I wake up most mornings wondering why I still exist, when my soul aches to be free. When I run away it feels like I'm free, like an angel. I can't do anything right and when I try to I do it the wrong way. My Gran's cancer was discovered on my birthday and I can't say anything about this because I'm the one who has to hold my family together.'

Case study continued

Why is she upset?

Source: Pearson Education Ltd/Melinda Podor

Background

If we have an upset in our private lives, as mature adults we have the capacity to control our feelings and carry on 'as normal' in our professional lives. We are able to separate our personal and public persona. Most children do not possess this ability. It is a skill that has to be learned. As adults we have the capability to understand our feelings and control our emotions and, if necessary, to articulate them to a third party. Children do not comprehend the link between feelings and emotions and, as a result, may express their angst in inappropriate ways such as temper tantrums, bullying or self-harming.

Many issues relating to challenging behaviour have their roots in social deprivation of one type or another. The problems manifest themselves as emotional issues due to basic needs not being met outside of school, and while as teachers we are not in a position to affect a child's private life, we can educate them to be able to come to terms with their feelings and deal with them in a manner that is not destructive to the rest of their life. As teachers we may (rightly) question where we are going to find time to 'teach' these skills in a curriculum that is already full to bursting and hidebound by one new initiative or another.

Developing social and emotional skills in children is not so much a case of doing as it is of being.

How we as teachers interact with the children and deal with their day-to-day issues is how we develop these skills.

Possible signs of social and/or emotional behavioural issues

Social and emotional issues affecting children tend to manifest themselves as either physical and/or emotional neglect. Whereas physical neglect is there for all to see, emotional neglect is not always so obvious. Signs of physical neglect may include:

- dirty or soiled clothing
- being malnourished
- being obese
- being underweight
- bruising and/or signs of physical abuse
- being hand shy (veering away from physical touch).

Signs of emotional neglect may include:

- oppositional behaviour
- being withdrawn
- attention seeking
- poor attendance
- being unhappy
- being hand shy (veering away from physical touch)
- being clingy.

Emotional aspects of behaviour are one part of a broader perspective relating to social issues. The whole picture has been summarised in Maslow's Hierarchy of Needs. Maslow's Hierarchy identifies the needs that have to be satisfied before a person can 'function fully'. Maslow calls this self-actualisation. It is presented as a hierarchy because a person cannot operate effectively at a higher level until the levels below have been satisfied.

At the base of the hierarchy are physiological needs. If a child is feeling ill they are unlikely to be able to concentrate in class, and they may become lethargic or tetchy. The teacher may send them to the medical room or even send them home. However, other basic physiological needs that have not been attended to may not be as easy

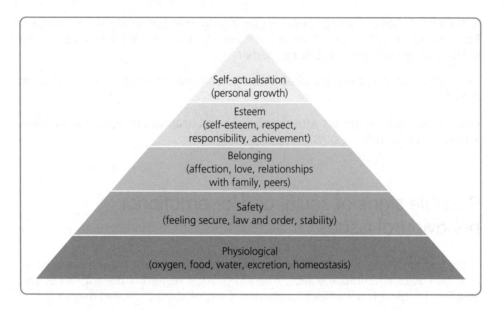

to identify. Maybe a child has been sent to school without having breakfast or they arrive in sub-zero temperatures without a coat and jumper. Until their basic physiological needs are satisfied their capacity to function in class is going to be compromised. This may lead to confrontation and conflict. The child may not (be able to) articulate what their needs are and may be locked into an approach where they have learned (through bitter experience) that shouting out or being aggressive is what is needed to get themselves noticed.

Task

Below are a number of common complaints that children utter.

a) What physiological needs are not being met?

b) Should the teacher take action in the classroom to accommodate each complaint? (And if so, how?)

- It's too bright by the window.
- I forgot to go to the toilet at break.
- I can't concentrate with all this noise.
- I've not had any breakfast.
- This room is too stuffy.
- I'm freezing, can I keep my coat on?
- I'm tired, I stayed up late to watch a DVD with my older brother.
- I'm really thirsty.

(Answer: all are as a result of physiological needs.)

Complaints like this are not always so clear cut, but they form the basis of excuses for not complying or are utilised as avoidance tactics to escape work being done in class. As a teacher we do not know for sure: denying them may exacerbate a needy situation and conceding may be playing into their hands. The clue lies in the frequency of the requests over time.

The structure of the school day, the buildings and the environment may also have a bearing on a child's basic physiological needs.

Task

Study the information in the chart.

This school has a five-period day with two half-hour breaks. The data shows the number of children sent out of class for poor behaviour over a 12-month period.

	Lesson 1	Lesson 2	Break	Lesson 3	Lesson 4	Break	Lesson 5
Number sent out	50	75		55	170		110

1) Account for the variation across the school day.
2) Compare the behaviour of the class(es) you teach across the school day. Is there a connection between their ability to concentrate and the time of day?
3) How might you adjust your teaching to take account of any variation?
4) Does the length of a lesson affect a child's basic physiological needs?
5) If a lesson is 1 hour long (or more), how might a teacher ensure that a class's basic physiological needs are attended to?

(Answer: 1) Tiredness, lack of correct nutrition, lack of water or oxygen. 3) Less sitting, more activity, vary the stimulus in your lesson, open the windows, have mini-beaks. 4) The ability of children to concentrate is dependent on age, ability, the work they are asked to undertake and homeostatic balance of the body. 5) Ensure proper hydration for each child, room is airy, room is at an even temperature.)

School management teams have a responsibility to ensure that the school environment does not compromise a child's physiological needs and teachers have a similar responsibility within the confines of their own classroom. How safe do you feel in your school? Is the school open plan with rolling fields or does it have a high perimeter fence and CCTV on every corridor? Do these make you feel secure?

(!)

How safe do you feel?

- at break times
- on the corridor at lesson changeover
- on your own after school.

How confident are you that the children you teach feel the same at these times? Are there any 'no-go' areas around the school?

School rules and regulations should be designed with basic health and safety in mind. Attendance to such needs is quite dry and boring but is essential if staff and children are to feel safe and secure within the school environment. Imagine trying to teach in a building where the roof is in danger of collapse or windows are broken. Likewise, in the classroom, it is the teacher's responsibility to make sure that basic health and safety is attended to, whether in a science laboratory or in a plain classroom. Chapter 4 looks at some of these issues relating to the classroom.

Feeling safe and secure is also about the people you interact with.

(!)

Do you know how safe your school is? How frequently do the following occur in your school/classroom?

- assaults
- fights
- arguments.

Are there children in your class who make you (and others) feel anxious? On a scale of 1 to 10, how confident are you that you are in control of the class you teach?

Strategies for dealing with social and emotional issues in the classroom

Classroom order does much to put children at ease and the more confidence that they have in the teacher, the safer they will feel. Bullying is dealt with in Chapter 14, but it is another aspect that influences the sense of security children feel within the school environment.

Something as simple as classroom routines helps engender a feeling of security. Even the most challenging children take comfort in accepted routines. For some children stepping outside of a routine or trying something 'new and exciting' can cause behaviour to deteriorate as anxieties rise. However, change is a fact of life and so exposing children to change should be part of a teacher's style, albeit a managed one.

Managing change

If a class does not cope with change easily, try to introduce changes sensitively. For example, rather than take up a whole lesson on a new activity use only half a lesson or the last few minutes of the lesson, making changes manageable. Priming the children beforehand may cause some anxieties, but throwing them in at the deep end could be much worse.

(!)

- List the routines you have in your classroom.
- Identify when you have done things 'out of the ordinary'.
- How did the children respond to the change?

Once a child's basic needs are attended to, it will be possible to look at a child's emotional issues.

'Emotions are the building blocks of relationships'

(e.i. intelligence central)

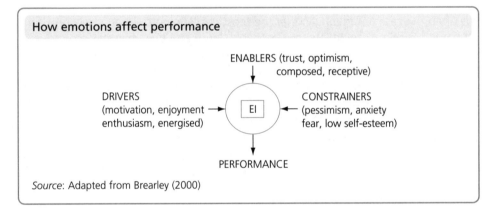

How emotions affect performance

ENABLERS (trust, optimism, composed, receptive)

DRIVERS (motivation, enjoyment enthusiasm, energised) → EI ← CONSTRAINERS (pessimism, anxiety fear, low self-esteem)

PERFORMANCE

Source: Adapted from Brearley (2000)

Task

Match the following needs to Maslow's Hierarchy:

- That girl does not like me.
- I'm too fat.
- I'm rubbish at Maths.
- My work is really scruffy.
- My mum and dad have just split up.
- My dog's died.

(Answer: safety, belonging, self-esteem; self-esteem; self-esteem; self-esteem; safety, belonging; belonging.)

Aspects such as self-esteem are dealt with in Chapter 12, however the next stage in Maslow's Hierarchy deals with 'belonging'.

Case study

Mike was an intelligent if somewhat laid-back boy. He was an aspiring athlete with lots of potential. He was expected to do well in his examinations. He sat in the room staring at his mock exam paper, doodling. The teacher went over to chivvy him but she had barely spoken a word when he shot out of his chair, tipping over the desk, strode towards another student, a girl, who was busy writing, and screamed and yelled expletives at her before storming out of the room. He stood outside in the cold air, hands clasped tight and flushed with anger, tears in his eyes.

The teacher managed to coax him into an adjacent room and put the exam paper in front of him. He stared blankly at the paper before putting his head in his hands and sobbing. His girlfriend had just dumped him.

- What needs had not been satisfied that prevented Mike from attempting the exam paper?
- How might the teacher resolve the situation?

It is often the case (infuriatingly) that the most challenging children rarely take time off school. They may arrive late (but probably don't) and they may stay around after school (detentions are a good way of making sure you don't have to go home straight away). Even though the child appears to be constantly in trouble they turn up, day after day, for more of the same. Such a scenario says a lot about what goes on in their private lives. The reason for this apparent anomaly is that the school provides the child with a sense of belonging.

The need to belong can manifest itself in many ways. It may be a child who 'clings' to a teacher or a child who misbehaves in class but is 'perfect' when it comes to playing for the school football or netball team. Challenging children find comfort in extra-curricular activities because they satisfy most of Maslow's Hierarchy, allowing them to function fully in that environment.

(!)

If a child is challenging in and around school but is picked for a school sports team, should they be allowed to take part?

Carry out a PMI on the issue.

(Comment: this debate centres on the argument that a child who has transgressed should not have the same privileges as those who have not and so they should not be allowed to take part until they modify their behaviour. However, the counter argument is that for many challenging children who have little that is positive in their lives, being part of something may lead to them tempering their behaviour eventually, and that if this positive in their life is removed they will become even more disaffected.)

Being overtly critical of a child in class does not help to foster a sense of belonging. Where a child feels that they are not accepted by a teacher it is likely to result in conflict. The child may disrupt from the outset knowing that they will be removed (and in some cases teachers engineer such scenarios knowing that the child will 'kick off' and will no longer be their responsibility).

'She is always picking on me.'

It is important to be even handed when dealing with children and to try to avoid bias. This is especially the case when working with challenging children. They are quick to apportion blame or use a number of techniques to deflect responsibility onto others.

'I am targeting your behaviour (be specific). You are so good at (XY and Z) but I cannot allow the poor behaviour to go unchallenged.'

Of course, children can also gain a sense of belonging by joining a gang. Gangs can be very intimidating and tend to draw like-minded individuals to them. There is empathy in a group, especially if it is formed out of adversity, that can satisfy each individual's need for acceptance. Once established, the sum can become greater than the parts. With peer support they are likely to test boundaries that, individually, they would not normally go near. If this occurs in a classroom situation, for example the creation of a 'sink group', they can be near impossible to teach. Being placed in the same group sends a message that they do not 'belong'.

A school that engenders a sense of belonging is less likely to suffer from petty vandalism. Vandalism is usually a reaction by individuals designed to exact 'revenge' because of the rejection they feel.

(!)

Do you know how much vandalism occurs in your school? Is it persistent or incidental? Does the level of vandalism reflect the welcoming nature of the school?

It is significant that children who exhibit challenging behaviour are often described as lacking social skills. Social skills, like other skills, can be taught. In Chapter 20, where cognitive ability is discussed, the concept of multi-intelligences is introduced. When dealing with situations that occur as a result of emotional problems it is useful to utilise the principles of 'emotional intelligence'. It is well documented that many people with high IQs are often lacking when it comes to building positive and lasting relationships.

Emotional intelligence is the ability to:

● recognise and manage your feelings (emotions)
● understand the feelings of others you interact with.

Emotionally intelligent people are subjected to the same hardships as everybody else but what makes them different is the way they react and deal with problems they face. Emotionally intelligent people are more resilient.

The first step in developing emotional intelligence is to get a child to recognise how thoughts, feelings and actions are connected.

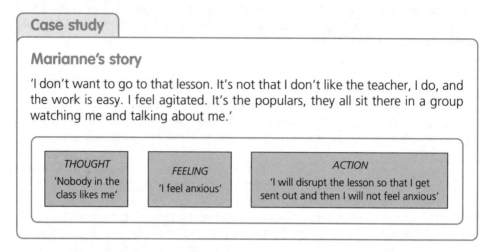

Case study

Marianne's story

'I don't want to go to that lesson. It's not that I don't like the teacher, I do, and the work is easy. I feel agitated. It's the populars, they all sit there in a group watching me and talking about me.'

THOUGHT	FEELING	ACTION
'Nobody in the class likes me'	'I feel anxious'	'I will disrupt the lesson so that I get sent out and then I will not feel anxious'

By disrupting the lesson the child antagonises the rest of the class (including the teacher) and so the thought that 'nobody likes me' is reinforced. This type of scenario is played out in the minds of many children, but especially those with emotional and behavioural issues.

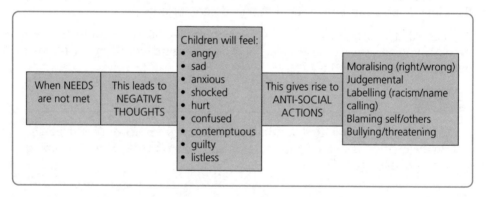

| When NEEDS are not met | This leads to NEGATIVE THOUGHTS | Children will feel:
• angry
• sad
• anxious
• shocked
• hurt
• confused
• contemptuous
• guilty
• listless | This gives rise to ANTI-SOCIAL ACTIONS | Moralising (right/wrong)
Judgemental
Labelling (racism/name calling)
Blaming self/others
Bullying/threatening |

To create a permanent change in a child's perception can be a long and exhausting business. The more 'damaged' a child is, the harder it will be to effect change. A child who has had a lifetime of not having their needs met is likely to have negative thoughts and emotions heavily ingrained. Much of the work needed will be beyond the remit of a class teacher, but teachers can (and should) play their part in bringing their concerns about a child to the 'experts' within the school and in creating an inclusive environment that not only endeavours to accommodate a child with emotional issues but also tries to educate them in dealing with their problems. To achieve this, the teacher must also be emotionally intelligent.

The emotionally intelligent child:

● takes responsibility for their feelings
● is resilient
● is confident

- is optimistic
- is self-aware
- shows self-discipline
- is courageous
- cooperates
- communicates
- has long-term life goals.

(!)

Use criteria from information from signs of neglect bullet points and from the emotionally unintelligent child and the emotionally intelligent child to study selected children whom you teach. How might you alter your approach to help them in class?

Try out the criteria on yourself. How do you fare?

'Emotions are like waves, we can't stop them coming but we choose which one to surf.'

(Jonatan Martensson, Swedish footballer)

TOP TIP!

1) GIVE THE CHILD A VOICE.

Ask them why they behave in the way they do.

2) LISTEN TO WHAT THEY SAY.

They are likely to express their negative thoughts.

Because:

'She's always picking on me.'

'I'm rubbish at Maths.'

'Nobody likes me.'

3) Treat this as a hypothesis to be studied by getting at the facts (done sympathetically).

BE EMPATHIC.

'List what the teacher has said to you (good and bad).'

'You can add up, take away and multiply.'

'List the people who have spoken to you in the class. What have they said?'

4) ENCOURAGE.

It may not be possible to get all children to leave school as balanced human beings who have achieved the pinnacle that is self-actualisation. All that can be hoped is that the teacher has at least placed them on the road where they are willing to listen and are beginning to recognise the process of action and reaction in terms of how it affects them and others around them. The affective domain of Bloom's Taxonomy is helpful in allowing a teacher to see where on the road each child is.

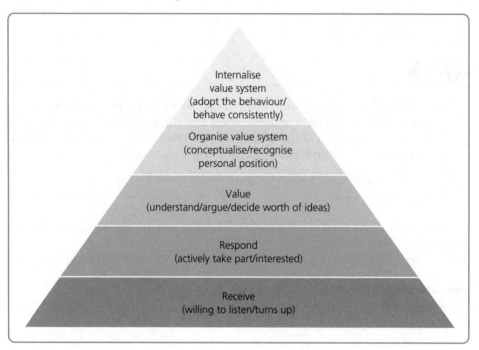

In conclusion

Case study

Maia's story

'I keep arguing with my stepdad. He tries to tell me what to do, but I tell him he's not my real dad and I don't have to listen to him. My mum stays out the way. She's never at home much anyway, she works shifts. My mum and dad split up a few years back, they're always slagging each other off. I don't like it so I don't say anything. I'd like to spend more time with my dad but I can't. He's always promising to take me places but he never does, he's such a twat. Mum kicked him out because he drinks a lot. He's moving away soon. He's got another girlfriend. I want to go with him but mum said if I go she'll never speak to me again.

I want to do well in school but sometimes I just can't concentrate, there are too many things going around in my head. I'm always angry and I get into trouble for having a go at them. I just wish somebody would listen to me.'

In society, children who exhibit behavioural issues as a result of social and emotional issues are the least 'sexy'. Many people may be sympathetic to their needs, but few people are prepared to take on board their problems because to do so demands a lot of the person in both time and energy. These children are often quite damaged, difficult to get through to and are high maintenance. Society seems to be able to accept a child's challenging behaviour if the root cause is cognitive (as with autism or dyslexia) or if it is physiological (as with a disability), but there seems to be a dearth of compassion if the cause is social or emotional. There is a stigma attached. If a classroom is to be truly inclusive it must find a way to accommodate these 'damaged' children. This does not mean that challenging behaviour should be condoned in any shape or form; it means that oppositional behaviour should be tackled with tact and with the needs of the child foremost. This may well mean the creation of an individual behaviour plan that all who come into contact with the child follow. Examples of such an approach may include an anger card to allow the child to leave the room if they feel themselves getting angry, a quiet place where the child can go to regain their composure, or possibly an understanding that a teacher does not raise their voice if the child transgresses but gives a signal that they are to leave the room.

Emotional intelligence often lags behind intellectual capability. As teachers we assume that bright, articulate children can express what they feel easily, but this is not always the case. Children often come to school carrying more baggage than the one on their back. Children learn to bury trauma. They do this for a number of reasons, but principally it is to avoid drawing attention to themselves. Others are not so adept at disguising their worries, but their cry for help may manifest itself in a temper tantrum, or bizarre behaviour such as hiding under a desk, or inappropriate noise designed to attract attention. The skilled teacher who understands each of the children in the class will learn to recognise these signals and act upon them unobtrusively so as not to draw too much attention to the child.

Further reading

www.sealconsultancy.com

www.businessballs.com

www.emotionalintelligencecentral.org

Blake, S., Bird, J. and Gerlach, L. (2007) *Promoting Emotional and Social Development in Schools*, Sage Publications.

Brearley, M. (2000) *Creative Learning Strategies*, Crown House Publishing.

Chapter
10

Attention seeking

Case study

Calinda's story

'When I am upset I suck my thumb. If I am really worried I will go and hide under a table. It's something I've always done since I was little. I do it to make problems go away. My dad knows where to find me and he will know something is wrong and he will speak nice to me. When I do these things at school some teachers shout at me and the children laugh. That makes me really angry so I shout and scream back at them until the teacher has to get rid of me. When I am at home alone, I feel a lot safer. I'd rather get suspended and stay at home than come to school.'

To gain a teacher's attention a child may put up their hand, ask politely or use welcoming body language such as a smile. Most children in a class will use these techniques only when they need help – perhaps they don't understand a question or they are not sure whether they are doing the work properly. Whatever their reasons, their demand on the teacher's time is much the same as the rest of the class and so the teacher can spread their time evenly among the children. Although not all of us enjoy being the centre of attention, we welcome acknowledgement of work well done. Problems occur if the teacher is not so forthcoming with their time, possibly trying to do other jobs while the children are working, in which case a backlog of requests builds up and the class become unsettled.

> **(!)**
>
> **How often do you carry out marking and other administration tasks while the class are working?**
>
> **How often do you move around the class and give them your attention?**
>
> **At what point does your preoccupation with another job impinge on your teaching commitment?**

Possible signs of attention-seeking behaviour

Negative attention seeking is a classic sign that all is not well with a child. Tactics used might include:

- repetitive tapping or drumming
- strange noises, guffaws and calling out
- constantly up and out of a seat
- swinging dangerously on a chair
- hiding under a desk
- feigning illness or injury.

Background

Some children, despite being given the same amount of attention as the others, seem to demand more. They will go to any lengths to satisfy this need and they don't care whether the attention they get is positive encouragement or negative admonishment. At home they may be starved of attention, possibly by parents who have to work long hours to make ends meet, or maybe they are neglected. Attention-seeking behaviour is not just a problem with children from socially deprived backgrounds – affluent families may lavish money on their offspring, expensive holidays, designer clothes, the latest computer games, but the one thing the children don't get is hugs, cuddles and quality time with their parents.

A baby cries to gain attention because it lacks the language skills to tell its parents that it is in distress. The next stage in that child's development may be a grunt or a continual pointing at an object that they want. Some children may continue in this vein if it gets them the results they desire. How many children can be seen in the local supermarket screaming the place down because they want a certain packet of sweets? Drawing negative attention gets them what they want, it is an important lesson that they learn, early on, and if not addressed it carries on into their teenage years and beyond. Having learned that this type of behaviour works, it is then just a case of finding the right button to press or to up the ante until the adult gives in and they get what they want.

As children grow up their ability to communicate usually develops so that they will tell a teacher that they are too cold or that the chair is uncomfortable or that the room is stuffy, but very few will say that they are unhappy, worried or frightened. They will endeavour to keep these feelings under wraps. Rather than explain what they are feeling, children may resort to obtuse attention-seeking displays to get an adult's attention. Why? Is it a cultural thing like the British 'stiff upper lip' or is it to avoid embarrassment? The reasons are many and sometimes complex and often beyond the scope of the classroom teacher. However, persistent attention seeking on the part of a child is a sure sign that there is an underlying issue. Depending on how ingrained the behaviour is, a teacher can wean them away from such habits as long as:

● they recognise the signs
● they have a strategy agreed with the child for dealing with the behaviour.

'The only way I ever feel like someone knows I exist is if I stand out.'

(Schoolgirl)

'If you've got a big mouth and you're controversial, you're going to get attention.'

(Simon Cowell)

Disruptive behaviour is often used to gain attention

Source: © Jenny Hart/Alamy

Attention seeking is not peculiar to emotional neglect. Other social and emotional issues such as

● drugs
● low self-esteem
● attachment

and cognitive impairments such as

● ADHD
● autism

may also bring with them attention-seeking traits.

Children who seek extra attention may be loud and silly, often to excess. They may even indulge in bizarre antics such as hiding under the desk or in a cupboard. Ultimately, they get the attention not only of the teacher but also the class, reinforcing their perception that such behaviour is acceptable because some children in the class laugh, nervously, as they make a fool of themselves.

> 'I've been (disrupting) like this since Year 4. It's what I do, everybody expects me to mess around and so I do.'
>
> *(Boy)*

In the classroom the attention-seeking child has a captive audience, misreading their peers' laughter at their embarrassing antics as genuine laughter. Such outbursts satisfy their need for recognition, acceptance and belonging.

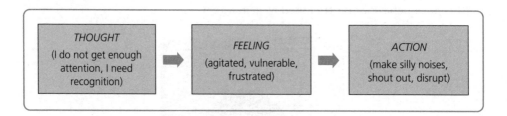

Strategies for dealing with attention seeking in the classroom

During question-and-answer sessions the attention-seeking child is likely to be keen to take part. Their hand will go up enthusiastically every time, whether they know the answer or not; they may even blurt out a reply in an attempt to be first and get the customary recognition. It then comes as a shock when the teacher ignores their outburst or, worse still, chastises them for not following protocols. They may perceive their efforts as being positive, taking part when others do not bother and maybe even getting the question correct.

TOP TIP!

Managing Q & A sessions

Try no hands up, the teacher chooses who will answer. Use a 10-second pause before choosing.

- This allows the teacher to spread the question evenly, differentiating the students based on the degree of difficulty of the question.
- It gives control of attention-seeking behaviour.
- It allows for 'think time'.

Some advice in respect of negative attention-seeking behaviour is to ignore it and to encourage positive behaviour. When negative attention-seeking behaviour stops and positive responses occur is when they get the attention they crave. While tactical ignoring is suitable for low-level disruption, it is likely that a serial offender will 'up the ante' in order to satisfy their needs. This may manifest itself as an increase in frequency of a particular display (tapping ruler more often) or it may be that the intensity increases (silly noise gets louder). The exhibition continues until the teacher is forced to stop what they are doing and intervene. Job done! What started as a low-key affair has now mushroomed into something a lot more serious and has taught them a new lesson: that persistence pays and that all they have to do if they are ignored is to increase the frequency or volume of the disruption to get the attention.

(!)

What is your tolerance threshold?

Place the attention-seeking tactics in order of least disruptive to most disruptive. Which of the following would you either tactically ignore or intervene against?

- shouting out answers
- making silly noises
- swinging on a chair
- interrupting conversations
- hitting another child
- calling another child names
- wandering around the classroom
- hiding under the desk
- dangerous behaviour with classroom equipment
- verbal bullying of the teacher.

(Comment: the key to dealing with attention seeking is to be aware of it but tactically ignore it, choosing an opportune moment to stop it. Pausing your teaching to admonish a child is giving them the type of attention they seek. At some stage it is likely the teacher will have to intervene as the interruptions will increase in frequency and/or volume.)

To reduce the impact an attention-seeking child has on a class it is moot to plan for that very eventuality. The teacher can be proactive by acknowledging the children as they arrive in the class, ensuring that they spend quality time with the attention seeker, making them feel welcome as they settle, possibly by asking about their interests (done sincerely).

If they shout out during question-and-answer sessions, acknowledge the child's enthusiasm but seek to modify their outbursts.

'Thanks for that but please don't shout out. Now listen carefully because I am going to ask you a question in a moment.'

Make sure you include them. This can be repeated a number of times. The attention-seeking child perceives that they are getting recognition and will show some patience. It is a careful balancing act keeping the attention-seeking child gainfully occupied and actively encouraging them without displaying to the rest that you are showing any bias.

TOP TIP!

Source: educational-psychologist.co.uk

(This may be useful where a child is taught in one class for a long period of time.)

- Tell the child that they will get a 'special time' each day.
- Each day tell them that the special time will start in 2 minutes.
- Tell them the special time will start now.
- During the special time do something reasonable with the child (watch a video, make cakes). Do not teach, watch the child and help only if they request it. Engage in praise every now and again – this shows that you are paying attention.
- Tell them that the special time will end in 2 minutes.
- Tell them that the special time will end now.

Make sure the balance between positive and negative attention is at least 3:1.

Catch them being good and praise them accordingly (as you would with all the others in the class!).

'Well done for not shouting out.'

'Do you know you have sat still for 5 minutes? Have a house point.'

'I value your contribution to the lesson, just try to remember to give others a chance.'

If the work carried out in class is captivating, it is likely that a child who resorts to attention-seeking activities will not disrupt (at least while the work is being carried out) as they will be so absorbed in what they are doing. It is by making work active rather than passive that attention-seeking behaviour will begin to diminish and the child learns self-control. Attention-seeking behaviour will manifest itself when work does not engage the child (perhaps it's too difficult, too easy, not interesting). To occupy one child to the exclusion of the rest is not good practice, but if the teacher produces work that excites all the children in the class that is another matter!

'A good teacher, like a good entertainer, first must hold his audience's attention, then he can teach his lesson.'

(John Henrik Clarke, American writer, 1915–1998)

The teacher must intervene if the attention-seeking child:

- prevents others from learning
- is a danger to the wellbeing of others in the class.

If the attention-seeking behaviour becomes too disruptive, the best option is to remove the child from the classroom. Avoid placing them in the corridor outside as they are likely to cause a furore to get attention even outside the room. They are best placed where their capacity to get attention is minimised – maybe a supervised room else-where (it is illegal to place a child in isolation and/or in a locked room, unsupervised).

(!)

Do you know of a place near your room or elsewhere in the school that might serve such a purpose?

In conclusion

Attention-seeking behaviour is perhaps the most prevalent of all behaviour traits witnessed in a classroom. Depending on its intensity, to ignore it may prove to be counterproductive, yet to acknowledge it reinforces the behaviour. The process of tactical intervention (Chapter 6) is perhaps the best way of approaching the problem as it manifests itself in the classroom. However, if a lesson is active and engaging, an 'attention-seeking' child is less likely to seek attention if they are gainfully occupied; it is only when they get bored or have a chance to dwell on personal issues that the challenging behaviour surfaces. (It may be the case that they are attention seeking at the start of the lesson, in which case tactical ignoring may be a good plan in order to get them started on the work at hand.) It is also the case that a positive working relationship between child and teacher will help modify a child's outbursts because the child is comfortable in the teacher's presence and reassured that they are being acknowledged or will be if required.

Further reading

www.specialed.about.com

www.slc.sevier.org

Glenn, A. (2005) *Behaviour in the Early Years*, Routledge.

Iwaniec, D. (2006) *The Emotionally Abused and Neglected Child*, Wiley-Blackwell.

Leaman, L. (2009) *Managing Very Challenging Behaviour*, Continuum International Publishing.

Anger management

Kylie's story

'I've got a rotten temper, my mum says I get it from her. What makes me really angry is when teachers shout at you. They treat you like dirt but when you shout back you get in trouble. It's not fair. Mrs Harrison gets so close to you, you can smell her stinky breath, and sometimes she spits at you. She doesn't like me and I don't like her. She once sent me out for no reason. I'd done nothing wrong but got blamed for shouting out. She tells me off for wearing my rings. I can't stand her, she just has to come near me and I start screaming and yelling at her to go away and leave me alone. Sometimes I feel sick inside when she comes towards me, I just know she is going to have a go at me for something, she's always picking on me.

After I've shouted at her I go to the girls' toilets to calm down. My hands shake. I often skip lessons until I feel right. Thinking about my gran helps to settle me down. She died a couple of years ago. I feel sorry that I've lost my temper but Mrs Harrison deserves it.'

Possible signs of anger

The signs that a child is getting stressed include:

- heart pounding
- flushing of skin
- tight chest
- butterflies in stomach
- muscles tense (fist clenching)
- feeling hot and sweaty (palms)
- head buzzing
- wanting to urinate
- fidgeting.

Background

What kinds of things make you angry? Perhaps somebody queue-jumping or an incompetent colleague? In a classroom environment, what actions by the children really get under your skin?

(!)

Score the following on a scale of 1 to 10 in respect of how angry they make you.

- Children talking across you when you are speaking.
- Scruffy written work.
- A child swearing at you.
- A child farting loudly.
- Children arriving late.
- Children arriving without equipment.
- A child eating gum.
- Being ignored by a child.
- A child spitting.

How would you react in each situation?

- Would you feel stressed?
- Confront them by giving them a piece of your mind?
- Assess the situation before dealing with it calmly?

The emotionally intelligent person would likely do the latter. If an intervention was made, the tone of voice, body language and vocabulary would be carefully choreographed without inflaming the situation. As emotionally intelligent adults we should be able to:

● recognise our emotions
● control them
● transfer these skills to most stressful situations that we are faced with.

In an inclusive classroom it is essential that a teacher not only keeps their emotions under control but also knows what type of things really make them hot under the collar. Some challenging children push the boundaries with the intention of finding out what makes a teacher angry. Once they have that information they will keep pressing the button to get a reaction. It's a subtle form of teacher baiting and if teacher and child end up in conflict, the child justifies their actions with the excuse that they were provoked by the teacher.

TOP TIP!

Avoid doing the hairdryer treatment.

Angry children may mirror your aggression

Source: © JPageRFphotos/Alamy

It is common for people to mirror another's behaviour. If you are calm, the other person tempers their anger; if you exhibit anger or aggression, it will be reciprocated.

Children are unlikely to possess the ability to recognise and control their behaviour, nor do they have the vocabulary to express what they are feeling and so they simply get angry. In their daily lives they step in and out of many groups, each with their own customs. These include home, out with friends, school and possibly other clubs and associations. What is acceptable at home may not be acceptable at school. How they interact with their peers may not be how they conduct themselves in a formal club. Boundaries and rules differ so that a child may have difficulty adapting. It may be the 'norm' at home and with peers to get angry when somebody annoys them, so when they are at school they do the same. In their world this is acceptable and maybe even expected; to stay calm may be seen as a sign of weakness. If a teacher is to endeavour to control a child who is prone to getting angry, they must seek to:

- recognise the signs
- know how to deal with the child if they lose their temper
- know how to deal with the child in the aftermath of the situation.

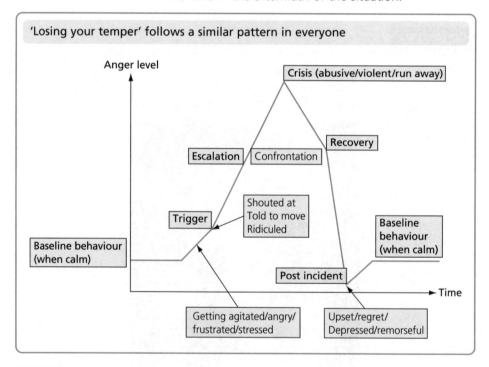

'Losing your temper' follows a similar pattern in everyone

Anger level

Crisis (abusive/violent/run away)

Recovery

Escalation | Confrontation

Shouted at
Told to move
Ridiculed

Trigger

Baseline
behaviour
(when calm)

Baseline behaviour
(when calm)

Post incident

Time

Getting agitated/angry/
frustrated/stressed

Upset/regret/
Depressed/remorseful

Task

Use the graph to identify the stages in Kylie's story.

(Answer: the mere presence of the teacher is the trigger for Kylie. She sees the teacher, expects trouble and gets it. Escalation occurs as the two argue and then Kylie reaches crisis when she tantrums and screams at the teacher. She runs away to help her recover, feeling nauseous as the adrenaline rush subsides.)

Usually children become slowly more stressed over time. Little things irk and irritate them. Perhaps the teacher has been 'nagging' them to get on with their work, another child in the class is making faces at them, they are finding the work difficult and they want to go to the toilet. Stresses are adding up until there is a final 'trigger' that sets them off.

Stress Bucket

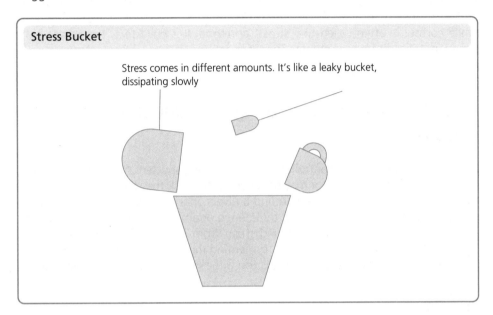

Stress comes in different amounts. It's like a leaky bucket, dissipating slowly

(!)

Make a list of things that make you stressed (try to get 20 or more). Categorise them as:

a) a spoonful of stress

b) a cupful of stress

c) a bucket full of stress.

Try this exercise with the children you teach.

For some children there is no gradual build-up of tension but rather a sudden trigger – possibly an insult – that sparks a temper tantrum. The next stage happens very quickly. Their stress levels escalate to the point of crisis, when they will lash out verbally or physically at anything and/or anyone standing in their way. At this point the child and those nearby are in some danger. It is likely that the child will run off. Eventually they will calm down, reflect and possibly be remorseful. They will probably remember what it was that tipped them over the edge, but they may not remember what they did or said while in crisis (this is not a lie but rather a case of 'redding out' as opposed to 'blacking out').

'Anger is what makes a clear mind seem clouded.'

(Kazi Shams)

Children may undergo therapy for their anger, but it is the teacher in the classroom who has to face the outburst and deal with it initially. Knowing that anger follows this pattern is helpful as a starting point because it allows the teacher to recognise where a child is and as a consequence put in strategies to reduce tensions.

From a physiological perspective what occurs as a child gets angry is that adrenaline and cortisol start to flow. Adrenaline is described as the 'fight or flight' hormone while cortisol is often called the 'stress' hormone. If a child feels threatened by a situation, these hormones prepare them for action.

Useful strategies for dealing with anger in the classroom

At this point anger can be controlled if these signs are spotted. A child may be asked to go and get some fresh air or may be taken off the task they are doing to do something more mundane. The idea is to find a diversionary task that will allow them to regain their composure and not feel threatened or anxious. If the teacher knows the reason for a child's anxiety, separating them from the stimulus is recommended. Perhaps other children in the class are tormenting them or they are getting frustrated because the work they have been set is too difficult and they feel embarrassed.

(!)

What techniques do you use to de-stress? Could they be adapted for use with children in the classroom?

'The greatest remedy for anger is delay.'

(Seneca, Roman philosopher, 1BC–85AD)

TOP TIP!

Do not ask someone who is getting angry to 'calm down'. It is likely to have the opposite effect!

The trigger for an angry outburst can be something quite innocuous. A child might be asked, politely, to move seats or hurry along and finish a question. There is a sudden rush of the hormones in the child's system and they reach crisis point in a second. At this point the part of the brain that controls emotions (neo-cortex) is put on hold as the amygdala takes control. This is a primitive part of the brain that deals only with protection and is activated under severe stress. The child's basic needs (possibly physical, safety or belonging) are not being met.

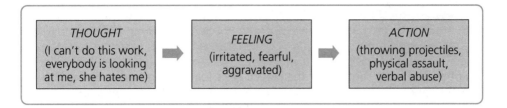

Once aroused, anger is very powerful and almost impossible to control. This is when the child will lash out. They are literally not thinking but just doing. They may subject the teacher to a tirade of abuse, they may throw things around or even hit people. Their action is designed to protect them from harm and is not a premeditated assault.

Often, when they have calmed down, they may not even recall what they have said or done, but everyone else will. If a child loses self-control, it is important that the teacher:

- stays calm (do not shout or yell – remember, they may mirror your behaviour)
- ensures the safety of the rest of the class
- ensures the safety of the angry child.

'Never argue with a man who's drunk!'

(Anon)

If the child seeks to leave the room, let them go – blocking their exit may be dangerous. A teacher can either follow them or send for assistance to make sure that they are safe. Most times when children run away, they do not actually go very far. They find a quiet place, hidden from the public eye, and start to calm down; they may even return. Once they have calmed down they may be tearful, exhausted, emotionally drained. Perhaps a school may utilise this process and create a place where 'angry children' can go in order to calm down.

(!)

Does your school have a quiet place where children can 'chill out' if they get angry?

Could you design a place in your classroom where an angry child might calm down (somewhere without an audience)?

Case study

Robert's story

Robert had been sent out of the French class for refusing to do any work. He had also refused to leave and so a senior had been called to get him.
'I've done nothing wrong. It's him, he just picks on me all the time, he hates me!'
'Just sit there and get on with your work,' he was told.
Robert did sit but he was not doing his work, he just doodled on a piece of paper.
'What are you drawing?'
'Suitcases, I've drawn 120 already.'
'Why are you doing that?' The teacher thought he was bonkers.
'It helps me calm down.'

When children are really stressed they are unable to concentrate. Trying to give them 'meaningful' work may prove counterproductive. It would be easier to give them something mundane to do, such as:

- a wordsearch
- colouring a picture
- doodling
- reading.

The first graph on page 128 does not show the true picture of how people act after a crisis because even though they have gone beyond the crisis point there is still a lot of cortisol in their system and if threatened once more they will tantrum again. It can take anything from an hour to the rest of the day before a child has settled down properly. Consider a child who had an angry outburst in the car just before they were dropped off at school.

Information

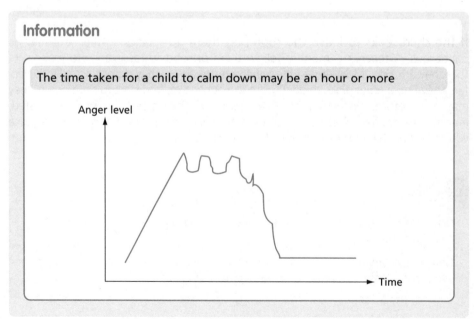

The time taken for a child to calm down may be an hour or more

(!)

What techniques do you use to calm down?

- **Relaxation techniques**
- **Slow breathing**
- **Counting down**
- **Stress doll**
- **Punch bag**
- **Exercise.**

How might you incorporate some of these in managing anger outbursts in the classroom?

It may seem odd, but dealing with angry outbursts in a class should not be sanctioned but dealt with sympathetically and treated properly by experts. At no time should a teacher shout or chastise the angry child. Such actions will appear as aggression and will serve only to antagonise and prolong the situation. It would also be useful to carry out a debrief once the student is calm to explore issues such as triggers and putting in place contingency plans to help.

Some children seem to be constantly 'in a mood'. The stereotypical 'Kevin' made famous by comedian Harry Enfield is a reality. They are fractious, on edge and the teacher feels as though they are 'walking on eggshells'. Every time they try to engage with the child they are growled at. If this hostility carries on over a period of time, there are likely to be underlying issues. These may be:

- physiological (illness, hormones, addiction, hunger)
- psychological (self-esteem, attachment, perfectionism)
- cognitive (autism, ADHD)
- social (neglect, family trauma).

'Holding on to anger is like grasping a hot coal with the intent of throwing it to someone else; you are the one who gets burned.'

(Siddahartha Buddha)

As Maslow's Hierarchy illustrates, the child will not be able to function effectively until their needs are met. Again, sanctioning a child in this frame of mind may just tip them over the edge. In a classroom situation it is wise not to address the issue with the child directly but rather to monitor it and refer or choose a time when the teacher can speak quietly to them in confidence so that they can express what they are feeling. Knowledge is power.

In conclusion

Anger can be such a destructive force. Many serious crimes occur as a result of people losing their temper. Trying to maintain our composure is a skill that many adults have difficulty mastering, so demanding that a child do so is asking a lot. There are those who are naturally calm and unflustered whatever the provocation and there are those who 'lose the plot' at the drop of a hat. Knowing which students have anger issues is crucial to maintaining a healthy working atmosphere in class, as is recognising the signs when they are beginning to lose self-control. Of equal importance is the way in which the teacher interacts with the children. Teachers who lack empathy are most likely to be on the end of a temper tantrum. Children tend to be sanctioned for what they say and do when they lose their self-control, but if they are not 'in control' should they be sanctioned at all? In an inclusive school classroom there should be contingency plans for anger outbursts and education to help children build up their resilience to tackle their anger-management problems. If the frequency and terror of the attacks are too much to bear, a child may require a period of time away from the mainstream classroom while they undergo therapy and treatment. In a teaching environment there is the health and safety of others to consider.

A few children with anger issues tend be 'blowers'. For much of the time they are calm, friendly and approachable, but on occasion their temper explodes in a volcano of violence that can be shocking. These children are hardest to deal with. They disguise their angst until it is too late. Cruel as it may seem, they may also need to be 'helped' away from the mainstream environment if their angry attacks threaten the safety of others.

Further reading

www.educational-psychologist.co.uk

Alsop, P. and McCaffrey, T. (1993) *How to Cope with Childhood Stress*, Longman.

Ledbeater, J. (1999) *Applying Psychology in the Classroom*, David Fulton Publishers.

Traxson, D. (1999) *Destressing Children in the Classroom (Applying Psychology in the Classroom)*, David Fulton Publishers.

Chapter 12

Self-esteem

Case study

Silvia's story

'Miss Price says that she knows me but she doesn't and I don't want her to know me either. She doesn't know that my dog died in February this year, the day after my Gran's birthday. My mum and Rhiannon are the only two people who remember my birthday. I put three foundations on every morning so that I can mask my feelings.

I hate swimming coz I'm too fat to fit in my size eight jeans. Everybody's just trying to label me with ADHD or something, it's so embarrassing. Everyone thinks "she's just being Silvia", but I don't know what Silvia is or even who I am or what I am doing here. Do you know how hard that is?'

Case study continued

Leave me alone

Source: © Jenny Matthews/Alamy

Self-esteem is the value we place on ourselves. It is how we perceive ourselves against others. It is not the same as self-confidence, which is more about what we think about our abilities to do particular tasks, although the two are inter-related. For example, a person may have high self-esteem but may not have the self-confidence to get up and speak in public; conversely, a person may have low self-esteem but is confident enough to get up and speak in front of a large audience (many performers fall into this category).

'I am afraid to show you who I really am, because if I show you who I really am, you might not like it and that's all I got.'

(Sabrina Ward Harrison, Canadian artist, 1975–)

The stereotypical image of a child with low self-esteem is one who is shy, withdrawn and sits in a corner cowering, speaking only when spoken to. Any child exhibiting such behaviour is likely to have low self-esteem, but low self-esteem also manifests itself in other ways. Many children mask their self-esteem issues by using disruption as a tactic.

Possible signs of low self-esteem

- Social withdrawal.
- Refusing to work (can't do, won't do) or take part.
- Anxiety.
- Lack of social skills.
- Egotistical behaviour (emphasis on I, me, mine).
- Lack of social conformity.
- Eating disorders.
- Self-harming.
- Emphasising the negative.
- Reluctance to take on challenges or do anything in public.
- Worried about what others think.

'Low self-esteem is like driving through life with your hand brake on.'

(Maxwell Maltz, creator of Psycho-Cybernetics, 1899–1975)

Background

> **Task**
>
> ### Rosenberg's Self-Esteem Scale
>
> | | Strongly agree | Agree | Disagree | Strongly disagree |
> |---|---|---|---|---|
> | On the whole I am satisfied with myself | | | | |
> | * At times I think that I am no good at all | | | | |
> | I feel that I have a number of good qualities | | | | |
> | I am able to do things as well as most other people | | | | |
> | *I feel I do not have much to be proud of | | | | |
> | * I certainly feel useless at times | | | | |
> | I feel that I am a person of worth, at least the equal of others | | | | |
> | * I wish I could have more respect for myself | | | | |
> | * All in all, I am inclined to feel that I am a failure | | | | |
> | I take a positive attitude towards myself | | | | |
>
> Strongly agree score 3, Agree score 2, Disagree score 1, Strongly disagree score 0
>
> Those with an asterisk score the opposite way
>
> Try out the Self-Esteem Scale on yourself and others you think may have self-esteem issues

Maslow's Hierarchy shows that high self-esteem is crucial if a child is going to be able to function fully in their everyday life. However, there are situations where high self-esteem, especially a fragile one, can be harmful. It was once thought that bullies disguised their low self-esteem through their violent and aggressive actions. It is now thought that bullies (and criminals) often have an inflated opinion of themselves, giving rise to exaggerated tendencies in order to defend their self-worth (self-promotion, exaggerated stories, etc.). This unhealthy high self-esteem gives rise to violent outbursts (such as blaming others for their own mistakes, verbal and physical attacks) as they seek to compensate for their self-doubt. A healthy high esteem gives a child the courage (confidence) to try new challenges and make the right choices even in difficult circumstances.

The indication that a child has low self-esteem rather than just lacking confidence is in the range of situations where they are reluctant to participate. A child may not bring their PE kit but they may be adept at playing the guitar. A child with low self-esteem will rarely display confidence in any activity and this will be apparent over a long period of time.

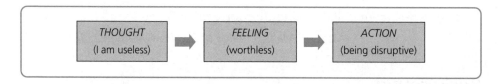

There is a perception that children with low self-esteem are unsure of themselves; in fact, the opposite is true. They are certain of their own lack of self-worth. A child low in confidence can be 'chivvied' into taking part; this is less likely if a child has low self-esteem. A child low on confidence will gain encouragement if they take part and if they are successful. A child with low self-esteem will put any initial success down to 'luck' or that 'somebody else did most of the work'.

Any fleeting success will not alter their perception that they are inadequate. If the teacher seeks to be positive by lavishing praise on them, 'fantastic', 'excellent', this can have the opposite effect of what it is intended to do as it casts doubt on the comfort a child with low self-esteem takes from the conviction that they are useless. (This is why an abused child stays in the home and goes back for more because their abuser empathises with their perception of themselves as being 'no good').

A child with low self-esteem may come from a background that includes:

- parents with a low self-esteem
- an environment where they are not valued as a person
- abuse (home or peers) involving sex and/or violence
- an environment where their emotional needs are not being met
- a death in the family
- being a looked-after child.

These environments reinforce the child's perceptions that they are just an 'object' and that they are of little intrinsic 'value'. Bearing this in mind, how do you think the statements following the case study made in the classroom might affect a child with low self-esteem?

Case study

Tom's story

'The teacher doesn't like me. He always picks on me. I can't do Maths. I don't understand any of it so I just sit there and chat with my mates. If the teacher has a go at me I argue with him. He can't touch me, he can't make me do the work. I don't care if he sends me out. Sometimes I disrupt the class so that he does send me out, then I don't have to do the work.'

Task

Consider the effect of the following comments:

'You are good for nothing!'

'You could do better.'

'You are useless!'

'You are a waste of space!'

'You will never amount to much.'

How might a teacher put across their concerns without resorting to comments like these?

(Answer: each of the above statements focuses on what a child cannot do. The comments are also personal. The intent of such comments is to shame a child into performing better. However, comments like these tend to have the opposite effect, possibly reducing a child's self-esteem further to the point at which they cannot function. For a child with low self-esteem, they reinforce what the child already believes: that they are worthless. It is better to acknowledge progress made and then build on that. For example, 'You have tried really hard, well done. Now think about doing x or y.')

We all have to deal with criticism, but for a child with low self-esteem harsh words can be devastating, especially if this is all they get outside of school. If a child's work or behaviour is not what it should be:

- criticise only the behaviour, not the child
- sandwich any criticism between some positive comments (two stars and a wish)
- be calm and reassuring when delivering the comments that have to be made
- if a criticism has to be made, think about saying it in private (not in front of the class).

Dealing with low self-esteem issues in the classroom

It is not beyond the bounds of possibility that a child may receive little or no encouragement in their home life and is struggling academically at school. They may be in all the bottom sets or are in need of specialist support to deal with literacy or numeracy problems. They may have issues with their weight or have hygiene problems that make them the focus of attention by others in the class. Any combination of these is likely to reinforce low self-esteem.

Taking a child away from the 'norm' can help – maybe a day trip or an outing or new and interesting activities where all the children can 'enjoy' themselves and express themselves without the need for self-reflection. In the classroom, recreational activities that do not involve competition or team games (to avoid the possibility of rejection, unless sensitively managed) will also help the child 'forget' themselves.

> **TIP**
>
> Games like Heads down thumbs up are non-competitive and fun.

Non-competitive activities include:

- craftwork, art, design, etc.
- skipping
- play.

Children with low self-esteem need prolonged nurture and concrete proof that they are making progress. Persistent failure to succeed reinforces deep-seated perceptions. A star chart on the form notice board will be of use only if they are towards the

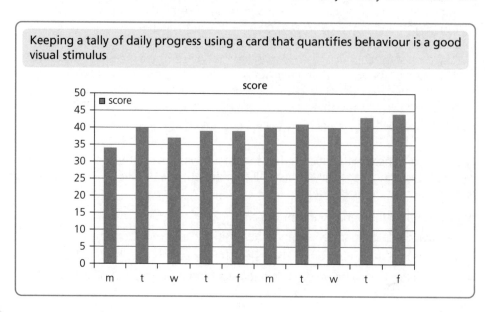

Keeping a tally of daily progress using a card that quantifies behaviour is a good visual stimulus

top – anything lower will prove counterproductive. If a child is on a behaviour card, tally the daily totals and show them what progress is being made. Making the evidence quantitative is a way of proving unequivocally that they are getting better, which improves confidence and starts to raise self-esteem. If progress can be sustained in a variety of aspects of the child's school life, they will begin to change their perceptions of themselves. However, such progress is likely to be fragile at best and it can take only one unforgiving teacher to undo all the progress that has been made.

'Nothing builds self-esteem and self-confidence like accomplishment.'

(Thomas Carlyle, Scottish writer and historian)

Creating a 'can do' culture based around differentiation (make sure the steps from one level to another are not so big that children cannot progress) and scaling is something a teacher can put in place in order to try to help raise the self-esteem of children in the class. If this is done by everybody then a child with low self-esteem will not feel exposed.

TOP TIP!

Get the child to:

- list 10 good things about themselves
- then see if they can get another 10
- follow this with another 10.

This type of scaling will start to raise their self-esteem. Refer to it when they are feeling negative (remember the 10, the 20, etc.).

Also:

- get them to keep a log of things they did well at the end of the day. This will build up over time and provide evidence of having done well.

In conclusion

Self-esteem is more deep-rooted than self-confidence. Low self-esteem usually develops over time and can become entrenched in a person's psyche. Continuous failure to live up to expectations (personal or other people's) deepens a child's feeling of low self-worth, so it is imperative that teachers create a culture in the classroom where children see themselves progressing. This helps to raise self-esteem and build self-confidence. Any criticism should be constructive and depersonalised.

'The problem is the problem, not the child.'

(Solution focused)

It is possible that a child with low self-esteem will carry the burden with them for their whole life. All a class teacher can reasonably be expected to do to counter the concern is to endeavour to avoid stereotyping the child in terms of the child's self-perception. This means not openly criticising children, especially in front of the whole class. This is particularly the case when dealing with children with social and emotional behavioural issues. They are frequently in trouble and are used to being made an example of, reinforcing their view that they 'do not fit' into a school environment. The more that they are sanctioned, the more they realise that they are unwanted. This leads to disaffection, truancy, further disruption ('well if they don't want me then I'm not going to try and behave, am I?'). They may start to target the school with acts of vandalism, bullying and such. Driven so low, there is little chance of redressing the problem and so the child is likely to be permanently excluded. It is a path trodden by many SEBD (social and emotional behaviour disorders) children. Beyond school it may lead to anti-social behaviour and eventually crime. Trying to prevent the slide is no mean feat – it takes persistence, perseverance and much tolerance on the part of the teacher and the school. Few are capable of such a feat.

Further reading

www.bbc.co.uk

www.webmd.com

www.self-confidence.co.uk

Deci, E. and Ryan, R. (1985) *Intrinsic Motivation and Self-determination in Human Behaviour*, Plenum Press.

Shunk, D., Pintrich, P. and Meece, M. (2007) *Motivation in Education*, Prentice Hall.

Chapter
13

Attachment

Case study

Charlotte's story

'I don't like change because it is always for the worse. My dad left because of me and I always make the wrong decisions. Everyone I tell things to moves away and the only place I felt safe was in my old house. Everything I ever get attached to gets taken away. I don't have many friends as they will judge me and it's easier to cope on my own. I get migraines coz I stay up most nights cuddling my teddy. I prefer the company of younger kids because they agree.

I did what I did [threw the book at the teacher] because she was shouting at me for ripping up my group's work. They're all stupid! They said it was a level seven when it was only a level three. What does it matter? It was rubbish anyway. I prefer to work on my own but she (the teacher) won't let me. If we do group work I've got to be in charge or else I won't take part. I like being in charge. So what if I did take Jessica's pen, it's a pen. I know it was her Grandad's, she told me. I gave her it back, didn't I?'

As we go through life we make many attachments to both animate and inanimate things. As a child we may have had a favourite soft toy or a pet that we still remember with fondness. As adults we perhaps have had attachments to friends, family and even the house or area we have lived in. All these attachments have one thing in common: an emotional tie that has been severed, leaving us with a sense of loss. For some, that loss leaves a void that has never healed and they carry the pain throughout their daily lives. For others, the loss develops into something much more pernicious, influencing emotions, feelings and ultimately relationships with everyone they meet.

> 'Some of us think holding on makes us strong, but sometimes it is letting go.'
>
> *(Hermann Hesse)*

Nobody loves me

Source: Daniel Atkin/Alamy

Attachment disorders are characterised by a child's inability to form lasting relationships. This could manifest itself in terms of indifference and lack of remorse and/or in violence and abuse. The main issue with attachment disorders is one of safety, which spills over into the areas of belonging and self-esteem in Maslow's Hierarchy.

Children with attachment disorders remain on the periphery of social groups because this is where they feel safest. They have erected a barrier to protect themselves from being emotionally hurt, which means they neither give nor accept love and affection. Their world is one where they must be in control so that they can feel

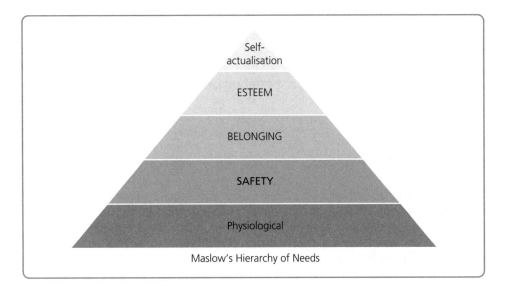

Maslow's Hierarchy of Needs

secure. If a class has a child who is extremely disruptive, it is possible that the child will have attachment issues. Children with attachment problems can be extremely demanding, involving many hours of a teacher's time, outside agencies and a lot of stress along the way.

Possible signs of attachment issues

Children with attachment disorders can exhibit a range of behaviours in the classroom.

- They have difficulty making lasting friendships. They will make and break friendships with alarming frequency, sometimes allying themselves to others of a similar ilk or joining a 'gang' to satisfy their need for belonging.
- They can chatter incessantly, to the point of rudeness, cutting across or ignoring requests to be quiet so that they remain in control.
- When they transgress they may show no remorse or an indifference to any harm they have caused, characterised by the 'I don't care!' statement. They may deny that they have done anything wrong.
- Superficially they may be charming, but they may flinch or jump away from physical contact. 'Get off!' 'Leave me alone!'
- They can be cruel and hurtful, either by direct physical and verbal abuse or by using more subtle methods such as theft or spreading malicious rumours. What separates them from others is their lack of remorse when called to account.
- They have a desire to be in control of every situation, either by persistently arguing and being defiant or just being stubbornly disobedient, thus putting themselves rather than the teacher in charge of the situation. If they surrender control, this will leave them exposed and so they feel threatened.
- They are likely to have low emotional intelligence and will be below their peers in terms of play and social interaction. They may gravitate towards younger children in the school or others who possess poor social skills.

Attachment disorders can manifest themselves in a number of ways. The most challenging children are those who exhibit oppositional behaviour. They are constantly angry and aggressive and may even be violent. The anxious type are clingy and insecure, but another type use avoidance tactics, often appearing agreeable and compliant and trying to please, but their efforts are not genuine and they are soon exposed.

Background

Attachment disorders usually have their source somewhere between birth and the first three years of life. This is the period when the child bonds with its mother, allowing it to feel empathy, love and trust. If the bond is broken, emotional trauma may ensue and affect the child for the rest of its life. Reasons for severance of the maternal bond can be many:

● postnatal depression
● unwanted pregnancy
● abuse or neglect
● illness of mother
● frequent change of day carer or unsatisfactory day care
● fostering/change of parents.

(!)

Consider the pros and cons of placing a child in a nursery before it reaches its third birthday. How can parents compensate for the need for day care?

(Comment: this could be quite a contentious subject, bearing in mind the rights of both mother and father to go out to work. The government has set aside money to fund nursery places. However, there is a cost to having both parents at work and this comes in terms of a possibility that a child may develop attachment problems if the parents do not work equally as hard at building an emotional bond with their offspring. They may be too stressed in the morning to give their children quality time and/or too tired in the evening to spend quality time with them. On the flip side, a child who is encouraged to mix with other children will build better social and communication skills.)

Issues with attachment can occur later in a child's development. Perhaps their parents separate and get divorced, possibly leaving them unable to get in touch with one parent or the other. A death of a loved one, not necessarily a parent, can initiate attachment problems, as can moving house too often, leaving a child without a sense of belonging.

'Dysfunction sets in when you seek yourself in it and mistake it for who you are.'

(Eckhart Tolle, Writer, 1948–)

Case study

Jaryd's story

'I hate my dad, he left us years ago. When he went he smashed everything up and he hit me. I think about it a lot, often on my way to school. I still see him sometimes, he scares me. He says he will meet me, then never turns up. He gives me things but I don't want his money, I just want him to spend time with me on our own. My favourite moment is when he taught me to ride, properly, without those stabiliser things.

If I woke up tomorrow and everything was different I would be happy.'

Dealing with attachment issues in the classroom

Because a child experiencing attachment problems has trouble forming trusting relationships they can present a particular problem in a classroom environment where social interactions are vital to the wellbeing of all the class. A smaller group unit will appear a lot less threatening, but even then the child may not want to 'fit in', seeking to disrupt and make others as miserable as they feel. There is no doubt that the teacher will require a lot of patience and tolerance as the child may prove very testing.

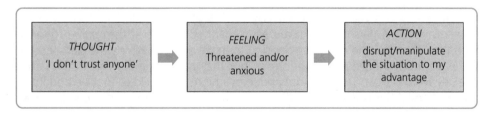

TOP TIP!

Include the child in as many aspects of their learning as possible (critical skills, A4L). This will help to satisfy their need for control yet still include them in the lesson.

- Deal with any transgressions calmly and assertively (aggression is likely to be viewed as threatening and the child may choose to disrupt in order re-establish control). Showing that the teacher can control without recourse to aggression is important.

- Set clear boundaries that are enforceable ('Please sit still while I give instructions' rather than try to keep them quiet all lesson).
- Be consistent in maintaining boundaries (and routines) as this provides the child with structure, which in turn gives them a sense of security.
- Set necessary consequences and apply firmly but fairly (sit in the naughty corner for 5 minutes).
- Once a sanction has been completed, accept the child back without rancour and re-establish empathy (smile, reassure, welcome, be friendly).

Task

Think of applications of the 'naughty step' technique that could find a use in:

- primary classrooms
- secondary classrooms.

(Answer: the concept of the 'naughty step' is to give a child a place to go that becomes synonymous with having transgressed. It takes them away from the situation and allows them time to reflect on what they have done wrong, as well as giving them time and a quiet space to compose themselves. It is also a way of showing an errant child who is in control. In school this could be a lone desk to one side of the class, possibly near to the teacher, or possibly a desk adjacent to the class door, indicating that the next step is to be sent out of class. A teacher may have the opportunity to use room dividers to section off a small area for such a purpose. When the child is allowed to return, they do so without any comment and start afresh.)

Attachment issues can be repaired over time but only when the child is either reunited with the person they have been separated from or if they come to terms with their situation and make the decision to move on. It is unlikely the class teacher will have much influence on the former, but they can play a key role in the latter. The key word is trust. This will not happen overnight. The child cannot be bought or tempted and if this is tried they will seek to manipulate it to their advantage in order to maintain control.

'Trust is like a vase . . . once it is broken, though you can fix it, the vase will never be the same again.'

(Anon)

Trust is best achieved on a basis of respect, even-handedness and knowledge that the teacher actually cares. However, be mindful not to be a pushover because the child is likely to test the teacher at each and every juncture, pushing stress levels to the maximum. Trust will develop over time when the child feels safe and secure in the teacher's company; in fact, they may come to rely on one teacher alone (which should be avoided if possible). Focusing on achievement both in and out of the classroom will build confidence and raise self-esteem; measuring this quantitatively is useful.

Children with attachment disorders often lack a sense of humour, so having activities that are fun and enjoyable will help to break down barriers. They may refuse to take an active part, but even watching from the sidelines helps to draw them in as long as they are included.

How often do you use 'fun' activities in your lesson? Think of a range of activities that you might use to bring an aspect of laughter into the classroom.

In conclusion

Attachment issues are behind many challenging situations in class, from creating low self-esteem, to anger problems to bullying. A solution-focused approach may be the best option because children with attachment issues are rooted in the past and are desperate for love, affection and recognition. A bond of trust has been broken, traumatically, and until it has been repaired or the child is able to move on, problems (severe problems) are likely to persist. As a teacher in the class the issue must be acknowledged because to understand the hurt a child feels is to share the burden and that in itself can bring some form of closure. But the child must be told:

'We cannot change the past but we can alter the future.'

If a child can start to rebuild their life and if they are really committed to moving on then they have a chance. However, many children with attachment issues may want to change but lack the support or the skills to do so. An emotionally intelligent classroom that encourages a child to progress and to achieve will go a long way in addressing this most traumatic of disorders. So many children get swallowed up by insidious attachment issues through no fault of their own and the scars can remain with them for a long time. It is issues like these that make the job of teaching so frustrating.

Further reading

www.attachmentdisorder.net

www.attachmenttherapy.com

Fonagy, P. (2001) *Attachment Theory and Psychoanalysis*, Kamac Books.

Holmes, J. (1993) *John Bowlby and Attachment Theory*, Routledge.

Chapter 14

Bullying

Case study

Gareth's story

'All we did was trip him up, we were only having a laugh. So what if he is different? He's a retard. Sorry? Why should I be sorry? Once people never noticed me and I was bullied but now I get respect. He should toughen up like I did. When I come into a room people look up to me, even some of the teachers are frightened of me. He tried to make me look stupid so I did him over, it was funny. I'm a winner he's a loser, he has to be put in his place. Yes I am proud of myself, I've got lots of mates, it's more than he's got. Anyway it's not as if he got hurt, you heard him say that he was all right.'

It is natural when a group of people work together that they will align themselves in some sort of pecking order. There will always be an alpha male or female wanting to take control and organise others in the group. It is when someone uses coercion to get others in the group to do what they want them to do that bullying begins. Bullying is the persistent physical, mental and/or emotional abuse over a period of time by one or more people towards another person.

In a classroom environment bullying can take on a number of different guises. It may be overt, possibly taking the form of physical assaults, or it can be more subversive, utilising techniques such as spreading rumours or intimidation.

Examples of bullying that may occur in the classroom include:

● verbal abuse (name calling, poking fun)
● physical abuse (hitting, slapping, punching, nipping, tripping)
● racial abuse
● sexual abuse (including homophobia)
● cyber bullying (using text messaging, internet, social networking sites)
● pressure bullying (forcing others to do something they do not want to do)
● peer group exclusion (getting others to refuse to speak to one child)
● serial bullying (moving from one target to another)
● secondary bullying (others in a class taking their lead from a principal bully).

The capacity for bullying is endless but the outcome is always the same: the victim is made to feel miserable and frightened.

How can a teacher recognise the signs that bullying is taking place?

(!)

Do you know for certain if there is any bullying taking place in your classroom? If so, what strategies have you put in place to:

a) Stop it?

b) Prevent it from occurring again?

If not, how can you be sure?

Background

Bullying affects the areas of safety, belonging and self-esteem within Maslow's Hierarchy. A child who is being bullied will feel threatened and anxious.

Case study

Jeannie's story

'They keep going on about how small I am, they call me an oompa loempa. They always poke me and yesterday they drew pictures on my arm. One said when I grow up I will die alone. He keeps staring at me and it makes me feel very uncomfortable. I want him to move out of our class, he doesn't let me learn. I feel scared to enter our classes. Some of the classes I like but can't enjoy because of them. The girls are nasty to me. They randomly ring me and get me on Facebook, MSN and text me so I did not want to come to school. I even moved away but then came back. When I walk past them they give me the evils.

I was on my way down to the toilet and some year nines came in and they switched off the light. I was trying to get out but they would not let me. One of them pulled my hair. They kept turning the lights on and off. When they left I ran to find my friends. They asked if I was ok but they could see the tears so they told me to find Miss.'

A victim's perspective

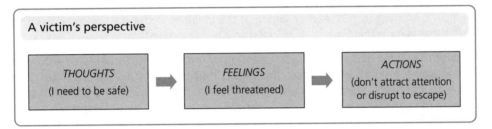

'Violence was currency passed from the strong to the weak.'

(Angus Watson)

For some victims of bullying, especially those with low self-esteem, bullying reinforces what they already believe, that they are worthless, and so they may accept what a bully does without complaint. They may even do anything the bully asks of them, including misbehaving in class.

Possible signs of bullying in the classroom

Alternatively, the child may keep their feelings under wraps as to expose them will draw attention not only to their weakness and thus reinforce their lack of self-worth but also to the bully who may, in turn, seek vengeance, thereby making matters a whole lot worse. If they stay quiet then maybe the problem will go away, but it rarely does. However, it is difficult to bury the strong emotions that are elicited as a result of being bullied, so it is pertinent to recognise when unusual behaviours in a child appear.

- They may start arriving late to class or play truant.
- The quality of their work may start to slip.
- They may appear more distracted than normal.
- They may start to behave badly when previously they were well behaved.

As their self-esteem slips they may become more withdrawn:

- avoiding speaking to others in the class
- refusing to take part in group activities
- choosing to sit alone
- looking fearful and nervous.

Children may exhibit these behaviours for reasons other than being bullied, but what should raise the concerns of the class teacher is if these observations are new to the child and/or occur over a prolonged period of time. It is the change in a child's demeanour that is the first sign that things are not as they should be. With children who are naturally shy and reticent, recognising a change in behaviour is not easy.

Signs of bullying are not just the domain of the victim. A child who is actively targeting another child in the class may give themselves away by paying abnormal attention to someone in the class they do not normally socialise with. This may be over-exuberance in the child's vicinity, back-slapping, ruffling their hair. It may involve asking to borrow something and taking it before the child can give an answer or it may be staring in their direction for an inordinate length of time. The signs will be there – it is down to the teacher knowing the children in the class and recognising that there is something amiss, they need to be ever vigilant.

Children bully for many reasons. At one time it was thought to be a consequence of low self-esteem, but the latest thinking is that it is for the very opposite: high self-esteem. New evidence suggests that bullies tend to have a 'fragile' high self-esteem (recognised as narcissism at its most extreme). Their over-inflated opinion of themselves is not built on solid foundations (as per Maslow's Hierarchy), so when a perceived threat to their self-esteem occurs their fragility is exposed and they act to cover up the cracks by imposing their will on the perpetrator, even though the person may be completely unaware that they have (supposedly) transgressed. The bully has a reputation to maintain and so the victim has to be punished.

> 'The bigs hit me, so I hit the babies: that's fair.' In these words he epitomised the history of the human race.
>
> *(Bertrand Russell, Philosopher and mathematician, 1872–1970)*

In order to maintain the illusion of superiority bullies may target those perceived as weaker than themselves. This is the basis for racist, sexist and homophobic attacks. In many cases the bully gains 'bravado' from being part of a gang. There is strength in numbers and being able to manipulate a group to follow their lead can make a bully very intimidating. From the victim's perspective, there is no escape.

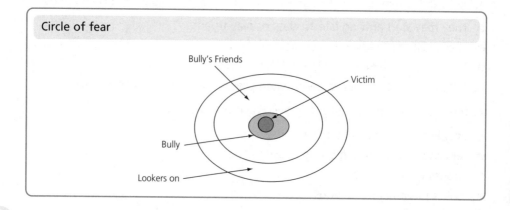

Circle of fear

Bully's Friends

Victim

Bully

Lookers on

Bullies target others whom they perceive as weaker than themselves

Source: © PhotoAlto/Alamy

Case study

Melissa's story

'It's not just me that does it, we all join in. Someone takes her coat and throws it to me and I chuck it to someone else. When she asks me to stop it makes me do it even more. It's fun. She deserves it. She annoys me. She made stuff up about me last year and I got into trouble when it wasn't even me. She thinks she knows all about my family but she knows nothing.'

A child may be singled out because they are:

- more intelligent (swot, nerd, geek)
- weak (they deserve what they get) to enhance the bullies' need for control and power
- more popular (taking attention away from the bully and making them feel insecure).

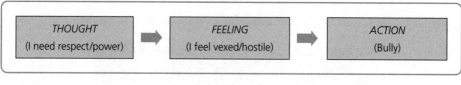

Task

How do a bully's thoughts, feelings and actions satisfy their needs in respect of Maslow's Hierarchy?

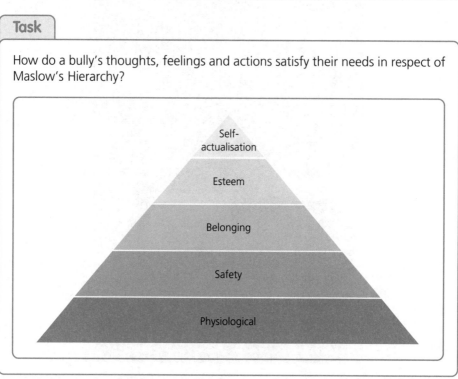

A bully's self-actualisation is one of power and control, but the pinnacle is built on a negative view of Maslow's Hierarchy. Even so, if the bully is in a commanding position, a measure of self-confidence will follow and it may prove challenging for the teacher in the classroom to wrest control of the situation.

Bullies can be identified not just by their actions (which may be clandestine) but also by their presence in a room. Signs that a child is an aspiring bully include:

- hangers-on gravitating towards them
- others careful not to antagonise them
- they are unlikely to be achieving to their potential
- they are confident in class to the point where they may even challenge the teacher.

The stereotypical view of the class bully being a swarthy, intellectually challenged child is not the norm. Bullies come in all shapes, sizes and levels of intelligence.

Bullying has its origins in socio/emotional issues. A child may have suffered emotional and/or physical abuse at the hands of others and as this is the norm, they copy what is done to them without viewing it is wrong. In other circumstances it acts as a psychological tool for an unhappy child to dump their emotional 'baggage' onto someone else – making somebody else miserable somehow makes them feel better. Those who are part of the bully's entourage give the bully the sense of belonging they need as well as a sense of security as there is 'safety in numbers'. As a bully they get the respect and acknowledgement they crave and so their self-esteem is enhanced.

Bullying works a little like terrorism. Spasmodic acts of malevolence put others on their guard, creating an atmosphere of fear and intimidation. Their mere presence in a classroom may be enough to instil paranoia in their target's mind. Once in control, such is the power of the bully that they hardly ever need to 'flex their muscles', thus it is often difficult to get hard evidence with which to tackle them.

Useful strategies to deal with bullying in the classroom

In the classroom the teacher can do much to prevent bullying occurring in the first place and to act decisively (yet sensitively) if an issue of bullying arises. Where large groups of people congregate for long periods of time the opportunity for bullying to occur is high, so it is important that the class teacher attends to the emotional needs of the class as well as their academic needs.

It is useful for a teacher to engineer where children are placed when in the classroom. This could be a seating plan and/or within group work. Keeping an eye on social grouping may help alleviate stress. Critical skills groups require children to be managers, gofers, ideas people and scribes. Rather than children volunteering for certain jobs it would be a good idea to get the children to take turns, thereby preventing the dominance of one individual while giving those with lower self-esteem the opportunity to build their confidence.

Good classroom discipline, well-organised and interesting lessons will all help reduce incidences of bullying. If children are gainfully occupied they are less likely to think about hurting someone or being a victim. Structure and routine also help to provide a feeling of security in a classroom. It is important that the teacher is not complacent, moving around the room frequently, being vigilant without appearing supervisory. Sitting behind a desk, attending to a pile of marking, allows subversive bullying to take place with impunity.

Knowing the children who are being taught – their personalities, fears, concerns and hopes – helps to create a picture of possible vulnerable children and those who may possibly start to domineer. This may not be so easy if a teacher sees the class only once a week, so background research will help.

If a teacher suspects a child of bullying then their first move should be to ensure the safety and wellbeing of the victim. This could be achieved by:

- placing the bully and victim well away from each other
- putting the victim in a place where they feel secure (ask them where they would feel safest)

- ensuring that the two are never alone together (making sure the teacher is always present and alert).

Once the immediate safety of the victim is sorted out, longer-terms solutions can be sought to:

- build up the victim's resilience (see Chapter 12 on self-esteem)
- break down the bully's resistance.

'The bullying stopped when I claimed myself and proved I wasn't afraid.'

(Randy Harrison)

Bullying is usually a secretive pursuit and it is best dealt with by exposure. To do this, however, is to expose the victim and possibly place them in a more threatening situation, so the victim needs to be an active (and controlling) part of the solution.

TOP TIP!

Get the victim to keep a diary of events.

Let the bully know that their actions are being monitored and reported.

Monitoring of a bully's actions by the victim gives the victim more control over the situation, empowering them to 'fight back'. However, this will work only if the victim is confident that the teacher will act decisively.

Restorative action and/or conflict resolution are also possibilities, but having a bully and a victim meet face to face may prove too daunting for the victim and present the bully with an opportunity to impose their will on the victim. This route would be advised only if the teacher is a skilled negotiator.

Avoid humiliating the bully because this may prove counterproductive as the bully will be so angry that they are likely to seek revenge.

TOP TIP!

Have an honesty box on the desk in which children can put notes voicing their concerns about issues in the classroom.

In an emotionally intelligent classroom the teacher will play an active part in making sure that the learning environment is one of calm, promoting positive interactions between children and nipping any altercations in the bud. It is not just what the children bring into the classroom that matters but also how the teacher maintains order and discipline. Intolerance fosters bullying. If the teacher displays such behaviour then the children may copy this role model.

(!)

Do you suffer fools gladly?

- **How do you react to/deal with (gross incompetence) by a) children in class, b) colleagues? Do you:**
    - **blame ('It's your fault')**
    - **find fault ('That's just not good enough')**
    - **threaten ('If you do that again I will . . .')**
    - **belittle ('Alice's work is much neater than yours, you should be more like her')**
    - **mock ('What do you call that?')**
    - **become sarcastic ('It looks like you've dragged it through a puddle')**
    - **make an example of ('Look at John's work everybody, this is what you should not do!')**

If you use these types of strategies to effect good discipline/improve standards, you are bullying.

- **How might you get the same result by being positive and encouraging rather than resorting to coercion?**

(Answer: recognising good practice and encouraging are far more powerful than using negative, bullying comments when trying to get a child to work better/ harder. Even where it is hard to find something positive to say there will be a positive, and the skill is to seek it out and use it as a focus for improvement. A teacher using coercive tactics justifies the potential bullies in the class to do likewise.)

Ultimately a school should have an effective policy relating to bullying. Without such a policy any class teacher's good intentions will be effective only inside their classroom; elsewhere a child's safety may not be ensured and so a bully will be able to exercise their influence in the classroom with impunity.

(!)

Does your school have an anti-bullying policy?

Can you recite what it is?

Have you ever had occasion to put it into action?

How effective is it in tackling the problem of bullying?

In conclusion

(!)

Do you shout at children when they transgress?

Do you step into their personal space?

Do you use hand gestures that are threatening?

Do you use threats of sanctions as the mainstay of your behaviour management?

If the answer to any of these is yes, then you are a bully.

It is easy to say that in a position of authority you have to sometimes 'bully' people to get things done, but do you?

It may be that managers in the school in which you teach use similar methods to coerce staff into doing as they are asked. If this is the case, they too are bullies.

When working with children (and colleagues!) it is important to convey positive ways of communicating wishes and expectations without resorting to bullying. Children will mirror how adults behave. A child who witnesses excessive use of force, verbal threats and intimidation will observe that it gets results and will copy to try to impose their will on others. While the teacher cannot control what goes on at home, they can offer an alternative, so it is important that they do not resort to bullying tactics in the classroom. A sanction-based approach reinforces a bully's perception that intimidation gets results. Short term, sanctions may have their uses in stalling a bully, but long term a more constructive policy is needed. This must remove the need for the bully to use scare tactics to get respect, and this is best done by creating an environment where the bully (and all the rest) can be successful by working hard. This will supersede their need to exercise muscle.

Further reading

www.stopbullyingnow.com

www.bullyonline.org

www.direct.gov.uk

Olweus, D. (1993) *Bullying at School*, Wiley-Blackwell.

Smith, P., Pepler, D. and Rigby, K. (2004) *Bullying in Schools*, Cambridge University Press.

Chapter 15

Drugs

Case study

Gael's story

'I started smoking in year 5. I have a smoke with my friends at break times and before school. Sometimes I have a smoke in the toilets during lesson time. I've been caught a couple of times but it's no big deal. If I don't have a ciggie I get ratty and I can't concentrate in class. I can stop when I want. I have done a couple of times, it's easy, you just do it. I came home hyper at the weekend, my mum thinks I was drinking or had taken drugs, she's stupid.'

Case study continued

What

- is more addictive than heroin?
- has withdrawal symptoms worse than cocaine?
- causes more deaths than most other drugs put together?
- and is used by 1 in 10 of 11–15 year olds?

The answer? Smoking tobacco.

Source: © Bubbles Photolibrary/Alamy

Every day 450 children start smoking (*source: The Independent* on Sunday, July 2006). Schools have been trying to eradicate smoking on their premises probably since there were schools, without much success. Children can be excluded, even expelled, but the problem never seems to go away. Children will forever find some nook or cranny in which to secrete themselves and partake of a habit that has them hooked on two levels:

- physiological addiction
- psychological attraction.

To many children, cigarettes (and alcohol) are seen as a rite of passage from childhood to adulthood, forming part of an itinerary of rebelliousness that defines their teenage years. To smoke (and drink alcohol) is to emulate adult role models (parents, public icons, etc.). Even putting up signs telling children it is forbidden to smoke (and to drink) is like telling them that to be grown up they must do exactly this. Children are a resourceful bunch and adept at finding their way around most obstacles.

'Sticking an over-18 label makes cigarettes more attractive.'

(Ian Willmore, ASH)

(!)

Do you know where children in your school go to smoke? Do they confine themselves to that area?

Should smoking cigarettes be banned on a school's premises? Should staff turn a 'blind eye' in the direction of children smoking?

How might a school resolve the issue of children needing a cigarette yet balance this against the need to satisfy health and safety demands?

(Comment: The law demands that there should be no smoking inside public places. Schools will fall into that category. However, this may not dissuade the active smoker. In effect, they will be breaking the law and so smoking in school needs to be tackled robustly. In terms of dealing with cravings in class, an innovative school might supply nicotine patches for use during the day as part of a health education programme. If this is not feasible then just being aware of why a child may be irritable will have to suffice. This is a case of being pragmatic in the face of possible class disruption; it is not making allowances for under-age smokers.)

Much is made about cannabis as a stepping stone to 'harder' drugs, but cigarettes and alcohol for some children are themselves 'gateway drugs' and unlike cannabis, which is illegal, both drugs are legal and an accepted part of modern society. A child's need to push the boundaries will determine whether they step through the gate or not. Today's world is one that embraces the pursuit of new trends and crazes and this is why ever younger children mirror adult fashions. As a result, smoking tobacco, drinking alcohol and experimenting with illegal drugs are creeping down the age scale as the notion of what is acceptable and what is not is pushed further backwards.

Task

Study the chart below from a survey showing why children start taking drugs.

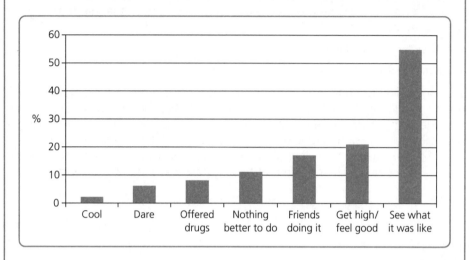

(Adapted from 'Drug use, smoking and drinking among young people in England in 2005', NHS)

a) Which part of Maslow's Hierarchy does experimentation with drugs target?

b) Which part of Maslow's Hierarchy does addiction to drugs affect?

c) What is the significance of this in terms of classroom teaching?

(Answer: a) Experimentation usually goes hand in hand with belonging and/or self-esteem. It is well documented that peer group pressure is the main cause of children starting to smoke tobacco. Low self-esteem creates a self-harming scenario where a child seeks comfort in taking drugs, knowing that they cause physical harm. b) Physiological needs, therefore drug dependency will mean that a child will not be able to function properly if their 'addictive' needs are not met. c) The significance in terms of classroom teaching is to understand that if a child is addicted to or dependent on any form of drug and they are late getting their 'fix', be that a cigarette or alcohol or something much harder, their ability to work in class is going to be compromised.)

While a teacher delivering Mathematics second lesson on a Tuesday may think that societal problems such as these have nothing to do with the lesson, they need to be aware that drug taking, either on the school premises or off them, will impact on the behaviour and performance of the children who indulge. Each and every teacher has a responsibility (*in loco parentis*) to report any concerns in respect of a child's wellbeing.

Information

In medical terms a drug is any substance that can modify one or more of a person's functions.

In terms of effects on the body, drugs can be grouped as shown in the table below.

	Effect	Examples
Stimulants	Make you more alert, competitive, aggressive	Caffeine, cocaine, amphetamines
Sedatives	Help you to relax	Nicotine, alcohol, cannabis
Analgesics	Block out pain	Opiates including heroin, aspirin, paracetamol
Hallucinogens	Make you see things differently	LSD, cannabis, inhalants

Information

Ritalin is a drug that is used to treat ADHD. It contains a stimulant that is similar to amphetamine, but in the doses used it has the opposite effect. It acts to increase the amounts of dopamine in the brain, which allows the user to control their behaviour and attention.

Possible signs of drug use in the classroom

The general signs that a child is taking drugs are:

- mood swings (from hyperactivity and silly behaviour to depression)
- unreliability
- lack of motivation (lethargy, underachieving, late to class, truancy)
- dishonesty
- secretive behaviour
- resentment, hostility and irritability
- loss of appetite
- distinctive odours (bad breath or on clothes).

While some of these traits are typical of adolescent or socio-emotional issues, it is the sudden or progressive change in a child's personality that will attract attention. It is sometimes described as a 'drug personality'. On its own it is likely to be only a concern, but if aligned with other observations or facts, a fuller picture can be built up.

Background

Each drug has its own specific effect on a child's 'personality' and these are summarised below. The signs and symptoms of drug use may not be confined to physiological and/or psychological changes – there is a culture that is built around drug use which includes language and paraphernalia.

Marijuana (dope, weed, grass, pot)

- Compulsive eating (munchies)
- Bloodshot eyes
- Trouble keeping eyes open
- Uncontrollable giggling
- Forgetfulness
- Delayed motor skills
- Sickly sweet smell on body and clothes
- Strong mood changes

Inhalants (rush, poppers, snappers)

- Flushed face
- Giggling
- Headaches
- Dizzy (fainting)
- Bad breath
- Odour on clothes
- Sneezing/runny nose
- Watery eyes
- Lack of coordination

Methamphetamines (speed, crystal meth, bennies)

- Dilated pupils
- Excited
- Talkative
- Aggression
- Agitation
- Mood changes

Cocaine (coke, crack, blow, snow, rocks)

- Anxiety
- Dilated pupils
- Scratching
- Impaired thinking
- Short-tempered
- Panic attacks

LSD and magic mushrooms (acid, tab, blotters, shrooms)

- Dilated pupils
- Loss of coordination
- Hallucinations
- Self-harming
- Skin discoloration

Alcohol (booze, juice, sauce)

- Slurred speech
- Euphoria
- Lack of coordination
- Aggression
- Talkative
- Over-affection

Case study

Mandy's story

'Tina stayed overnight at my house because we had an exam the next day. When mum went to work we dared each other to have a drink of vodka. We ended up walking to school in our pyjamas, totally wasted. One teacher tried to stop us going into the exam but we ignored him. Then another one came and started shouting at us, so we gave her a mouthful and threatened to punch her lights out. She chased us off site. Next thing we know a police car turned up as we staggered down the road back towards my house. They stayed with us till mum came home. I was grounded for ages afterwards.'

- Might the teachers have dealt with the situation better?
- Were the two girls put at risk as a result of the teachers' actions?

Task

How do you differentiate between high spirits and a drug 'high'?

Should an adult challenge, enquire or just monitor a child if they are unsure?

(Answer: a child under the influence is likely to behave oddly for a prolonged period of time. High spirits is usually a passing phase. There are also likely to be other physiological signs. If a teacher is suspicious, they should not react immediately unless they fear for their safety or the safety of others. It is better to be low key, monitor the child and possibly get help to take the child out of class before questioning them.)

Children bring cigarettes into school and so they may bring other drugs into school. The lists above provide the teacher with visual evidence that they may wish to use in recognising some of the most commonly used drugs. Inhalants are worth a special mention at this point because they are found in everyday items such as aerosol deodorants, hairspray and lighter fluid. Other items can include glue and correction fluids. Their presence in a child's bag could be completely innocent, but if a teacher has a concern about a child then such items are not above suspicion. If there is a real worry that such items may be being abused, they should be confiscated and returned to a responsible adult, thereby sharing the concern with parents or guardians.

Drugs act on the central nervous system, principally the brain, in a way that is described accurately as 'mind altering'. A child under the influence of a drug still sees what a 'sober' person sees, but it is how they perceive what is happening that is different. This makes them a significant risk to themselves and others in the classroom, including the teacher.

Strategies to deal with drug-related issues in the classroom

Information

- In 2006 17 per cent of pupils reported taking drugs in the past year.
- Cannabis was the drug most commonly taken during 2006 when 10.1 per cent of pupils reported using it.
- In 2005 39 per cent of pupils reported ever having been offered drugs.

(*Source*: www.ic.nhs.uk/statistics)

If a child is known to have taken drugs and is causing concern, a teacher should act to deal with the situation in the same way they would deal with a sick child. There is no point being judgemental as any display of antipathy towards the child may result in a serious escalation of the situation. It is best to get support to help remove the 'intoxicated' child and put them in a place of safety until they are fit to be dealt with. Simply throwing a child out of the lesson puts them at risk.

(!)

Are you isolated in your classroom?

In case of an emergency in the room, what procedures are in place to ensure your safety and the safety of the children in the classroom?

Some schools have an emergency 'on-call' system. Does your school have something similar?

(Comment: This is a situation where all staff need to be sure that there is a procedure for dealing with such an eventuality.)

Being in a drug-fuelled state is only one part of the problem when it comes to dealing with drug abuse. There is also the more likely situation of the teacher in the classroom having to deal with the onset of cravings due to drug dependency and addiction.

The withdrawal symptoms of smoking tobacco include:

- irritation
- anger
- problems with concentration
- anxiety
- restlessness
- fatigue.

There may be a number of children in the class you teach who are desperate for a cigarette.

- How may their craving affect their performance in the classroom?
- Should the class teacher acknowledge this and alter the way they treat the children?

If as a teacher you suspect a child of being under the influence of drugs you should:

1. Monitor their behaviour in the lesson without causing alarm. If they are quiet and not being disruptive, it may be best to avoid confronting them personally.
2. Seek support from another teacher or management to 'ease' them out of the lesson with minimal disruption.
3. Write an incident report explaining your observations and concerns.

It could be that your fears are unfounded, but it is better to be safe than sorry for the sake of the child and of the class. If you are incorrect in your judgement you can always apologise after the event.

Possession of illegal drugs for personal use or with intent to supply is likely to result in permanent exclusion from school as well as acting as an impetus for criminal proceedings. It may be the class teacher who inadvertently stumbles on the incriminating evidence.

Information

Drugs, children and the law

If a child is caught in possession of a controlled drug they have committed a criminal offence.

For a first offence a child may receive a formal warning or formal caution. If they are between the ages of 10 and 17 and commit further offences, they could be charged and dealt with by a youth court.

If illegal drugs are taken from a child they must be destroyed or handed into the police. By having drugs in your possession, you may also be committing an offence, even if you have no intention of using them.

(*Source*: www.drugrehab.co.uk)

Class	Drugs	Possession	Dealing
A	Ecstasy, LSD, heroin, cocaine, magic mushrooms, amphetamines	Up to 7 years in prison	Up to life in prison
B	Amphetamines, cannabis, Ritalin	Up to 5 years in prison	Up to 14 years in prison
C	Tranquillisers, some painkillers, ketamine	Up to 2 years in prison	Up to 14 years in prison

Class A drugs are considered to cause the most harm.
The Misuse of Drugs Act 1971 states that it is an offence to:
- possess a controlled substance unlawfully
- possess a controlled substance with intent to supply it
- supply or offer to supply a controlled drug (even if it is given away for free)
- allow a house, flat or office to be used by people taking drugs.

(*Source*: www.homeoffice.gov.uk)

Task

If, as a class teacher, you stumbled on a suspicious package in a child's possession:

a) What should you do?

b) What would you do?

c) Would your choice be any different if the child was
- a normally reliable child?
- one who was often in trouble?

(Answer: As with a child who may be intoxicated, such a situation is best dealt with by tactically ignoring the suspect package but getting support straight away to remove the child and have them searched in the privacy of an office. If they refuse to comply, the senior teacher may then call the police and/or the child's parents.)

If you stumble on a cache of drugs in a child's possession it is your duty to report it. As when dealing with a child under the influence of drugs, it is important not to confront the child in situ but to call for support, remove them from the lesson and get a member of the senior management to carry out a search.

In conclusion

Children may initially take drugs just to experience their effects. This can develop into a long-term dependency as they discover that the drug is an escape from the stresses of life, be they emotional, social, physical or psychological. In this respect their drug of choice acts as a 'painkiller', blocking out their true feelings. Although school may not appear to play a major part in this process, its role in creating a safe environment where the child feels acknowledged and successful may help to prevent a child from straying too far.

Ultimately, dealing with issues surrounding drugs and drug abuse is about a broader education within PSHE and is largely beyond the remit of the subject teacher, but in creating a classroom that is vibrant, interesting and motivating a subject teacher offers each and every child an alternative to the temptation of drugs. Using Maslow's Hierarchy as a template, a subject teacher can offer a child everything they require for self-actualisation, from a place of safety and belonging to one where their self-esteem is raised. This may sound a touch twee, but the influence a good teacher exerts on children is profound and as such should not be understated.

Further reading

www.drugrehab.co.uk

www.drugs-info.co.uk

Caulkins, J. (2002) *Drug Prevention, What Kind of Drug Use Does It Prevent*, Rand.

Noble, P. (2002) *Safe and Drug Free Schools*, Nora Biomedical.

Chapter

16

Nutrition

Case study

Eddie's story

'I don't eat breakfast, I get up too late. Mum's so fed up she leaves me to it. She has gone off to work by the time I get up. She only gives me enough money for the bus so if I don't pick up my packed lunch, which I usually leave because I don't like what's in it, I don't eat anything all day. The teachers at school think I cadge money for cigarettes but I don't, even though I do smoke. I get ten pence off as many as I can so that I can buy a chip butty at lunch.

I get sent out of class a lot because I can't be arsed doing the work. It's not that it's too hard, most days I just can't be bothered, I'm too tired.'

There has been much written about the influence diet can have on the behaviour of pupils in the classroom. From the effects of additives on hyperactivity to the claims that omega 3 can directly improve a pupil's intelligence. Some of the evidence is misleading but has been leapt upon by the daily papers and has been claimed as fact by many, without proper studies having been carried out. However, there is evidence in relation to eating habits and pupil performance that is unequivocal.

Without sounding too much like a school science textbook, a healthy, balanced diet should include carbohydrate, protein, vitamins, minerals and water in the recommended daily allowance. Too much or too little of one nutrient or another makes a diet unbalanced and this can lead to physiological (and psychological) problems that affect a pupil's behaviour in the classroom. If a child has an unbalanced diet, they will be suffering from malnutrition.

Malnutrition occurs when a child does not receive the correct nutrients in their daily diet over a prolonged period of time; feasting on junk food often means that essential nutrients are lacking in their diet. Malnutrition is perceived as a third world problem, conjuring up images of emaciated children with distended bellies who are starving. While this perception is true, it is not the complete picture. In the first world, where obesity levels are reaching chronic proportions, malnutrition is also prevalent.

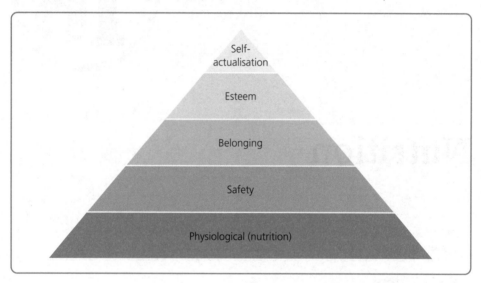

Approaching the subject from Maslow's Hierarchy it can be seen that the need for nutrition occurs at the base of the triangle. That we all need sustenance to keep us functioning is evident without any need for scientific study. As adults we can suppress our hunger for a time and carry on working, but that is because we are, by and large, well fed and watered. Eating and diet influence a pupil's capabilities on many levels:

- physiological
- emotional
- social.

Malnutrition may occur as a result of:

- poverty (lack of food, preponderance of less nutritious, cheap/junk food
- cultural influences (males may focus on muscle enhancement via protein-rich diets)
- religious/ethnic influences (some religions do not condone certain foodstuffs or feature fasting as part of their rituals)
- poor parenting (allowing their children to eat what they like, when they like).

Source: Peter Dazeley/Getty Images

Malnutrition is not the preserve of the less fortunate in society. It is easy, as busy parents, to reach out for easy-cook meals or to ignore (not be aware of) an offspring's snacking, opting for an easy life rather than have World War Three over whether they are going to eat the carrots on their plate.

Possible signs of malnutrition:

- Poor health (frequent minor illnesses coughs, colds, etc.).
- Extreme body shape (obese or too thin).
- Lethargy (lack of energy, unmotivated, disaffected).
- Poor concentration (inability to focus, low tolerance levels).

'1 in 4 children are obese by the time they reach primary school.'

(The Guardian, December 2010)

A book could be written dealing just with the effects of the lack of one nutrient or another on a child's performance in class. However, two nutrients are worth mentioning in some detail: water and glucose.

Water is essential for hydration. Lack of water can lead to tiredness, irritability and lack of concentration as the pupil becomes dehydrated. If you have ever had a hangover then you will appreciate the effects of dehydration. You will also be aware of how hard it is to function effectively when hung over.

Caffeine-based drinks such as cola increase the dehydration process as they act as a diuretic and should be avoided. Other fizzy drinks are high in sugar and may adversely affect blood sugar levels. It is recommended that a child drinks around 1.2 litres of fluid a day.

TOP TIP!

Encourage pupils to bring a bottle of water to class every day in order to maintain good hydration.

Signs of dehydration

- Headache.
- Nausea.
- Dry mouth.
- Fever.
- Tiredness.

(!)

- **Which (if any) pupils in your class are malnourished?**
- **What food do they eat (and do not eat) regularly?**

Case study

Bradley's story

'I've got ADHD but my mum doesn't want me to take any tablets, she says they're dangerous. I'm always hyper like this, most teachers can't handle me. My mum's always being called into school to see the headteacher when I'm getting suspended. I'm thick. I'm rubbish in class and can't wait to leave school. I don't eat breakfast. My mum gives me money to get something from the shop on the way to school. I usually buy a litre bottle of coke and a large bag of nachos, they don't last long. At lunch I always have chips and a burger and then a doughnut if I've enough money left. I don't care if they call me 'Blobby', I just smack 'em when I get hold of them.'

Background

Blood sugar (glucose) is the nutrient that provides us with energy. Glucose does not come just from eating sugary foodstuffs, it is obtained by converting other nutrients such as carbohydrates, fats and, in extreme situations, proteins. If we lack glucose in our system we soon begin to feel tired. This in turn reduces our ability to function effectively. Think about situations where you have felt 'exhausted' because you have not eaten – perhaps 'shopping till you drop' or overstretching yourself trying to keep (get) fit. Notice how you become irritable, unable to concentrate for any length of time – all you want to do is relax and put your feet up with a strong cup of coffee (a stimulant) and a biscuit (carbohydrate). Now apply that to a child who has been sent out of the family home without any breakfast and has no money to buy any-thing at the corner shop on the way to school. They will have to wait until lunch before they can have their free school meal and they will be in your lesson the one before lunch. It is not just a case of what a child eats but also when they eat and if they eat that affects their ability to function.

How will their low glucose level affect:

- their ability to concentrate in class?
- their behaviour in class?

Number of weekdays on which breakfast is eaten by children aged 5–17 years (source HPA N. Ireland)

No. of days	% 5–11 boys	% 12–17 boys	% 5–11 girls	% 12–17 girls
0	2	6	2	16
1	2	0	1	1
2	1	1	2	7
3	2	4	3	4
4	1	1	0	3
5	93	87	91	70

The information in the box above has been taken from a study of eating habits in Northern Ireland. Notice that almost a third of teenage girls do not have breakfast every day. In fact, the habit of eating breakfast seems to deteriorate across both genders as children move into the teenage years. Primary children appear to fare much better, but even at this age around 10 per cent of girls and 7 per cent of boys go to school without breakfast at least once a week. The creation of breakfast clubs could account for some of the shortfall, but there will still be some pupils arriving at school hungry. Religious fasting may also result in a pupil coming to school feeling hungry.

(!)

Do you know which of the pupils in your class are of the Muslim faith?

The holy month of Ramadan in the Muslim religion forbids any eating or drinking between the hours of dawn and dusk. The fast is broken in the evening after dark. How might this affect their work in class?

(Answer: lack of carbohydrates may make them lethargic and unable to concentrate.)

We gain glucose most easily via the carbohydrates that we consume. However, some foods are easier to metabolise (convert to glucose) than others. Foods are given a GI (glycaemic index) rating based on how quickly they can be converted to glucose and consequently how soon they can provide us with energy. Foods with a high GI will give a pupil a sudden spike of energy but for only a short period. While foods with a high GI are useful for giving a quick fix of energy, once their energy is used up the pupil will begin to flag once more. A child who snacks on sweets throughout the day will operate on a cycle of boom and boost. Such inconsistency can lead to swings in mood that a child may find difficult to cope with, leading to behavioural problems. Foods with a low GI work more slowly, providing as much energy but over a longer period of time – there are no peaks and troughs. Low GI foods make for a much more settled temperament.

High GI foods (index >70)	Intermediate GI foods (index 55–70)	Low GI foods (index <55)
Chips 75	Soft drinks 68	Wholewheat spaghetti 37
White bread 70	Wholemeal bread 69	Banana 53
Doughnuts 76	Brown rice 55	Apple 36
Jelly beans 80	Mars bar 68	Crisps 54
Cheerios 74	Shredded Wheat 69	Porridge 49
Rice Krispies 82	Muesli 56	Peas 48
Cornflakes 77	Shortbread 56	Carrots 39
Baguette 95		Baked beans 48
Gatorade 78		Semi-skimmed milk 34

Task

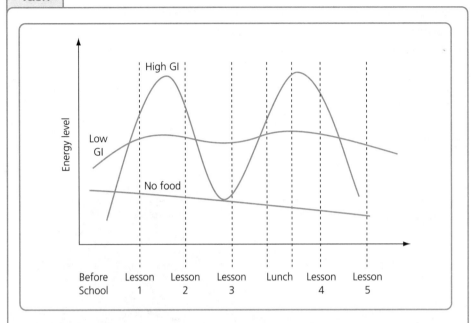

Consider the school day above.

a) In which lessons is the pupil who has not had breakfast going to function at their best/worst?

b) In which lessons is the pupil who has had a high GI diet likely to be i) hyper-active, ii) lacking in energy, iii) functioning effectively?

c) In which lessons is the pupil who has had a low GI diet going to function effectively?

d) How might a school day be altered to ensure the energy levels of its pupils are in harmony with all of the lessons?

e) How does your school day compare?

(Answer: a) Best in lesson 1, worst in lessons 2–5. b) i) Lesson 1, ii) lesson 3, iii) lessons 2 and 3. c) Lessons 1–5. d) Move lunch to midday)

Eating habits do not occur just as a result of socio-economic factors, they may also emerge as a consequence of psychological problems developing into eating disorders. Detecting eating disorders is not just a case of observing extreme body shapes, it also requires a high degree of psychological profiling by experts before a diagnosis is given. People may have extreme body shapes as a result of illness or other medical complaints, so it is important not to jump to conclusions based on observations alone.

There are many types of eating disorder, but the most common are:

- anorexia (eating too little, resulting in a Body Mass Index (BMI) of less than 15)
- bulimia (eating too much and then purging)
- obesity (caused by binge eating and having a BMI greater than 30).

'The number of children with eating disorders has increased 80 per cent in the last ten years.'

(BBC Newsbeat, *February 2009)*

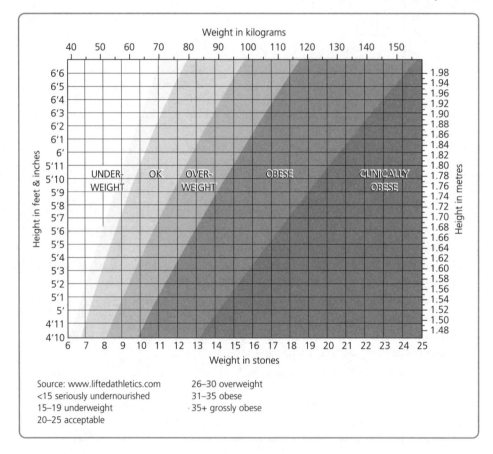

Source: www.liftedathletics.com

<15 seriously undernourished

15–19 underweight

20–25 acceptable

26–30 overweight

31–35 obese

35+ grossly obese

Possible signs of anorexia

- Dramatic weight loss.
- Hiding behind baggy clothes.
- Preoccupation with body image (too fat).
- Frequent illness.
- Anaemia/bruising.
- Dry hair, nails and skin.

- Lethargy.
- Secretive/avoiding social events.
- Low self-esteem.
- Self-harming.

'Nothing matters when I'm thin.'

(Anonymous anorexic)

Possible signs of bulimia

- Secret stashes of food.
- Constant 'grazing' on food.
- Expressing disgust at appearance.
- Low self-esteem.
- Self-harming.

Possible signs of binge eating

- Obese.
- Stomach aches.
- Mouth infections.
- Diarrhoea.
- Constant 'grazing' on food.
- Lethargy.
- Low self-esteem.
- Illness.
- Withdrawn.

Eating disorders can be triggered by many factors, including:

- stress caused by family break-up, bereavement, injury and illness
- peer pressure, such as wanting to look like public icons and role models
- bullying
- high expectations from parents and teachers.

Eating disorders are a mental health issue stemming from negative thoughts and feelings.

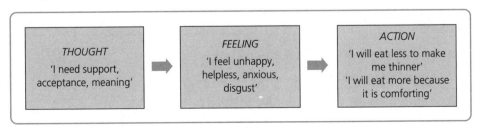

Eating disorders have their roots in low self-esteem, whether it is a sense of not belonging or a feeling that the sufferer has a poor body image. The result is that the child will endeavour to alter their body in a search for an ideal. It is a search that has no ending, pushing their body to the limits of its endurance until eventually it starts to break down. In terms of Maslow's Hierarchy it can be seen that low self-esteem instigated by trauma affects a child's basic physiology and this in turn reduces the child's self-esteem further as they are unable to function properly. It is a dangerous, positive feedback system that all too easily spirals out of control. While a class teacher may appear to be able to play no part in dealing with eating disorders, their role in initially detecting a growing problem can be crucial in effecting a swift diagnosis. Eating disorders are a creeping illness that develop over long periods of time and a class teacher is ideally placed to observe subtle changes as they begin to manifest themselves.

Useful classroom strategies to deal with nutritional issues

Most schools allow pupils to take a bottle of water with them into lessons. This is helpful in ensuring that all children are properly hydrated. Other than this a class teacher should not give any foodstuffs to children, principally because the child may have food allergies. For example, a teacher may have a stock of sweets as rewards or to give pupils a 'sugar boost' if they appear to be flagging. Even this simple treat is not without its dangers.

Research funded by the Food Standards Agency (FSA) has suggested that the consumption of certain mixes of artificial food colours and the preservative sodium benzoate could be linked to increased hyperactivity in some children. The following colours are used in a wide range of foods that tends to be brightly coloured:

- sunset yellow (E110)
- quinoline yellow (E104)
- carmoisine (E122)
- allura red (E129)
- tartrazine (E102)
- ponceau 4R (E124).

(*Source*: www.food.gov.uk)

(!)

Do you give sweets as a reward in class?

Do any of your pupils have food allergies?

What other treats could you give instead?

If the teacher thinks a child is malnourished they should report their concerns to a higher authority. Issues relating to malnourishment should be dealt with at a higher level, involving parental contact. On a broader level the school should pursue a healthy eating policy. This may involve limiting what is sold in the school canteen or even checking the contents of a pupil's lunch box.

Talking to, nagging or lecturing pupils about their obsession with body image is not likely to prove helpful. Working in class to create an environment that is both supportive and gives a sense of belonging can do much to allay the effects of low self-esteem (see Chapter 12). As with many emotional issues, creating avenues to lift a child's self-esteem through success can have a profound effect on other areas of their life. Sometimes it is these oases of excellence that help turn the tide when it comes to children with emotional problems.

A classroom teacher can control what pupils eat and drink only in the confines of their classroom. Outside of this environment what occurs is down to whole-school policies. This is an area where school/parent liaison can work. Advising parents on what their children should (and should not) eat and seeking their cooperation can help in trying to get pupils better prepared for learning. Working in conjunction with parents helps to deal with situations involving special dietary requirements. Any work on healthy eating should have been agreed with a specialist dietician.

> **(!)**
>
> Do you know whether your school has a healthy eating policy or not?
>
> If so, what is expected of you as a class teacher?

In conclusion

There is little doubt that nutrition (or the lack of) plays a significant part in the behaviour of pupils in the classroom, but to what extent can (or should) a class teacher or even a school influence what children eat and when they eat outside of offering general advice with a broader educational brush?

> **(!)**
>
> Do you have breakfast before going to school?
>
> Do you eat healthily throughout the day or are you so busy all you have time for is a snatched cup of coffee at break times or a sandwich while on duty?
>
> If the teacher is not properly nourished, their effectiveness in the class-room is also going to be compromised.

Further reading

www.nhs.uk

www.food.gov.uk

www.eatingdisorderexpert.co.uk

Bryant-Waugh, R. (2004) *Eating Disorders: A Parents' Guide*, Routledge.

Morris, J. (2008) *ABC of Eating Disorders*, Wiley-Blackwell.

Chapter 17

Self-harming

Case study

Corey's story

'She told me to take my coat off so I said, "No! I like my coat and I'm keeping it on". She said if I didn't take it off I'd get a sanction. I said, "Go for it, I'm still not taking my coat off, if I put it down somebody might nick it". She sent me out of class and to the head of year. I told him the same, that I wasn't taking my coat off, they couldn't make me. He asked to see my arms, I told him to sod off and mind his own business. He said if I took my coat off he'd give me a jumper to put on for the day and that I could collect my jacket at the end of the day. I agreed but I still wouldn't let him see my arms.

I get so angry. I'd do anything for mum but she doesn't do anything for me. She makes me stay in on my own and then goes out with her friends. My parents are always on my case, they want me to do well at school. The teachers say I'm clever but lazy, I just don't f***king care. I feel like I'm going to explode. Pressure builds up inside of me. I get a roaring in my head. The only way to stop is to do something to myself. I wind up and then down, hitting the wall harder and harder till my knuckles bleed and the stuff inside my head stops and then I can stop. Afterwards, for a while it's quiet and the pressure is gone but I feel so ashamed and disgusted with myself.'

As adults we have a perception that self-harming is all about children mutilating their bodies with broken glass or rusty razor blades. In some cases this may be true, but in the majority of situations self-harming is a far more complex issue and one that has a direct association with the school classroom.

Task

Would you describe the following as self-harming?

- Body piercing.
- Drinking to excess.
- Smoking cigarettes.
- Picking at an unsightly scab.
- Removing unsightly body hair.
- Cosmetic surgery.

If not, when would each of these actions constitute self-harming?

Self-harming is the deliberate use of any material to damage the body. This may involve cutting, but it can also involve burning, hitting inanimate objects with intent to cause personal injury and taking drugs to excess (including alcohol). Even eating disorders can fall into the sphere of self-harm because, like all the other scenarios, the action is premeditated and prolonged.

Research has shown that self-harm tends to begin around the age of 11 (although evidence has shown that some very young children self-harm) and tails off around the age of 25.

Possible signs of self-harming

There are distinct physical signs that a child is self-harming. These include:

- cuts and scratches
- burns
- picking at wounds until they bleed
- sticking objects into the body (puncturing)
- imbibing toxic substances (drugs, alcohol)
- covering parts of the body to disguise wounds
- refusing to change in public (for PE or drama)
- thumping walls or banging their head with intent to hurt themselves.

On occasion children will do some of these things, possibly when angry or very anxious, but this does not mean that they are repeat offenders.

Background

Information

About 1 in 10 children will self-harm (source: www.rcpsych.ac.uk).

An outward sign of inner turmoil

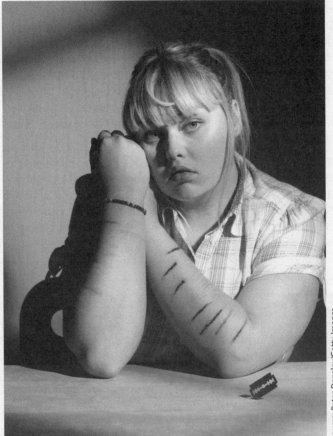

Source: Peter Dazeley/Getty Images

Self-harming becomes a real issue when a pupil indulges repeatedly and the action not only constitutes a physical danger to the child but is also a sign of inner emotional issues that need to be resolved. Children may resort to self-harming for a number of reasons:

- They may be being bullied in class.
- They may feel under pressure to achieve academically.

- They may have no friends and feel isolated.
- They may have problems at home.
- They may have issues with their sexuality.
- They may be part of a subculture (Goths, Emos) where self-harming is an accepted ritual.
- They may be suffering from depression.

Some of these causes can be dealt with directly by the classroom teacher while others require the skilled intervention of a therapist.

The fact that self-harming is prevalent around teenage years is indicative of the inner tensions that push a child to injure themselves. At this age puberty begins and the body starts to change physically as well as emotionally. This is when sexual relationships begin and when a child starts to flex their independent muscles, causing arguments in the home. Amidst all this turmoil the child is under pressure to achieve at school with the dreaded GCSEs appearing on the horizon. For children in the upper years of primary the problems are likely to be just as intense. Puberty may have started and they are under pressure to do well at school.

What distinguishes a child who self-harms from those who do not is their lack of emotional intelligence, manifesting itself in their inability to deal with their inner feelings, to the point at which they choose to self-harm as a way of expressing what they feel inside. There may be a feeling of desperation because they feel trapped. Their emotions are all bottled up and there is often a feeling of being detached from the real world or a feeling of shame or guilt. These create strong emotions that require release and self-harming provides that release, reducing inner tensions.

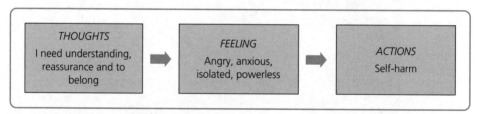

Children who self-harm are often impulsive and have difficulty in expressing their emotions properly.

As such, self-harming is best described as

'an inner scream.'

(Source: www.harm.me.uk)

A pupil who has a tendency to get angry may thump walls or headbutt furniture as a way of releasing their pent-up anger. Others may do the same as a form of self-punishment (some religious sects use self-flagellation as a way of reparation for sins committed). The act of self-harming is a way of turning emotional trauma into physical pain, which the child can understand more easily. It is also true that inflicting pain stimulates the body's natural painkillers, which help to allay the hurt. Once released, the child feels better.

Some children may use self-harming as a way of drawing attention to themselves (although most self-harmers are secretive). This can be troubling for other pupils, who may not comprehend why a classmate could do such a thing to themselves. Those who do are sending a clear message that they are distressed and are looking for help.

It has been thought that children who self-harm have suicidal tendencies. While this may be the case for some, for the majority it is not – the action of self-harming is just their way of dealing with inner turmoil. This is not to play down the seriousness of self-harming because such actions can lead to permanent injury, such as paralysis, infection and scarring, but rather to put it in perspective and not allow our anxieties to exaggerate what is already a sensitive issue.

Useful strategies to deal with self-harming issues in the classroom

If a teacher discovers that a child in their class is self-harming, possibly in full view of the rest of the class or quietly at the back of the room as the lesson unfolds, there is a natural tendency to either express horror and disgust or to take the pupil to one side and voice concerns by criticising the pupil's actions. These reactions are not helpful to the child because doing so is to reinforce the pupil's core belief that they are not worthy or that they are in a hopeless situation. Criticism is likely to exacerbate their problems.

> 'I like the thought that it is *me* causing the pain for once and not some-one else. It makes me happy.'

Self-harming is an outward sign of inner turmoil and this is where a class teacher can best effect change. In terms of Maslow's Hierarchy, self-harming fits into the areas of belonging and low self-esteem and so focusing attention on these will do more to help a child who self-harms. Chapter 12 deals with raising low self-esteem, but a classroom that provides a safe and secure environment will help to deal with any issues relating to bullying or safety issues that have their origin outside of school. An inclusive classroom that attends to the emotional needs of the pupils by involving all the children and by encouraging a positive working atmosphere will go some way to giving a pupil a sense of belonging and help raise self-esteem. Such practices seem to lack specificity, but a teacher should not underestimate their capacity as an agent for change, particularly when it comes to vulnerable children. Children are always drawn to 'good' teachers for a reason. They take strength from being valued as an individual and draw comfort from knowing that they are in 'good hands'. Beyond this, a school's anti-bullying policy and attention to the pupils' social and emotional welfare, possibly as part of a personal and social educational programme, should contribute to raising awareness of the issues around self-harming.

There is one aspect relating to self-harming that teachers can influence directly and that is the issue of examination preparation. Education, at present, is heavily exam-ination driven as schools compete for positions in local and national league tables.

It is well documented that classes at all levels stop 'educating' and start teaching towards success in examinations, whether it be KS1 SATs or GCSEs. In many respects the pupils are innocent victims of combined pressure from parents, teachers and government, all desperate for them to show improvement. Raised expectations at home will put children under pressure and if the class teacher adds more, this is a breeding ground for self-harm as a child feels unable to cope yet is fearful of conveying openly their anxieties because they do not want to upset adults whom they care for. It is the job of the class teacher to protect all the pupils under their tutelage from such pressures, at least in a classroom setting.

(!)

Do you know how much pressure you put on your pupils to succeed?

Do you know which pupils bottle up their emotions because they don't want to show how they are really feeling inside?

Simply trying to play down the importance of the pending examinations may not be enough. What is required is a well-managed and planned strategy designed to alleviate anxiety. The fear is one of failure and what that will bring, so it is up to the teacher to create an atmosphere where the pupils feel successful and confident – a 'can do' culture. While this may not eradicate all their worries, it will reduce them to a level at which they are tolerable. For more information on how to do this, read Chapter 20, which deals with cognitive development, Chapter 2 relating to differentiation and Chapter 3, which looks at active learning.

In conclusion

Case study

Laura's story

'I started by writing all over my arms but this didn't help release the feelings that were inside of me so I began cutting myself. I self-harm when I feel things aren't in my control, like when I get into a fight with my boyfriend or I feel that no one cares about me, like my dad. I want to show everybody how I feel inside. I get depressed if anything goes wrong at school or at home, if I forget my homework or the teacher shouts at me. I love to watch myself bleed.'

Self-harming is not one of those behavioural issues that is likely to affect the smooth running of a lesson. However, the impact of a teacher's relationship with the children they teach may have a profound effect on whether those children will resort to self-harming or stop self-harming if they are already doing so and as such the role of the teacher could turn out to be pivotal.

Further reading

www.harm.me.uk

www.selfharm.net

www.mentalhealth.org.uk

Sutton, J. (2007) *Healing the Hurt Within*, How To Books.

Spandler, H. and Warner, S. (2007) *Beyond Fear and Control*, PCCS Books.

Chapter 18

Truancy

Case study

Ryan's story

'I hate school. What's the point? It's better down town with my mates, nicking stuff from the shops and then hiding when the police chase after us. School's boring. Most of the teachers are crap, all they do is shout and when I shout back I get suspended so why should I bother? Last week I decided to go to school because the wag officer was pestering me. As soon as I sat down in class the teacher was at me so I told him where to go. Then I got put in the red room so I told them to f**k off and walked out.'

Task

Which of the following would you describe as truancy?

- A child taken out of school to go on holiday.
- A child refusing to come to school because she is being bullied.
- A child kept off school to look after their little sister while mum goes to work.
- A child kept off school to go shopping for clothes.
- A child kept off school because relatives from abroad are visiting.
- A child kept off school to attend a dental appointment.

Which of the above are authorised absences?

Technically speaking, truancy is when a child is absent from school without author-isation by the school, in which case all of the above are permissible as long as the school sanctions the absence. If the school does not sanction the absence then it is truancy.

Information

90 per cent attendance or better is the accepted norm.

80 per cent attendance equates to missing 1 day per week.

60 per cent attendance equates to missing 2 days per week.

40 per cent attendance equates to missing 3 days per week.

How many days do you think a child can miss before their education is seriously compromised?

Possible signs of a potential truant

- Absence rate gradually rising (attendance dipping below 90 per cent).
- Increase in minor ailments (headaches, nausea, etc.).
- Skipping the odd lesson (day).
- Frequently late to school.
- Reluctant to attend certain lessons (tantrums, avoidance tactics, poor punctuality).

Background

The perception of children playing truant is the one where the pupils decide to 'bunk off' from class for no apparent reason other than to escape the monotony of school life. In reality, absence from class can be a lot more complicated. Absence from school falls into three distinct categories:

1. **Wanton truancy** where a child chooses not to attend school for no other reason than they cannot be bothered or they have found something 'better to do' with their time.

2. **School refusers** (school phobia) where a child has severe anxiety issues when they are asked to go to school, often manifesting itself in the form of panic attacks (tantrums, nausea, tummy aches).

3. **Condoned absence** where parents actually encourage their child to stay away from school even though the child may be perfectly happy at school.

Information

- In 2009 absence rates in primary and secondary schools rose to 6.42 per cent from 6.26 per cent the previous year.
- The most common reasons given were sickness (58.9 per cent) and holidays (9.5 per cent).
- 60,700 pupils missed class on a typical day.
- 38,000 were persistent absentees.
- 17 per cent of pupils account for over half of all absences.

(*Source*: bbc.co.uk)

Truants: disaffected or disillusioned?

Source: JohnHarris/reportdigital.co.uk

Children 'bunking off' just for the hell of it is, in fact, quite rare; behind every absence there is likely to be an underlying reason. The wanton truant is likely to have started off as a child exhibiting challenging behaviour in class and, as the teachers have struggled to contain the behaviour, the child has started to skip the odd lesson where they know there is likely to be conflict. In some cases teachers actively seek confrontation in the knowledge that a child will choose to run rather than conform.

Task

Children are encouraged to be proactive and take responsibility for their actions, but when a child opts to stay away from a class because the chances of conflict are high, they are castigated. How might a teacher deal with such a situation in their class?

(Answer: in a situation like this it is useful to find out the underlying reasons why a child is absconding. Once this information is known, strategies can be applied to help alleviate the tension. It is important to act quickly and decisively so that bad habits do not form.)

Once a child has learned that running away removes the stress, they will do it again and again. If the child is told often enough that they are a 'bad person' and are made to feel unwelcome, they become disillusioned and disaffected. From there it is a short step to becoming a full-blown truant, joining the ranks of 'lost children' who hang around the periphery of society, choosing to go into town and cause problems because there is nothing better to do with the time they have on their hands. This is reflected on Maslow's theory at the level of belonging and self-esteem.

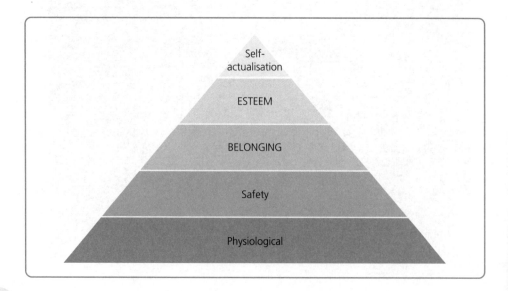

For the wanton truant it is very much a case of feeling that they do not belong to the school, coupled with low self-esteem made worse by the fact that they are falling behind the rest of the pupils in the class. By hanging around with like-minded peers, they gain that sense of belonging and safety absent from their time in school. The pressure of the peer group is significant in drawing them into petty crime and anti-social behaviour and so the delinquent is created.

If they are cajoled or coerced into school via threats of court action, etc., it is possible that the persistent truant will resort to confrontational tactics in an attempt to get themselves suspended, thereby legitimising their absence from school.

The sad fact is that truants who fall into this category want to learn and want to be successful, but they lack the wherewithal to remove the barriers that they have created to justify their actions and make them feel secure.

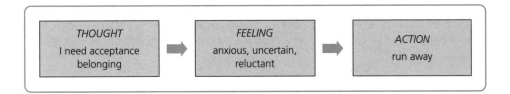

School refusers are quite distinct from truants, although they share a common feeling: one of anxiety at the thought of having to go to school. Where the two differ is in the trigger that creates the anxiety. Whereas wanton truants' actions are born out of a feeling of rejection, school refusers' actions stem from fear – a fear of failure in respect of the demands from teachers or a fear of being bullied.

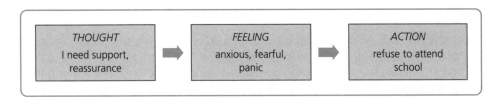

In the previous chapter the pressures of modern schooling (with its emphasis on examinations and league tables) were cited as one of the reasons for children's destructive actions – this is also the case when it comes to school refusers. While it is not healthy to wrap children in cotton wool and protect them from the pressures that life puts on them, neither is it in a child's interests to place them under undue pressure for the sake of hitting benchmarks. Class teachers (whole schools) can become so neurotic about hitting targets that their paranoia rubs off on their protégés, creating unnecessary worry. Examinations are a necessary evil, but how teachers coach their charges and how much emphasis is placed on succeeding at any cost can be a step too far for some children. A child who frets about doing well in an exam and does not want to let the teacher and/or their parents down can quite easily have a panic attack and refuse to set foot in school, even though every other aspect of their life is perfectly normal.

Anxiety attacks can be triggered by many other traumas, leading to a child becoming a school refuser:

- bullying
- family bereavement
- low self-esteem (body image, self-harming)
- lack of friends
- new school
- abuse in the home (bruising, fear of detection).

Condoned truancy is possibly the single most common reason for children not attending school on a regular basis. Condoned truancy ranges from parents who regularly take their children out of school to go on holiday during term time to those who keep their children at home to look after siblings or to indulge their personal needs for companionship, even though the child may be quite happy at school. Condoned truancy is a difficult nut to crack because the parents, with whom a school needs to work closely to get a child into school, are implicit in the subterfuge.

Information

- Parents have a duty in law to ensure that their child is educated. It begins from the start of term after their fifth birthday to the third Friday in June in the year in which they turn 16.
- There is a £2,500 fine for parents and/or a 3-month prison sentence for not making sure their child is properly educated.
- School is not compulsory – children can be educated at home.

Most schools have efficient computerised registration systems that allow an attendance officer to offer a same-day (often within the hour) contact with home service if children are absent, thus nipping potential truancy in the bud, but if the parent makes excuses for their child's absence, the rot can set in and getting the child back into school on a regular basis becomes problematic. From illness to bullying and possibly even criticising the very school that is trying to get their child back into class, some parents will use every possible strategy in a misguided attempt to defend their offspring. As with the wanton truants, court action may bring parents to heel temporarily, but long term it is likely that the child will continue to stay away for large chunks of the school term.

Useful strategies for dealing with truancy from the classroom

A child may choose to truant for a lesson or for the whole day as the result of intolerance on the part of a single teacher. Not all teachers are child friendly!

A child may truant simply because they have issues with a particular lesson. Perhaps they are embarrassed at having to change in front of their peers when doing PE, or because the teacher insists that they read aloud in class.

Knowing the fears and anxieties of the children we teach is important. The teacher's role is to support and encourage, not to coerce.

> **(!)**
>
> **Do you force children to take part in activities even when they refuse?**
>
> **Do you humiliate children when they transgress by showing them up in front of the whole class?**
>
> **Do you put children under extreme pressure to achieve at examination time?**

Tactics such as those above are commonplace as teachers seek to get the best out of the children, but such methods may result in creating anxieties in a child that make them want to run away.

- It is better to encourage children if they are reluctant participants, perhaps letting them perform in private or in a select group.
- It is more productive to chastise a child in private than in public (possibly outside the classroom door or at the end of the lesson).
- Examination technique is not just about driving children via test after test and criticising them if they do not come up to the mark, it is about building confidence and paying attention to anxieties that emerge as a result of the whole examination circus.

> **TOP TIP!**
>
> ## Revision technique in the classroom
>
> - Use differentiated questions for all the class, starting with very easy ones that all can do – this will build confidence.
> - Repeat skills (practice makes perfect) using a variety of angles to drive home the principles.
> - Use exemplar questions that are worded in the same way as the examination questions in order to familiarise the children with the language in the examination.
> - Keep everything low key and fun, always encouraging (solution-focused scaling) and remaining positive.

Case study

Christine's story

'Me and my mum yelled and screamed at each other for weeks. She took me to the doctor's and I had all sorts of check-ups and blood tests but they could find nothing wrong with me. Eventually she gave up and left me alone. There was no way I was going back to school. I had done my mocks and they were really scary, I failed miserably. I couldn't face the pressure even though the teachers told me that I was clever and would do well if I continued to work hard. One morning I woke up and couldn't face going to school. That's when the shouting started. I kept feeling sick and got terrible headaches. My mum thought I was making it up but I wasn't. The doctor said it was anxiety. When the final exams started I just stayed at home feeling disgusted with myself but I couldn't have gone to school. On the day of my first exam there was a knock on the door. I ignored it and scrambled into the kitchen and hid under the sink. I could hear voices outside so I phoned my mum. When she arrived she brought in the headteacher and the deputy head. At first I wouldn't speak to them but then I agreed. They said I could do my exam at home, in the front room, as long as the deputy sat in with me. I agreed. I'm not sure that this was allowed. It gave me the confidence to go to school and have a go at my other exams.'

It is important when trying to encourage a child back into full-time education to make sure that the classroom atmosphere is as welcoming as possible. There should be no fuss, just a workman-like return to lessons. Avoid making any disparaging or sarcastic comments. If they return mid topic, make sure they are given work that they can achieve – don't leave them sitting for ages waiting to be shown what to do or feeling that they are out of their depth. They can always catch up on lost work once they have settled back into class. Over time a timetable for catching up on lost work can be devised, but not straight away – it is essential not to over face the child at this sensitive stage.

Have a fallback strategy if they are unable or unwilling to participate in the lesson. This may be just helping around the classroom or sitting quietly doing something that is not taxing, such as drawing or painting.

Having regular contact with parents is useful when reintegrating a child who has been away from school for a long time. Maybe the parent actually comes into the lesson at first and then comes as far as the class door, then the school gates, always being just at the end of the phone in case the child becomes over-anxious.

It may be that the child is placed in a support unit and allowed into mainstream lessons only when they feel confident enough to do so, or a modified timetable may be created with the input of the child, meaning that they come to school for only an hour or so, gradually building up their time in school.

These processes help build a child's confidence and reduce anxieties. When aligned to a positive working atmosphere created by the teacher in the classroom, they will help integrate a child back into full-time education.

In conclusion

Getting all the children motivated to learn and focused in class is difficult enough, but a child whose attendance is intermittent creates lots of frustrations both in the teacher and within the class as a whole. It is natural to let that frustration show and be intolerant of the errant child, but as a teacher you may not be armed with all the facts and so it is important to maintain a professional integrity and not pass judgement merely because a child rarely turns up to class. A child will (eventually) come to school if they want to and so it is the teacher's role to make the class as inviting as possible.

Further reading

www.bbc.co.uk

www.channel4.com

www.growingkids.co.uk

Blyth, E. and Milner J. (1999) *Improving School Attendance*, Routledge.

Csoti, M. (2003) *School Phobia, Panic Attacks and Anxiety in Children*, Jessica Kingsley.

Chapter
19

English as a second language

Case study

Sohil's story

'When I came to England I was sad because I left my home. I got in a lot of trouble at first. I had a lot of bad behaviour. I kept hitting children because they called me names. I didn't know anybody. I never got into fights at my last school. I got angry. I am not in trouble now, I am a good boy. I can speak good English. I think the teachers like me because I smile a lot. Some people still call me names but I don't bother any more, I just laugh at them.'

If you have ever been on holiday to a foreign country, travelling outside of the usual tourist area to get a feel for the real country you are visiting, you may have experienced a little of what it is like to be a foreigner in a strange land. Chances are that you had family or friends around you to offer support and if it all turned sour you could jump into the nearest taxi and escape. Now imagine a child, possibly a seven or eight year old, or maybe even a teenager, pulled away from a life that was familiar to them and arriving at a new school, in a different country.

Arriving in a new country can be unsettling and traumatic for a child

Source: © Janine Wiedel Photography/Alamy

The school has bright, airy rooms, carpeted floors, lots of computers and other technology, such as white boards. The classroom they sit in might be a far cry from the dilapidated buildings of their last school (if indeed they went to school at all). Other members of the class arrive and there are many but not as many as their last school, where classes may have reached in excess of 40 pupils and took in all age groups. Facilities may have been meagre, just a blackboard, and possibly a few ancient textbooks to work with. Learning was all done by rote. As the other children come in they give sideways glances at the newcomer; one or two stare at the child threateningly.

Possible signs of English as an additional language (EAL) issues in the classroom

- Refusal to speak
- Withdrawn/shy
- Unable to read basic words and sentences
- Does not understand instructions given
- Ignores teacher instruction
- Will communicate with others in their first language

Background

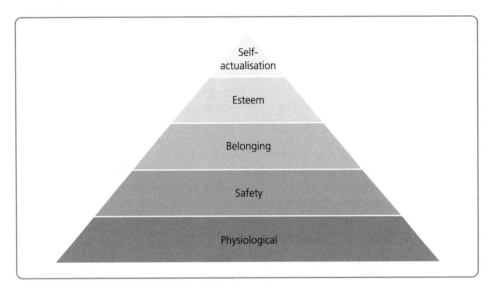

In Maslow's terms the child may have had their physiological needs attended to (you presume), but they do not feel safe, they have nobody familiar to turn to. Everything is so alien that they feel they cannot even communicate with the teacher because they don't speak the same language. They do not feel as though they belong. What self-esteem they had is lost in an overwhelming feeling of insecurity, and any past achievement is buried in a language in which they can no longer communicate. The child is left feeling isolated. The lesson begins and although the child wants to impress, they do not have the capacity to do so, fearful that they will look stupid if they get anything wrong, and because they do not wish to draw attention to themselves they sit motionless. All the child has to work with are facial expressions and other aspects of body language, assuming they are able to read them accurately – this is a different culture and they are young and inexperienced.

Useful classroom strategies for dealing with EAL children

What of the teacher who is presented with this new child in their class?

- What work can be given so that it is constructive?
- How does the teacher convey rules and procedures?
- How does the teacher know what the child's cognitive abilities are?
- What other 'special needs' does the child have?

On arrival it is important that the teacher makes the child feel welcome. This can be done by:

- smiling
- maintaining eye contact
- using soft voice tones
- talking to them slowly and clearly (not turning away)
- knowing a few words of their language (greetings, etc.)
- exchanging names.

It will help to buddy the child with a reliable class member, one who is a good role model and is confident. It is essential to get them actively involved straight away. The EAL child could be given simple tasks such as handing out equipment to get them used to the classroom environment. If they are left to sit, doing nothing, this will amplify their anxieties. Whatever class work is being done, they should be included. This will mean differentiating the work to suit their needs – it would be ridiculous to demand that the child does the same as the rest of the class from the outset. At this induction stage it is essential not to chastise but rather to instruct by role play or demonstration what is acceptable and what is not.

The child needs to make progress with the aim of assimilating them into everyday class life. The resolution lies in language acquisition because without the means to communicate, both teacher and child will be at a loss. It is useful to understand the stages in language acquisition so that the teacher can use strategies best suited to the EAL child at each juncture.

With a child new to school who cannot easily access the curriculum there may be a tendency to place them in a bottom set or to assume that they have learning difficulties. This may not be the case. Putting them with a group of students with behavioural problems will present them with inappropriate role models whose behaviour they may copy, unaware that they are transgressing. It may also be the case that they are academically able but simply lack enough English – putting them with children of a low ability can be demeaning and lead to disaffection and frustration on the part of the EAL child. Where possible, try to find out their capabilities before they arrive in the class. Otherwise carry out an induction (see the stages below) to try to gauge their capabilities.

Case study

Sylvia's story

'I came to England from Venezuela. When I arrived at the school they put me in the bottom sets with all the naughty children. I was scared and upset. I told my parents that I did not want to go to that school but they said that I had no choice. The school wanted me to start again in Year 10 but I did not want to stay in those classes with all that trouble so I said no. My parents told me to work hard and that maybe I could catch up at college after the GCSE exams. Towards the end of Year 10 a teacher noticed that I was doing well in French and Spanish as well as Maths, so she altered my timetable and got me moved to higher groups. She also got me extra help with my English. My reading age was below 8 years of age in the September, by December it was 11 years of age. I was doing Textiles and Graphics as my options and I took up Art GCSE in the January of my final year. I also went to Portuguese lessons after school. I passed all my GCSEs with a C grade or better, I got As in my languages, except for English, I got an E grade in that, so I repeated it at college and passed. I am going to university next year.'

When anybody arrives to live in a foreign country they progress through four identifiable stages. The time spent in each stage is dependent on age, ability and commitment.

STAGE 1 (the silent period)

(number of words 0–500) (time span, up to 1 year)

At this first stage, the child is unlikely to be confident enough to speak. They may say the odd word or repeat short phrases as they are spoken to them, but they are not thinking about what they want to say, they are just copying 'parrot fashion'.

The teacher might get the child to:

- respond to pictures
- copy key words in English and write the word in their own language (encouraging them to work in their first language will help them feel more comfortable and will give an indication of cognitive capabilities)
- build a vocabulary
- understand and copy gestures and movements
- listen to comprehension.

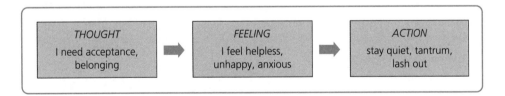

THOUGHT	FEELING	ACTION
I need acceptance, belonging	I feel helpless, unhappy, anxious	stay quiet, tantrum, lash out

STAGE 2 (early production)

(number of words 1,000) (up to 6 months)

At this stage the child will be able to speak in one- or two-word phrases and will be able to use short chunks of language that they have memorised.

The teacher might get the child to:

- answer questions that involve yes/no and either/or answers
- offer one- or two-word answers to questions.

The teacher may also:

- use pictures to support the child's learning
- modify sentences and focus on key words (see Chapter 1)
- allow the child to take an active part in group work
- use scaffolding to aid the child's learning
- get the child to use 'simple' books
- provide listening activities.

STAGE 3 (speech emergence)

(number of words 3,000) (1–2 years)

At this stage the child will be able to communicate using simple sentences. They will understand easy stories and be able to do some content-based work with teacher support.

The teacher may get the child to:

- complete simple cloze-type sentences
- read texts modified to their reading ability
- write brief stories based on their personal experiences (dialogue journals are useful at this stage).

TOP TIP!

Use dialogue journals

Dialogue journals are similar to diaries where the child will write about topics that they are interested in and develop at their own pace. They may include conversations held with the teacher, what goes on in the lesson and around the school. They can be written in their own language, interspersed with words in English to help them. They can also be used to express thoughts and feelings.

STAGE 4 (cognitive academic language proficiency)

(number of words 6,000+) (5–7 years)

In the first part of this stage the child will be able to use more complex sentences. They may ask the teacher to clarify details in class. Their comprehension of English literature will increase and they will use strategies from their native language to learn English. They will also be able to learn more complex concepts. As the child makes progress they will have a near-native ability to perform. At this point they are unlikely to need any extra support except with very difficult tasks as long as they do not possess any other learning difficulties.

Task

- How might you adapt your lessons so that they include a child who speaks no English at all?
- What would be the learning outcomes for the child?

Information

- 14.3 per cent of all primary school children do not have English as their first language.
- 10.6 per cent of all secondary school children do not have English as their first language.

(*Source*: DCSF, www.dcsf.gov.uk)

(!)

Do you teach any children with English as an additional language?

Do you know what their academic capabilities are?

If your classes are taught in ability sets, how many in the bottom set have English as a second language compared with sets at the top?

Another aspect of EAL relating to behaviour is that of group dynamics. If a multi-cultural class is not encouraged to mix, cliques will develop. This may develop into an 'us and them' scenario where racism starts to fester. Children can be targeted because of their ethnic origin. Claims and counter-claims about children talking about others in their native language may materialise. It is important as a class teacher to recognise tensions early on and nip them in the bud before they become a serious issue.

(!)

If children complain about others in the class talking about them in their native language, do you insist that everyone in the class speaks only English?

If so, could this be construed as being racist? (Or is it just being pragmatic?)

Based on the stages above, differentiating work with EAL students might follow this pattern:

1. Introduce key words and link to visual/pictures as well as to words in their own language.
2. Complete questions with a Y/N and either/or answer.
3. Use closed questions which are short answer or cloze in nature.
4. Complete larger sentences, short paragraphs using writing frames/scaffolding.
5. Complete open questions such as describe/explain.

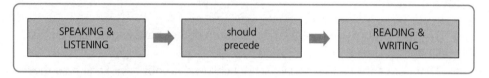

In conclusion

There is much political rhetoric made of issues surrounding immigration, political refugees and asylum seekers. Whatever a teacher's opinions, it is their professional duty to provide a safe, secure and stimulating educational environment for children in their charge. The Race Relations Act 2000 states that every school should have a race equality policy which should cover staff, pupils, parents and carers. However, the inclusive teacher should not need an Act of Parliament in order to carry out their duties responsibly.

When working with children whose first language is not English it is important to get the right balance between induction and inclusion, especially in the early stages. Too much emphasis on induction may lead to alienation, while too much inclusion without the necessary induction may result in a similar outcome. The key to inclusion is communication and that cannot occur effectively without being able to share a common language.

Further reading

www.primarylanguages.org.uk

www.nationalstrategies.standards.dcsf.gov.uk

www.everythingesl.net

Murcia, C. (2001) *Teaching English as a Second or Foreign Language*, Cengage ELT.

Chapter
20

Cognitive ability

Case study

Susie's story

'I was difficult in lower school. If the teachers were out of order I'd tell them. I still do sometimes, but nowadays I'm not so rude if they cross me. I've always been really good at sport. I was in all the teams: hockey, netball and rounders. I liked getting stuck in. Swimming was what I was best at, I was bordering on national standards. Then I got fed up. I couldn't be bothered getting up early all the time and practising every day for hours. I got in with a bad lot and became quite disruptive.

I got put into lower sets and began to wonder whether to even bother doing any work. My CAT scores weren't good and so I thought, what's the point? Most of the teachers seemed to think that I wouldn't amount to much.

When I got to Year 11 I started to focus more on my studies. I don't know why really, I kind of thought I'd give it my best shot, there was nothing to lose. At first I found it really tough but then the staff picked up on my hard work and encouraged me. I started staying behind after school to catch up and worked hard in class. I dumped all my old friends and made some new ones. I could not believe it when I got my results in August: I got seven GCSEs at C or better.'

▶

Case study continued

Susie's CAT scores

Verbal reasoning	Non-verbal reasoning	Quantitative	Mean
93	89	83	88

Susie's GCSE profile

	Maths	English	Science	ICT	Art	PE	French
Predicted GCSE grades	E	D	EE	DE	C	D	E
GCSE grades achieved	E	C	CD	BC	A	B	C

Background

Ability is not innate

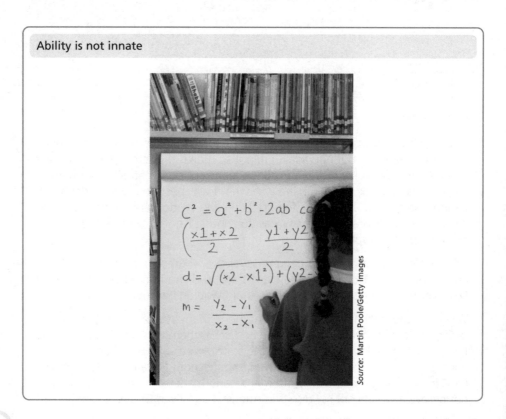

Source: Martin Poole/Getty Images

Task

What personal factors may have influenced Susie's academic achievements?

(Answer: commitment, ambition, self-confidence drawn from her achievements at sport, teachers who encouraged and supported her and did not give up on her.)

(!)

Do you know children you have taught who have achieved at a higher level than expected?

Does the number surprise you?

If these children have excelled, their achievement begs the question of how far they (and others) might go and what (if any) are their limitations.

As teachers we make assumptions about children's limitations, but are our predictions always accurate?

What factors limit a child's progress?

How many of these factors are cognitive?

Can all cognitive barriers be breached?

(Comment: With time commitment and excellent teaching, many academic barriers can be broken. Work by Reuven Feuerstein indicates that intelligence is not fixed.)

The reason for including a chapter on cognitive ability in a book about understanding behaviour is not to infer that low cognitive ability equates to a deterioration in behaviour. You are just as likely to get a gifted child who is very disruptive as you are to get a child with low ability exhibiting similar traits. Behavioural issues generally occur when the cognitive needs of the child are not being met. At the higher ability level children are prone to boredom if the work given to them does not challenge them. At the lower end of the ability range, challenging behaviour tends to emanate when the work set is too difficult.

'I used to get so bored in class I started to do all the work set and then kept demanding more to see how long it would take before the teachers lost their temper at me. Then I would have a go back.'

Setting physical impairment aside, children are generally placed in a mainstream school or 'special school' based on their cognitive ability as determined by their IQ (intelligence quotient) and other assessments. There is some blurring at the edges, but a general categorisation is shown in the table here.

IQ scores linked to cognitive classification – an IQ of 100 is used as the benchmark for students of average ability

IQ range	Intelligence classification
1–24	Profound cognitive disability
25–39	Severe cognitive disability
40–54	Moderate cognitive disability
55–69	Mild cognitive disability
70–84	Borderline cognitive disability
85–114	Average intelligence
115–129	Bright
130–144	Moderately gifted
145–159	Highly gifted
160–170	Exceptionally gifted
Over 175	Profoundly gifted

Areas shaded cover mainstream education

Another measure of cognitive ability used in education is the cognitive assessment test (CAT). This can be very influential in determining the route a child will take in the education system and what they are taught as well as being used as a predictor of future achievement. IQ tests and cognitive assessment tests measure similar aspects of cognition.

Examples of CAT scores as GCSE performance predictors

Mean CAT score	GCSE prediction English Language	GCSE prediction Maths
91	D	D/E
100	C	C/D
109	B/C	B/C

Information

CATs

- Verbal reasoning measures deductive and inferring skills.
- Non-verbal reasoning measures the ability to understand new information independently of language skills.
- Quantitative reasoning measures mathematical ability.

TOP TIP!

A high non-verbal score against a lower verbal score is indicative of a child with reading (e.g. dyslexia) or language difficulties.

There are those in education who believe intelligence levels are fixed and as a result children are pigeonholed for much of their school life with expectations that they are unlikely to achieve beyond a certain limit. This results in poor academic expectations for some children and higher expectations for others. The CATs predictions are based on probabilities and a closer look at how these predictions come about shows that they focus on the most likely outcome based on previous statistics.

Task

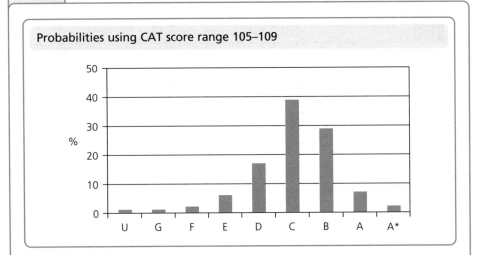

Probabilities using CAT score range 105–109

Using the tables:

a) Why is a score of 109 given a prediction of B/C?

b) What is the chance of getting an A grade?

c) What is the chance of getting a U grade?

(Answer: a) Nearly 70 per cent chance of this occurring. b) Less than 10 per cent. c) Around 1 per cent)

In some schools children are placed in sets on the basis of their ability. They may be streamed, banded or placed in a mixed-ability group.

- **Setting** is the process where children are placed in groups in order of academic ability.
- **Streaming** is where children are set across a narrow ability range.
- **Banding** is where children are set across a wider ability range.
- **Mixed ability** is where children are not set according to ability.

Some schools have a sink group. They occur either by engineering as a department seeks to deal with the challenging behaviour of a few weighed against the better behaviour of the many, or by default as children tumble down the setting system. They are the class everybody dreads. The children are feared, maybe even loathed. The children are united by an 'us against the world' mentality. Their very isolation is worn as a badge of (dis)honour. The group is a hotchpotch of the academically able children who are bright but disruptive and the low-ability children who have spent their life in the bottom strata of mainstream education. Some are actively aggressive, one or two are passively disaffected and likely to be the subject of persistent bullying. Someone has to try to teach them and the task is not for the faint-hearted. The children have low self-esteem, their confidence is shattered, they feel rejected by the school and they may also have learning difficulties of one sort or another.

(!)

- **What method of setting occurs in your school/department?**
- **What are the advantages and disadvantages of each method?**
- **Which would you prefer?**
- **Why would you prefer this type?**

TOP TIP!

If children are placed in sets in your department or school, it is important that all students are placed in a set commensurate with their academic ability in that subject. Dropping children down a set on the basis of poor behaviour is a recipe for disaster. If a child is proving disruptive in a set then it is better to deal with them in situ.

However, the precept that cognitive-based assessment tests are accurate presupposes that each child tries their hardest so that comparisons can be made, and this is often not the case. A child who has English as a second language may underperform, as might a disaffected child or one who is ill on the day of the exam. While such tests are an indicator of present performance and future potential, they do not provide the whole picture.

The work of psychologists such as Bruner, Piaget and Vygotsky has endeavoured to make sense of cognitive development. Vygotsky's social development theory is one of the foundations of constructivism and asserts that social interaction plays a fundamental part in cognitive development. This contrasts with Piaget, who believed that cognitive development precedes learning. Both theories can play a major role in enhancing cognitive development.

Piaget's theory is a useful tool when it comes to writing differentiated material for children. It is a simple and straightforward method of building schemas around which other styles of teaching and learning can be attached.

Piagetian stages of development

- **Sensorimotor** (0–2 years) Children gain an understanding of the world through sensory experience.
- **Preoperational** (2–7 years) Children learn to represent objects by using words and drawings. They are curious and gain lots of knowledge, but their reasoning skills are flawed.
- **Concrete** (7–12 years) Children are able to sequence objects and recognise logical relationships. They are able to classify groups and can manipulate basic mathematical equations.
- **Formal operations** (12–adult) Adolescents and adults can think abstractly, draw conclusions and reason logically. They can apply information to new situations.

At first glance a Piagetian view of learning would appear to support the perception of limits in a child's capabilities. How many children do you know below the age of five who can explain Einstein's theory of relativity? At a superficial level it also supports the notion that cognitive assessment is an accurate measure of cognitive development.

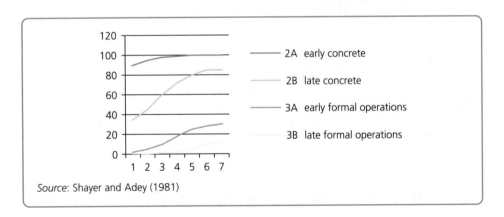

Source: Shayer and Adey (1981)

The graph shows the proportion of children at different Piagetian stages in a representative child population in Britain from the ages of 9 to 16 years. What it reveals is that only about 40 per cent of children at the age of ten are at or above the late concrete stage of operational thinking. This means that any task given to them that demands more complex 'thinking skills' will be beyond their ability. It would be easy to accept that we must wait for children to mature cognitively before we even attempt to ply them with more challenging and complex thinking tasks (a little like the idea of reading 'readiness'), but what is missing from this assumption is the fact that children can (and do) excel (frequently) beyond our expectations.

Task

Study these three maths questions. Notice the change in cognitive demand of each.

Piaget level 2A 2 oranges cost 4p, 1 orange will cost how much?

Piaget level 2B 2 sweets cost 5p, 6 sweets will cost how much?

Piaget level 3A 2kg cost 12p and 3kg cost 15p, which is the best buy?

(!)

- Check a textbook or worksheet that you use.
- Categorise it using Piaget's stages of development.
- Does it match the age of the children you teach?
- Do any of the children have difficulty with the work set?

'In a constructivist model of learning, nature and nurture do not compete, rather they work together.'

(John Abbot, Educationist, 2000)

If you look closer at the CAT graph it shows a range of predictions from U to A*. In any situation there is always a chance of a child scoring any grade, which means that predicted grades are not set in stone – they can be wrong! Yes, we need to be aware of where children 'are at' cognitively, but this should be just a starting point for a teacher as they plan for progress, not an acceptance that this is all the child is capable of.

Useful strategies for improving cognitive capability

So what can a teacher do to improve a child's cognitive ability and as a result enhance their chances of exceeding expectations? Factors such as motivation, attendance and commitment (from both parties) will all have a bearing on eventual success, but there are other specific teaching techniques that can have a direct effect on cognitive development. Differentiation (Chapter 2) plays an integral role in affecting cognitive development and it is this that forms the basis of a process called 'accelerated learning'.

The basis of differentiated work should include graded work that gets progressively harder.

Stage 1 – the work should be easy to complete and serve as an introduction or refresher.

Stage 2 – the work will build on skills/concepts introduced in stage 1 and be more cognitively challenging.

Stage 3 – the work will challenge the child even more using higher-level thinking skills such as analysis and evaluation.

Breaking an exercise into smaller chunks makes the task more accessible.

Accelerated learning is sometimes viewed as a methodology that might be used to improve a child's performance at examination time, given pressures to deliver 'value added' within a demanding curriculum and a tight time scale, but in reality the term 'acceleration' refers to the rate at which children improve cognitively compared with the more traditional methods of 'chalk and talk' or learning by rote. There are a number of methods that claim to provide accelerated learning, but this text will look briefly at two of them: multiple intelligences and cognitive acceleration.

The problem with CATs and IQ tests is that they test only one aspect of the brain, principally reasoning. They do not measure creative ability, linguistic skills, coordination or physical aptitude. These are examples of what are described as multiple intelligences. You may have heard of VAK (visual, audio and kinaesthetic learners), but there is a wider variety of ways in which we can develop a child's learning skills. Cognitive acceleration techniques (such as Bloom's Taxonomy and CASE – Cognitive Acceleration in Science Education) use a specific methodology to effect development.

The common features of accelerated learning techniques are that the role of the teacher changes to that of 'facilitator' and much of the learning process is child-centred. With the use of a multi-intelligences approach (including VAK) the emphasis is on varying the stimulus. Techniques such as assessment for learning, critical skills and cognitive acceleration utilise reflective strategies such as meta-cognition and application, as does Bloom's Taxonomy (p. 24).

Cognitive acceleration through science education (five pillars)

- Concrete preparation (stimulus for new learning).
- Construction (analysing information).
- Cognitive conflict (presenting information that does not fit patterns identified).
- Meta-cognition (reasoning how thought patterns have come about).
- Bridging (applying the knowledge to a new situation).

> **Task**
>
> a) The Yanomami tribe in the Amazon are largely illiterate. For this reason would you consider them less intelligent than yourself?
> b) If you were placed in their jungle environment and asked to survive on your own, would they consider you less intelligent?
> c) Who is correct?
> d) Which model of cognitive development does their study fit best?
>
> (Answer: a) Clearly they would fail to score on a standard IQ or CAT test. b) Most likely because we would not possess the knowledge and skills to survive in such a hostile environment. c) Neither. d) The observation would support Vygotsky's theory as it favours the principle of social development as a precursor to cognitive development, but this does not mean that Piaget's theory is incorrect.)

Multiple intelligences

- Verbal–linguistic (written or spoken words).
- Logical–mathematical (numbers, reasoning, logic).
- Visual–spatial (artistic, spatial awareness).
- Bodily–kinaesthetic (movement, physicality).
- Musical (rhythm, music, hearing).
- Interpersonal (extrovert, likes group work).
- Intrapersonal (self-reflective, introvert).
- Naturalist (sensitive to the natural environment).

> **(!)**
>
> **Do you know how Shakespeare's *Romeo and Juliet* might be taught using each of the multiple intelligences listed?**

A child who lacks academic ability in the classroom is showing only that their skills in the linguistic or logical–mathematical categories of multiple intelligences are lacking. That same child may excel at sport (bodily–kinaesthetic) or be a talented musician (musical).

Information

Savants are people who have impaired (often severe) cognitive disabilities, yet they may exhibit exceptional memory tasks, mathematical prowess or be musically gifted. These same people may not be able to tie their own shoe laces or make a cup of tea.

People like this challenge our perception of 'intelligence'. By being aware of the different ways that the brain works, which manifests itself in how children perform in various tasks, the teacher can provide differentiated material that draws on these other 'intelligences' in order to develop a child's cognitive abilities in the area of the logical–mathematical, which is what standard IQ tests measure.

The essence of all cognitive development is motivation. Whether it be scientifically researched strategies or just pseudo-science, if children are actively engaged in the learning process they will make progress. What dictates the level of their success is not so much a methodology (although it can be a key factor) but whether the child 'signs up' to the work. Once they commit, the job is made a lot easier. The skill is in getting them to 'sign up' in the first place.

No sign-up, no change!

(Solution focused)

With all the pressures of having to jump through the examination hoops put before teachers it is easy to rely on the tried and trusted methods to 'pass' exams. Making the shift to accelerated learning techniques can require a leap of faith because the cognitive gains, despite its title, are not immediate. Yet given time children will begin to exhibit a deeper understanding of the work presented rather than some superficial comprehension that is here today and gone the next. More fundamentally, the schemas created in the brain will serve to improve cognition further.

The simple truth is that there is no magic formula when it comes to improving cognitive capability. Effective teaching based on certain key elements that come together creates the optimum conditions for progress to be made. It is in this area that Vygotsky's work begins to take shape. How children are taught and the quality of teaching are pivotal in providing cognitive development. The key elements are highlighted below:

- positive relationships between teacher and child
- differentiated work that is challenging yet achievable
- 'active' as opposed to 'passive' learning techniques
- varying the stimulus (use of multiple intelligences)
- child-centred work that gives the child ownership of their learning
- development of 'thinking skills'
- creation of a 'can do' environment where a child is motivated to work

- commitment from the teacher
- high expectations of the child from the teacher.

In such a heady environment children will make significant progress.

In conclusion

As educationists we make many assumptions about the capabilities of the children we teach. We often make those judgements based on performance at examination time. Children are placed in sets and work is attuned to their needs based on such tests. With so many children to oversee it is easy to overlook their potential. A disaffected child is less likely to perform to the best of their ability, and nerves or self-esteem may also play a part in how well (or badly) they do. Children with English as a second language are particularly susceptible to underperforming, through no fault of their own. It is the classroom teacher working closely with their charges who detects potential. By structuring the work to attend to their needs and by motivating them to achieve, much progress can be made above and beyond the expectation of cognitive assessment tests. Alongside motivation must come a commitment from the child. If these are engineered to work together, a child will excel despite their circumstances. Learning is not just about cognitive ability.

Further reading

www.teachingexpertise.com

www.gl-assessment.co.uk

www.mindtools.com

Smith, A. (1998) *Accelerated Learning in Practice*, Network Continuum Education.

Pound, L. (2005) *How Children Learn: from Montessori to Vygotsky*, Step Forward Publishing.

Shayer, M. and Adey, P. S. (1981) *Towards a Science of Science Teaching*, Heinemann Educational Books.

Attention deficit hyperactivity disorder (ADHD)

Case study

George's story

Most of the class have arrived and are settling as George bursts into the room. He pokes or nudges every person he passes as he makes his convoluted way to his seat. He stops to share insults with a mate, laughing loudly and making rude gestures as he eventually falls heavily into his chair, all the while looking for potential interactions. Nobody takes any notice of him so he resorts to interacting with the child he has been placed next to, or behind him or in front of him, whether they want him to or not. After repeated requests to pay attention, George finally complies, swinging on his chair as the teacher introduces the work.

Case study continued

'Can anybody tell me the name of the Prime Minister?'

'Miss, you are going grey,' George observes.

The teacher tells him to stop swinging on his chair and he stops, but then he snatches a pencil from the person sitting next to him and starts to beat out a rhythm on the desk as the teacher is talking. George is looking everywhere except in the direction of the teacher. The teacher steps over and takes the pencil away. Irked, George starts to drum on the desk with his fingers. The teacher asks another question and hands shoot up, but George gets in first, shouting out the answer and grinning with satisfaction.

George is chastised for blurting out the answer and is told to stop drumming on the desk with his fingers. Frustrated, George takes a pen from his partner and starts to doodle on the desk while systematically nibbling chunks of plastic from the end of the pen and flicking them across the room at unsuspecting victims. Instructions given, the class start working in earnest. George reluctantly opens his exercise book but still does not begin work. The pen he pinched has been demolished and he has nothing to write with. The teacher gives him a pencil but it is not sharp enough so he gets up out of his seat and strolls over to the bin where he sharpens the pencil. He disturbs numerous students on both the outward and the return journey.

The lesson has been under way for a while and George has still not written a thing. His demeanour remains jovial despite the teacher being on his case, seemingly at every juncture. The teacher checks on his progress only to find that his book is in disarray. There are pages left blank, what is written down is not in sequence or complete and the handwriting is untidy. The teacher battles with George for much of the lesson, trying to prevent him disturbing others and get him to do the work that has been set. Eventually the teacher's persistent haranguing gets to George and he tells her to 'shut the f--- up!', sweeps his book off the desk and storms out.

(!)

Identify students you teach who exhibit similar types of behaviour.

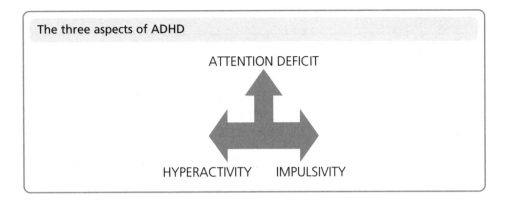

The three aspects of ADHD

ATTENTION DEFICIT

HYPERACTIVITY   IMPULSIVITY

Possible signs of a child having ADHD

To be truly ADHD a child must exhibit all three characteristics shown in the figure.

A child can be hyperactive without having ADHD. Even so, the strategies given later in the chapter will suffice for both.

Attention deficit

- Has trouble concentrating.
- Appears not to listen when spoken to.
- Makes silly mistakes.
- Skips from task to task.
- Forgets instructions.
- Disorganised.

Hyperactivity

- Restless.
- Fidgety.
- Always fiddling and touching things.
- Gets up and walks around.
- Talks excessively.
- Always on the go.

Impulsivity

- Interrupts.
- Intrudes on other people's conversations.
- Speaks and acts without thinking.
- Does not wait their turn.
- Outburst of temper.

There is little doubt that a child with ADHD will present a significant challenge to the teacher. Their actions are innately impulsive but are not attention seeking in design, however they can be very demanding on a teacher's time and patience.

Case study

Paul's story

'I still take my medicine. When I don't I concentrate less and don't do as much work. I just look around the room daydreaming. In primary school I was always getting told off for tapping my pen. I get in trouble a lot for saying stuff I don't mean to say. When I get angry I think 'oh ---- it!' and what I am thinking just comes out. Having ADHD has had a big effect. Without it I would have had better schoolwork. I'm good at Maths but because I'm always in trouble my grades are poor. My best subject is ICT, I'm looking to get an A grade in it. I don't like English much, there's too much writing.'

Task

Which of these children has ADHD?

a) The boy who always shouts out the answers in class.

b) The girl who fidgets in her chair.

c) The child who does both of the above.

(Answer: none of them or all of them. It is only by careful observation over a long period that a diagnosis can be given.)

Background

ADHD is a clinical disorder that occurs in about 3–5 per cent of the population. It is caused by an impairment of two main functions of the brain, namely attention and impulsive/hyperactivity. ADHD can be genetic in nature. It usually appears in early childhood some time before the age of seven. It can be influenced by diet. ADHD makes it difficult for a child to control spontaneous responses, from shouting out what they are thinking to ignoring something that catches their attention. To effect a diagnosis the symptoms must have been present in two or more different environments (usually home and school) for a period of at least six months. Other causes have to be discounted and the effects of the symptoms have to have had a negative effect on the child, their family and/or schooling.

If clinically diagnosed, the child can take medicines to control the problem. These medicines sometimes have side effects and so parents may choose not to medicate their children. Some of the most awkward students in school may have ADHD, and while some may have been clinically diagnosed, others may not. There is no cure for ADHD. The best that can be hoped for is that a child will gain the skills needed to control their behaviour or that by taking medication the worst excesses of their condition will be tempered.

Information

ADHD occurs most commonly in boys, but girls can also be affected by it. The ratio is around 15:1.

Possible strategies to deal with the ADHD child in the classroom

What separates the child with ADHD from the 'naughty' child is that their behaviour is likely to be persistent and difficult to control. In the classroom the teacher may not be concerned with the whys and wherefores of a child's ADHD but rather is in need of strategies to deal with the child. Many children with ADHD are innately intelligent, so it is imperative that they are given work commensurate with their academic ability. Putting them in lower ability groups or giving them work that is too easy will only compound secondary behavioural problems.

For all their lack of concentration, there will be times when the ADHD child is quiet and studious. This could be when they are asked to draw rather than write or perhaps work on the computer. They may work best when they are sitting on their own.

Students with ADHD can bring many skills to the classroom. They can be:

- creative, offering lots of ideas as their imagination lacks boundaries
- keen and enthusiastic, not limited in their outlook
- full of drive and determination when motivated
- interesting and fun to be around (never a dull moment!).

(!)

Observe a child you think may have ADHD. Jot down when they are being 'good'.

Note:

- the task they are doing
- where they are sitting
- who they are sitting with
- the time of day and the time in the lesson.

They are usually at their most unsettled at the start and end of the lesson.

TOP TIP

Using computers in class can often help children with ADHD focus for longer.

Getting the environment right

Trying to create an environment in a classroom that is free from distractions is impossible, but there may be an area that can be set aside for quiet study where a child with ADHD can be asked to work. Other strategies include:

- sitting the child near to the teacher's desk, so that they have a good line of sight
- Placing them away from a window or door where they may get distracted
- surrounding them with 'quieter' children who are less likely to distract
- Setting seats in rows facing forwards, which are better than tables arranged with seats facing inwards.

ADHD children are poorly organised. Their work is likely to be scruffy and disorganised, so good classroom structure and routine are helpful. Homework is unlikely to be done, not because they are lazy, it is just that they forget. A solution-focused approach is best at finding out by trial and error what works for the child.

'If it works, do more of it. If it doesn't, try something different.'

(Solution focused)

To organise a child with ADHD:

- maintain good eye contact with them when speaking to them
- make use of group work, no more than three per group and paired with an organised student
- use email to their home – it may help.
- keep all essential work in class
- encourage good practice but accept a task is complete rather than complaining about presentation
- catch the student being good, praise and reward (even if the good behaviour is brief, praise them immediately).

ADHD children fidget. Those who fidget may benefit from something (silent!) to hold and play with. Give them the opportunity to move around class (mini-breaks, class monitor).

Giving something to play with sometimes helps a child with ADHD

Source: Phototake Inc/Alamy

TOP TIP!

How to make a **quiet** fidget bean bag.

1. Fill a balloon with sand or flour.
2. Seal it.
3. Get the child to personalise it using stick-on eyes, hair, etc.

They can then hold the bag, squeeze and fiddle with it without making any undue noise.

ADHD students have a poor short-term memory. They rarely multi-task and are likely to flick from one question to another without actually completing any. If they wander off task, calmly remind them where they are up to.

Give them instructions one step at a time.
1) Write the instructions on the board
2) You may need to repeat the instructions more than once
3) If they wander off task remind them where they are up to
4) Use a stepping stone approach
5) Break larger tasks into smaller ones

TOP TIP!

Don't just say

'get on with your work.'

Better to say

'George, you should be doing page 26, question 5.'

Finishing tasks is a problem. Use praise rather than punishment to get the work complete.

Organising work in class to help a child with ADHD

Children with ADHD can pay attention when they are doing things that engage them, but when the task is boring or repetitive they are likely to lose concentration quickly.

- Give a brief outline of the work at the start of the lesson.
- Find a settling activity that works for them.
- Find the student's preferred learning style (many are visual learners).
- Work should be engaging, interesting and challenging (low boredom threshold).
- Set active, creative work rather than passive written work (avoid lots of note taking/copying).
- Use a stepping-stone approach to instructions.
- Structure work and routines (change causes distraction and over-excitement).
- Break larger tasks into smaller ones (use frameworks, no multi-tasking).
- Break the lesson into chunks (lots of variety as a stimulus).
- Get them to make lists, reminders, etc. (improves memory).

TOP TIP!

Make passive tasks more active by:

- annotating drawings
- using mind maps
- using colour to emphasise details
- underlining key words/phrases in texts that are being read
- acting out/role playing as a story is being read
- making tasks competitive (winner gets a house point or a sweet).

Information

Children with ADHD are usually visual learners.

TOP TIP!

Rather than use an open-ended approach to an activity, such as 'Write a story about your favourite food', break down the task into smaller parts, using writing frames or other guidelines.

a) What is your favourite food?

b) State five key features of your food.

c) Give three reasons why you like it.

d) Give two ways you might alter the food to make it even better.

(!)

Study one of your lesson plans. Design it to suit a student with ADHD.

Associated behaviours

As a consequence of the behaviours linked to ADHD a child may also:

- have other specific learning difficulties (reading, writing, etc.)
- be anxious or depressed

- be clumsy and lack coordination
- deliberately defy adults (Oppositional Defiant Disorder)
- lie, steal and damage property (Conduct Disorder).

Depending on the age of the child they are likely to have been consistently punished for not settling in class and for not completing work set. These secondary traits are generally learned behaviours resulting from constant criticism and sanctions. As the child gets older these defence mechanisms become more ingrained and are difficult to eradicate.

> 'The behaviour is the problem, not the child.'
>
> *(Solution focused)*

Dealing with poor behaviour associated with ADHD

It is important for a child with ADHD to have a clearly designated set of guidelines (Independent Behaviour Plan, Independent Learning Plan) that is followed by all teachers. This will help provide structure for the child as they strive to come to terms with their condition. While allowances are made to accommodate a child with ADHD in the classroom, it is equally as important not to lose sight of established boundaries when it comes to behavioural issues. Depending on the child's record of need they may have a teaching assistant assigned to help them in the classroom. If this is not the case, departments should target teaching assistants to support classes where ADHD issues are prevalent.

The child may deny any involvement in a misdemeanour and be quite vehement in that denial – short-term memory loss is likely to be the culprit.

- If a child is being excessively disruptive the teaching assistant can intervene and possibly remove the child for a short time.
- The child should be allowed to return without criticism, welcomed and allowed to get back to work.
- Ask them if they know what they are being punished for. Remind them if they do not remember and explain your reasons.
- Make any punishment immediate (time out, kept after class) – they will forget to come to a detention. Do not issue a prolonged punishment (banned for the next few lessons).
- Avoid getting trapped in arguments. Be assertive without resorting to shouting. Be calm even in the face of extreme behavioural outbursts (these tantrums are usually highly charged but brief). Give the child the chance to apologise once they have calmed down.
- If the child's behaviour is so difficult that you feel the need to remove them, use something like the three-strike rule, with clear warnings placed on the board. Send them to an agreed place within school that is managed by an adult and is quiet.

TOP TIP!

Cards that have to be carried from lesson to lesson are unlikely to get signed and will probably be lost. An in-class card is perhaps the easiest option, with the teacher taking responsibility. This should be clearly visible to the child.

In conclusion

ADHD appears to have emerged as a consequence of modern living – it was unheard of up until towards the end of the 20th century. Because of this there are those who question its existence, putting its symptoms down to poor parenting and other aspects of societal change. Those who believe in the existence of ADHD make reference to everything from food additives to air pollution as possible causes. In truth, the jury is out, although evidence is mounting that ADHD is 'real' and not a psychosomatic illness imposed on unruly children via the pseudo science fraternity.

Whatever the root cause, the fact remains that there are children all over the world behaving in a similar disruptive manner, which, at its most extreme, is almost impossible to deal with in a classroom situation without recourse to medication. Below the level of 'extremis' there are varying degrees in which ADHD will manifest itself and with careful planning and preparation the classroom teacher can deal with this in situ. Also, by getting to know a child and observing when they are actively engaged, a teacher can effect proactive control and begin to educate the child without straining their stress levels to breaking point.

Further reading

www.addnews.com

www.livingwithadhd.co.uk

DeRuvo, S. (2009) *Strategies for Adolescents with ADHD*, Jossey-Bass.

Lougy, R. (2007) *Teaching Young Children with ADHD*, Grown Press.

Chapter 22

Autism

Case study

Kurt's story

'It started when I was at primary school, the kids used to think I was weird. I didn't want to be in any of their groups because they always picked silly names. They used to sing a song to set me off and then that turned into them setting me off so that they could get out of doing a lesson that they didn't like. It carried on into secondary school. I would do anything to stop them, I would throw chairs, even fire extinguishers. I would look for the nearest weapon to try and kill them. In cookery I picked up a knife and in design tech I used a chisel, I was so violent and aggressive that I had to be physically restrained.

My record of need said that I should let the teacher deal with the situation but some didn't bother. I attacked one teacher for not doing anything to help. I wanted to make her pay so I punched her. In some lessons I felt safe and there wasn't a problem. I hated Art because the teacher told me to express myself more and I didn't know how to do that so I disrupted the lesson. She said use your imagination and I replied by saying I haven't got one! I didn't like Music because of all the noise. I had to have the lights on in class but another boy

▶

Case study continued

with autism could only work with the lights off so we used to argue a lot. When I came home at night I went to bed at 6 o'clock because I was so tired.

I had no friends at that school. When I moved to the other school it was completely different, I had so many friends it was stupid. I kept bumping into them in the corridor and they would always say 'Hello Kurt, how are you doin' mate!.' One boy sang the song at me but the headteacher dealt with him severely, justice was done. Before I was a shadow in a world of light but now I was just part of the crowd. When I started at the new school I had buddies to take me to class and to lunch, but eventually I didn't need them. I was in the lower sets to begin with but by the end I was flying. I got six Cs and one D in my GCSEs.

When some of the first lot see me they still sing the song but I just tell them that they are pathetic. I don't let them see what it does to me, even though it still takes hours to get over it.'

Background

The perception of a child with autism is often one of a flawed genius, oblivious to everyone around them, locked in a world in which few people are allowed to enter and one from which they cannot (or choose not to) escape. The reality, however, is that many children with autism are desperate to be accepted by society but they lack the skills to 'fit in'. Many people with autism go through life undiagnosed, even though one in every hundred is autistic – that means that almost every school in the country will have a child with autism in its midst.

Many children (and adults) with autism remain on the periphery of society, with few (if any) friends. To those who do interact with them they are likely to be viewed with disdain, bullied and/or rejected because they are perceived as 'odd'. As the child gets older, without the right support all they can do is look at society from the outside in, as barriers to their inclusion become increasingly insurmountable.

In class there may be one child who unnerves the others. They will be left to work on their own during group work or accepted grudgingly but still marginalised if the teacher intervenes. They may become overbearing in their fastidiousness, to the point at which the rest in the group start to complain, or, in an effort to make friends, they will be silly, over-acting and becoming a nuisance. Their presence irritates the group, thus behavioural issues start to emerge, and so the teacher accedes and takes the child out of the group to work on their own. The child has tried too hard to make friends and has failed again.

Possible signs that a child is autistic

Autism is defined by a child experiencing difficulties with:

- social communication (verbal and non-verbal)
- social interaction (the ability to make and maintain relationships)
- social imagination (the ability to think intuitively).

To be truly autistic a child should exhibit all three traits and they may also experience sensory problems as well as being compulsive when it comes to rituals and routines. Autism occurs as a spectrum, ranging from the severe, which is likely to include other learning difficulties, to what is termed 'high-functioning' autism (including Asperger's syndrome). Children with high-functioning autism are those most likely to be found in a mainstream school.

Information

Asperger's syndrome is a condition found at the high-functioning end of the autistic spectrum. The triad of characteristics that defines autism is evident in a child with Asperger's syndrome, but they tend to experience fewer communication issues and are often of average or above-average intelligence.

'Asperger's is a billionth part of who I am!'

(Teenager with Asperger's)

Social communication (verbal and non-verbal)

As with children who cannot speak English, a child with autism lacks understanding when it comes to language. Where the two differ is that an autistic child is capable of speaking the language but they do not comprehend the subtleties that lie behind the spoken word. They have a tendency to take things literally – colloquialisms, jokes and cultural slang are aspects that they fail to pick up.

'She's hot' (meaning pretty, sexy, good looking)

'He's cool' (meaning sophisticated, suave)

The autistic child may think the person being spoken about is ill. They may even go over to the person and touch them to find out whether they are actually hot or cold.

'What's up?'

(The ceiling? The roof? The sky?)

The autistic child may repeat what others say, possibly even out of context, without understanding the meaning of what is said.

'My mother's hot!'

It is not only verbal communication that sets them apart, it is their inability to recognise or read body language or facial expressions that may also get them into trouble.

We are conscious of people who step into our personal space or touch us, even gently on the shoulder. We tend to keep our distance when meeting people for the first time. We may proffer a hand to be shaken but our bodies are kept at arm's length, literally. A child with autism will not be aware of proximity and may step into a stranger's personal space. Friends play rough and tumble in the playground; an autistic child may join in even though he is not their friend, he may not even know them. In their teenage years boys will 'chat up' the girls and the girls flirt with the boys; when the autistic child copies these social interactions they get short shrift from horrified recipients.

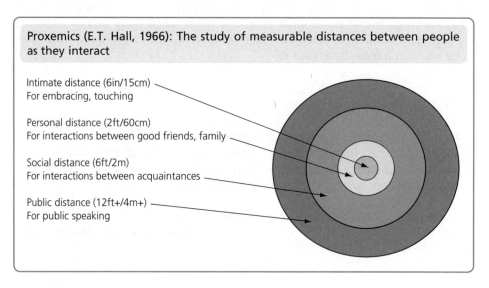

Proxemics (E.T. Hall, 1966): The study of measurable distances between people as they interact

Intimate distance (6in/15cm)
For embracing, touching

Personal distance (2ft/60cm)
For interactions between good friends, family

Social distance (6ft/2m)
For interactions between acquaintances

Public distance (12ft+/4m+)
For public speaking

TIP

Invasion of intimate and/or personal space leads to us feeling threatened, eliciting our fight or flight response.

Try placing a line on the floor and get two children to walk towards each other. Tell them to stop when they feel uncomfortable.

| 5 | 4 | 3 | 2 | 1 | 1 | 2 | 3 | 4 | 5 |

As teachers we use a lot of non-verbal communication to control a class of children – body language, hand gestures, facial expressions and tone of voice are an everyday part of our armoury. A child with autism may not know what these signals mean and even if they learn to recognise them, each adult they come across will use slightly different (or even completely different) expressions to convey mood, so the child will struggle. Recognising social signals is something that we learn intuitively as we grow from infancy to adult; children with autism are not able to learn this way.

'What neurotypical students know instinctively, students with autism usually have to learn scientifically.'

Task

Read some facial/body language expressions in class. Do you use the same ones?

Autistic children have difficulty making eye contact. They prefer to avoid looking at somebody directly and if asked to do so they will feel very anxious. This may make them appear shy or aloof.

Social interaction

If a child cannot read the social signals given by those around them and cannot comprehend the language of a subculture, they are going to find it difficult to mix. This will result in low self-esteem and low confidence to the point at which the child may become withdrawn. Alternatively the child, desperate to be accepted, may try too hard to get a friend and so not succeed. Even if another child does befriend them, sustaining the friendship may prove problematic.

(!)

Do you know how to make friends?

Do you know how to keep friends?

How would you explain these skills to a child with autism?

If another child shows an interest, the autistic child will talk at them rather than with them and so the conversation may become very one-sided, with the other child not able to get a word in edgeways. The child with autism is likely to have interests and hobbies that they are keen to share, but rather than allow their new friend to express an opinion they will talk incessantly about one topic, to the exclusion of everything else. We have all been at gatherings where one person dominates the conversation, possibly about their exploits, and we soon make our excuses and move away – children are no different.

Where young children play with toys, the autistic child may not engage in play as such but will rather fixate about one aspect of the toy. Rather than race cars around a track they may focus on how the wheels spin or put them in a line from largest to smallest. To other children such behaviour will seem odd. These aspects of autism make it difficult for the child to 'fit in' with their peers and so they become isolated.

In England there is a debate concerning the age of criminal responsibility, the age where it is felt children know the difference between right and wrong and the consequences their actions have on other people. Autistic children may not recognise the boundaries of acceptable or appropriate behaviour and so laying down a benchmark such as this is difficult where they are concerned. Consider the comment below.

'Hello, Orangina!'

A comment made to a teacher with a suntan, the inference being that it was a false tan. The child did not understand the full implication of what they had said. The intention was to have a joke at the teacher's expense. The child did not comprehend that the teacher might be hurt by such a comment. There was no remorse.

> **(!)**
>
> **What would you do? Do you reprimand or do you educate?**

An autistic child may laugh when told of a bereavement in another child's family or touch on any social taboo purely out of ignorance. We learn to regulate our behaviour through experience and by recognising the social signs; autistic children may be taught these skills as they occur but they might not transfer them to a new situation. In the same way, a child with autism may strike out at another child. This may be copied behaviour and although they may know that hitting another child hurts them, they are unlikely to be aware of the emotional damage it can cause.

Social imagination

Reasoning and logic are the tools of the autistic child. They will recognise patterns and sequences and be clinical in their assessment of what is presented to them, but what they have difficulty in doing is thinking intuitively. In Piaget's work and other approaches to thinking skills, abstract thought is at the higher end of the spectrum. The child may be able to predict by extrapolating a graph, but ask them to put themselves in somebody else's shoes or anticipate how someone might feel in a particular situation and they will struggle to provide an answer other than a logical consequence.

'If somebody is attacked, what might they feel?'

'Pain.' (Not 'upset' or 'scared' or 'anxious'.)

Play and role play are difficult. Children may create all manner of designs with building bricks, cars, houses, planes, etc. The autistic child is likely to place the bricks in piles of similar colour, shape or size. They prefer games that are logical in essence.

As well as not functioning in the three areas highlighted, children with autism may exhibit other characteristics.

Reliance on routines

The routines that they follow can be ritualistic in nature, straying into obsessive com-pulsive disorders. They may impose strict rules on themselves or place objects in a certain position before they can even function. To stray from these routines can be the cause of much stress and anxiety. Children with autism thrive on routines. Their obsessive behaviour can include stereotypical actions (like the animal caged in the zoo pacing to and fro), possibly swinging on a chair. They may feel they have to avoid the gaps in between pavement slabs or walk two steps up and one step back when climbing stairs.

Interests

Children with autism may have a particular interest in one or more subjects. They may recite long lists of facts and figures in incredible detail. At first their wealth of knowledge may prove exhibitionary, amazing all round, but it will not take long before the child 'bores the pants' off their peers because of their inability to recog-nise when others are tiring of their recital. Subjects can range from plane spotting to particle physics, comic book heroes to dinosaurs. Their insistence on paying attention to detail may be seen as 'geekish' by their peers.

Sensory sensitivity

In our daily lives we are bombarded by sensory stimuli: the sound of traffic on the road, car and house alarms blaring away, television, radio and music hammering out noise. Fridges, freezers and central heating thermostats click on and off. Our hear-ing detects not only sounds but changes in air pressure and balance as well. Visual stimuli, including lights that flicker and flash from computer monitors and television screens, can give us headaches. Science says there are five senses, but in fact there are many more. Not only does eyesight detect light and dark, it has sensors to detect all the colours of the spectrum, movement and much more. Our tongues are sensi-tive to a range of tastes and our olfactory system can detect myriad smells. On our skin we have touch, pain and heat sensors. As we grow up our brains learn to filter out the unwanted sensations, focusing only on those we want to take notice of, but just think what it would be like if we did not filter out all these sensations.

Children with autism can often have extreme sensitivity to one stimulus or another. They may be able to detect the buzzing of electrical circuitry in the back of a tele-vision or the frequency of the flicker of strip lighting. They may shy away from particular colours or jump at the texture of a specific material (remember how you felt when somebody scraped their nails down a blackboard!). The result of this heightened sensitivity can lead to anxiety and very challenging behaviour.

> 'Over 65 per cent of challenging behaviour associated with autism occurs as a result of sensory issues.'
>
> (R. Mills, National Autistic Society)

Case study

Katie's story

'I didn't want to go into the classroom. I can't explain why, except that it was something to do with the teacher. He shouts a lot. Last lesson he asked us to write what we thought about a poem. I wrote that it was too long. He said I had to explain why it was too long and so I said because it had too many words in it. He shouted at me and told me that I was being facetious. He asked us to write about the feelings that are represented by colours. I said that I did not understand. He asked me what red is associated with and I said danger. I knew this because it is on road signs. He then asked what I felt when I was in danger and I said "nothing" so he frowned at me and told me to stop being obstructive. He then started talking about blue being a colour that represents a feeling of cold. I said that people's noses go blue when they are cold, the class laughed but the teacher didn't. He asked the class what the emotion of coldness felt like and I said the opposite of being hot. The teacher sent me out of the room. Now he has sent me out I don't want to go back in.'

Task

How would you get Katie to write more about the poem?

How would you try to get her to understand the emotions associated with colours?

(Answer: children with autism have to learn by recognition rather than understanding, even when it comes to feelings. The teacher would have to teach them that red is for danger and blue is sadness so that if the question was asked they could answer as taught, but it would not be intuitive)

Useful strategies for dealing with autism in the classroom

The triad of impairments and their associated characteristics can result in all manner of challenging behaviour in the classroom, ranging from extreme violence to a simple refusal to do any work. At the back of the reaction is anxiety caused by sensory overload, confusion or distraction. The issues can be addressed in the inclusive classroom using the SPELL approach.

Structure of classroom routines, seating plans, rules for setting out work in their books. This does not necessarily mean a traditional approach to teaching in the classroom but that new and innovative work may have to be introduced within the daily routines so that the child can practise and so that there is not too much new material to be processed. Rehearsing new strategies may help.

Positive, even if the child is exhibiting challenging behaviour, in order to maintain their confidence and self-esteem. Correction should avoid negative chastisement in preference of encouragement and tolerance.

Empathy in respect of the teacher gathering as much information about the child and an awareness of what the lesson (classroom) looks like from the autistic child's perspective. This can then be built into their teaching and learning as part of their inclusive ambition. (For example, what are the child's interests and strengths? What makes the child anxious?)

Low arousal in respect of knowing what makes the child anxious (e.g. sensory sensitivities, compulsions, etc.).

Links with the community, within school and outside of the classroom. The use of a buddying system in class is useful in achieving this. The buddying system could even be extended to the playground and beyond.

(!)

Do you teach a child with autism?

Do you know what makes them anxious?

Do you know what their strengths are?

- Children with autism tend to be visual learners, so having tasks written down will help.
- It is important that they understand that instructions given include them, so make sure they know this by asking them to explain what they are to do to ensure that they are not simply repeating what the teacher has just said.
- Allow them time to process any instruction.
- Make sure that any task has a clear beginning and end, especially in more unstructured sessions (for example, telling them how they have to finish the task).
- Make sure they are seated where there is minimum distraction.
- Do not enforce eye contact as this requires extra processing skills.

Task

In a critical skills group, which role would best suit a child with autism?

- Manager
- Creative/Designer
- Scribe
- Facilitator.

Would any of these roles not suit them? Why?

'Stretch not stress.'

It is important not to make excuses for a child's behaviour because they are on the autistic spectrum; it is better to stretch their ability in order to improve their learning experience and develop their adaptive abilities. However, it is essential to avoid causing stress by being understanding of their condition.

In conclusion

Autism is usually viewed as a disability. Wendy Lawson described it, more appropriately, as

Difability

Children with high-functioning autism in particular can contribute significantly to society as a whole as long as intolerance and prejudice are put aside. Because children with autism tend to think objectively rather than emotionally they bring a dose of realism to any issue (imagine a prime minister with autism!). Their skills are analytical, dissecting any problem into its component parts and scrutinising it in detail. Their conclusion is likely to be clinical, based entirely on the facts presented to them. It will be judgement that is frank, honest and without equivocation.

(!)

Do you know what jobs might best suit a person with autism?
- Doctor.
- Lawyer.
- Counsellor.
- Teacher.
- Electrician.
- Computer technician.

In the inclusive classroom there is much talk of multiple intelligences, so why can autism not just be viewed as an alternative 'intelligence'? Neurotypical children (and teachers!) have a lot to learn from the autistic child, possibly as much as the autistic child has to learn from the neurotypical person. Their different way of thinking can be a boon rather than an obstacle, but only if we understand better how they function.

There have been many hypotheses in respect of what causes autism but none has been proven. The latest thinking is that autism occurs as a result of both genetic and environmental factors. There is no cure for autism (and many people with autism would react by saying that it is not a disease or a disorder and so it should not be perceived as something that might be 'cured'), but with expert guidance and support, children with autism can lead active and fulfilled lives.

Further reading

www.aspergers.org.uk

www.autism.org.uk

Cumine, V. and Dunlop, J. (2009) *Autism in the Early Years*, Routledge.

Moore, C. and Sicile-Rice, C. (2007) *Adolescents on the Autism Spectrum*, Vermilion.

Roth, I. and Barson, C. (2010) *The Autism Spectrum in the 21st Century*, Jessica Kingsley.

Vermueln, P. (2001) *Autistic Thinking*, Jessica Kingsley.

Chapter

23

Dyslexia

Case study

Jasper's story

'I have dyslexia and ADHD. I have always had a problem concentrating in class. I like maths, it's easy. The teacher gets angry because I always shout out the correct answer. She tells me that I have to show my working out in my book because in an exam I will get extra marks, but what does it matter if I get the answer right? I'm crap at English, my writing's scruffy. I don't like writing. The teacher showed me that my writing was better than some others in the class but he missed the point, I can't write! The teachers keep getting annoyed because I won't write and I mess about in class. When they shout at me I tell them to "F**k off" so I get suspended. I don't mind staying home, at least I don't get all that shit they give me at school.

I have had anger management and I have been working with the behaviour teacher. He got me a computer to use in class but I didn't use it, it made me look like a retard. I don't muck about so much these days, I just sit there and do nothing. They asked me if I wanted to go to a different school for kids with behaviour problems like me, I said bring it on, anything to get me out of this place.'

In most classrooms there is a child who seems to be something of a paradox. On the one hand they play an active part in class and appear to be quite bright, but this is in marked contrast with what they produce on paper. They may answer anything they are asked correctly or even offer extra detail, being impressive to the point of the teacher seeking to reward them for their contribution. On the other hand they may manifest a degree of antipathy towards the lesson (or the teacher), choosing to sit and doodle or chat with friends rather than engage in the lesson. It is only when they are confronted with a question about the work that they show their potential by glibly giving a correct answer, while the teacher thinks 'if only'. It is this disparity between the possible and the reality that indicates the presence of dyslexia. The child may excel in other areas of the curriculum that are less dependent on the written word, but when it comes to reading, writing and spelling they are found wanting. In truth, there may be many other reasons why a child shows such a disparity in their school work, but further analysis to confirm or deny dyslexia is worth pursuing.

> 'I was dyslexic before anybody knew what dyslexia was. I was called "slow". It's an awful feeling to think of yourself as slow – it's horrible.'
>
> *(Robert Benton, Screenwriter, 1932–)*

Dyslexia is a condition that causes children to have difficulties with the written word. They may have trouble reading text, spelling or actually putting pen to paper; for many dyslexics all three are evident. 10 per cent of the population is dyslexic – that converts to between two and three in every class.

Possible signs of dyslexia

Writing:

- Handwriting is scruffy and uncoordinated with lots of crossings out.
- Writing is very slow, often leading to unfinished or brief work.
- Work written is generally of a high quality, although brief.
- Uses upper- and lower-case letters inappropriately.
- Has difficulty with punctuation and grammar.
- Slow to write information from text, notes, etc.

Spelling:

- Spells the same word differently in the same piece of work (e.g. went, wnet).
- Cannot recognise the differences.
- Confuses letters that are similar (b/d, p/q, p/g, n/u, m/w), with many reversals.
- Writes phonetically.
- Cannot do rhyming or alliteration tasks ('round and round the garden the ragged robin ran').

Reading:

- Unfamiliar words misread.
- Adds or omits words (and whole lines).
- Reads but does not process the meaning/context of the text.
- Refuses to read or is hesitant.

Numeracy:

- Confuses x/+.
- Has trouble memorising formulae.
- Has problems sequencing data (including times tables).
- May think out high-level problems but needs a calculator for simple tasks.

Coordination:

- Laterality confusion (mixes up left and right. Does not use just one hand for a range of tasks).
- Clumsy/poor motor skills, holds pen awkwardly.

Other:

- Slow processing speed.
- Poor concentration.
- Has trouble following instructions.
- Difficulty in telling the time.
- Poor sense of direction.
- Sensitivity to black/white contrast.

Background

Information

Dyscalculia is a condition that affects the ability to acquire mathematical skills. It is like dyslexia but involving numbers. Children with this condition find it hard to understand simple number concepts and have difficulty learning facts and procedures. They learn methods mechanically without really understanding the principles, making it difficult to apply concepts to new situations.

- Can count in sequence but has difficulty navigating back and forth.
- Finds learning, recalling and using procedures difficult.
- Has difficulty with measures (telling the time, handling money).
- Has problems with special orientation (left/right, map reading).

According to the British Dyslexia Association, about 3–6 per cent of the population are affected, while 50–60 per cent of dyslexics show signs of dyscalculia.

A dyslexic child will show combinations or clusters of the above and although they may want to succeed in the lesson, setting themselves high expectations they may soon become disenchanted and/or frustrated at their apparent lack of progress. A teacher who is unaware of their condition may see the child as lacking effort or motivation and may chastise, criticise or threaten sanctions if the child does not comply with instructions given.

> A teacher sent the following note home with a six-year-old boy: 'He is too stupid to learn.' That boy was Thomas A. Edison.

The dyslexic child not only has to fight to keep up with others in the class, they may also have to deal with persistent pressure from the teacher. Imagine how anxious you would become if you were asked to paint a house inside and out in a day or write a 10,000-word essay in an hour. How would you react? Would you have a go, or refuse to do it? How would you react if you were pressured to complete the task?

Task

- Can you write with your other hand?
- Try writing a paragraph from this page with your other hand.
- Notice how much harder you have to concentrate to operate the necessary processing skills.
- How long did it take you?
- How neat is your handwriting?

Dyslexia is not a sign of high or low intelligence. However, it can be particularly galling for children of high ability as they may feel trapped by the condition. They will be able to cope with cognitively demanding work, but the insistence that most things they do have to be written down prior to assessment can be frustrating and ultimately disheartening in equal measure. This may lead to disaffection, withdrawal or excessive behavioural issues within the classroom.

It is not surprising that children with dyslexia find themselves slipping down academic sets or being placed with less able children. In this way the teacher inadvertently damages the child's self-esteem as they become disheartened.

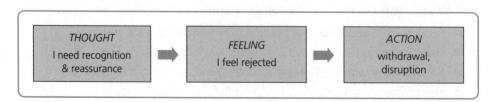

THOUGHT		FEELING		ACTION
I need recognition & reassurance	⇒	I feel rejected	⇒	withdrawal, disruption

The source of dyslexia is not known precisely, but a number of factors have been identified as possible causes.

Phonological deficit

To become fluent readers, children need to be able to link sounds that they hear with written letter combinations. In the English language there are 44 of these sounds, know as phonemes. Children without dyslexia pick up many of these intuitively, but dyslexic children have continual difficulty with these phonological processing skills. Recent research using brain scans has indicated that the dyslexic child does not process the phonological sounds that they hear fast enough. Children normally pick up these phenomes through experience or perhaps by rote learning. The dyslexic child has to be taught these rules – and there are more.

There are 44 phonemes in English

Vowel phonemes

Phoneme	Examples				
a	cat				
e	peg	bread			
i	pig	wanted			
o	log	want			
u	plug	love			
ae	pain	day	gate	station	
ee	sweet	heat	thief	these	
ie	tried	light	my	shine	mind
oe	road	blow	bone	cold	
ue	moon	blue	grew	tune	
oo	look	would	put		
ar	cart	fast (regional)			
ur	burn	first	term	heard	work
or	torn	door	warn (regional)		
au	haul	law	call		
er	wooden	circus	sister		
ow	down	shout			
oi	coin	boy			
air	stairs	bear	hare		
ear	fear	beer	here		

▶

Consonant phonemes

Phoneme	Examples			
b	baby			
d	dog			
f	field	photo		
g	game			
h	hat			
j	judge	giant	barge	
k	cook	quick	mix	Chris
l	lamb			
m	monkey	comb		
n	nut	knife	gnat	
p	paper			
r	rabbit	wrong		
s	sun	mouse	city	science
t	tap			
v	van			
w	was			
wh	where (regional)			
y	yes			
z	zebra	please	is	
th	then			
th	thin			
ch	chip	watch		
sh	ship	mission	chef	
zh	treasure			
ng	ring	sink		

(!)

Do you know how many blended sounds there are? (cl, pr, sch)

Do you know how many consonant diagraphs there are? (sh, ph, th)

Do you know how many vowel diagraphs there are? (ea, ow, air)

TOP TIP!

Children with dyslexia may find learning new languages difficult because the language uses a different arrangement of phenomes than English and sentence structures are likely to be different.

Children who are dyslexic often have difficulty processing visual information quickly

Source: © Emmeline Watkins/Alamy

Visual difficulties

These can be a factor in that children with dyslexia may not be able to process detailed visual information quickly. Many dyslexic children experience visual discomfort and are hypersensitive to strong visual contrasts, such as black writing on a white background or rapid flicker when looking at lines of parallel text. Words may also appear blurred or swirly on the page. Some dyslexic children experience a problem keeping their eyes steady when reading.

Genetics

There is evidence that dyslexia runs in families and is more common in boys than in girls (ratio of 3:1), although recent evidence suggests this may be closer to 50:50.

Short-term memory

Research has shown that children with dyslexia have problems with short-term memory. This can lead to them giving up part way through a task.

Cerebellum deficit

Many dyslexics have difficulty processing at speed. Tasks that are done automatically in respect of language learning may take longer and what is absorbed may take more time to become embedded. Even though they may be able to read what is written, they may not have the fluency to extract the meaning of the text at the same time.

Useful strategies for dealing with dyslexia in the classroom

Helping a child come to terms with their dyslexia is a specialised skill and has to be taught deliberately. The child will need to be withdrawn from mainstream classes at some point for specialist tuition and they are likely to have extra assistance in the lesson to help them access the work in class.

If a child is going to be treated for dyslexia then the earlier a diagnosis is made, the better it will be for all concerned. If dyslexia is not spotted until a child is well into their school career, other secondary issues, such as self-esteem and/or disaffected behavioural traits, may have been acquired, making any treatment more problematic. For example, asking a teenage child to wear glasses with coloured lenses or to attend 'special' lessons outside of the mainstream will draw unwelcome attention and so they may be reluctant to participate, even though they know that it is for their 'own development'.

While all these strategies are welcome (and necessary), to some children they will be a source of embarrassment and so the child may rail against the support given, especially a truculent teenager. This is why an early diagnosis is best. If a later diagnosis occurs, it is important to treat the child with sensitivity, taking into account their feelings as well as their educational needs (possibly discuss with the child how they prefer to have the support).

Case study

Denise's story

'I've had dyslexia since Year 3. When I speak it doesn't make sense to others but it does to me. I get the words all mixed, like was and saw. I did the NESSY (Net Educational Systems) stuff but I didn't like it because they took me out of lessons and I wanted to stay in, it was embarrassing. The others were always asking why I was going with the TA. My dyslexia definitely has held me back in English. I have the mind to speak what I say but I can't write it down. I can't seem to explain things properly like I can in Science. It hasn't held me back in Sports or Drama. In these subjects we write exactly what we want to say but sometimes when the teacher reads it back they can't make sense of it. People think that dyslexia people are dumb but they aren't. I was put in the bottom set for maths at first. Dad has dyslexia, we are in the same boat. I have had to push myself really hard to concentrate more and to check and read back, to get more confident in myself. I plan the work first and then tick off what I have done. I do most of my work at home. In the past I have written on a computer, as it shows up my errors. I have gone back and read it out to myself and worked on it.

If you say to yourself "why do I have it?", you put yourself down, but if you say "it's not bad at all" then that helps to boost your confidence. I'm going to the Commonwealth Games in June. Many sports stars are dyslexic – they are my role models.'

TOP TIP!

When helping a child with dyslexia, use the following strategy:

- see it
- say it
- hear it
- write it (from recall).

It is essential that a child with dyslexia is not set up to fail, therefore work in class should be designed with the dyslexic in mind. Written instructions should be:

- written clearly (large, bold, printed)
- brief and to the point (short sentences, few syllables)
- literal (avoiding the child having to infer)
- set out in a simple sequence (few steps, logical and in sequence)
- displayed using different coloured backgrounds (not just black on white)
- repeated frequently (it helps to refocus the child if they lose concentration).

The use of a multi-sensory, multi-intelligence approach may help, as will using scaffolding to put the work into manageable chunks.

In many classes the use of a 'fun' activity is offered as a carrot at the end to get them to finish the work. To the dyslexic child this is like having a 'punishment in reverse'. They will require more time than the others and so are unlikely to reach the fun activity as they soldier away at the task in hand. The same applies if the work is differentiated in tiers, where the work not only gets progressively harder but all the rewards occur at the end. This can be disheartening for a dyslexic child, who may be trying their best and would achieve at a higher level if only they had the time. Rewards are best given in situ. It is important that the teacher is aware of the work the dyslexic child has achieved – this will help to raise confidence levels and build self-esteem. This may mean setting individual (or group) targets with expectations that are different for each child in the class. Such an eventuality is fraught with problems and has to be delivered with a degree of sensitivity.

The dyslexic child is likely to be constantly comparing themselves with others, so the teacher should look to reinforce the positives in their work. The use of scaling may help (comparing what has been achieved previously with what they achieve at present). They may use assessment for learning criteria and/or critical skills, but it is important that such work has a sensitivity to their needs and does not become counterproductive.

The most productive approach is to train and encourage the dyslexic child to manage their own learning. The level to which this can occur will depend upon maturation and ability, but it is a useful exercise across the whole ability range. Their management could be as simple as:

- allowing time limits for each task and keeping to time
- breaking work into sections (read task, complete task, check work done)
- learning to recognise when they are losing concentration.

In conclusion

The likely dyslexic child will exhibit a disparity in their overall abilities. While they may experience significant problems with their classwork in a written format, they may excel in other aspects of their life, possibly at sports, art, drama or practical craft work. They are also likely to be adept orally.

Generally speaking, learning support units and lower ability groups have a higher percentage of children with dyslexia (diagnosed or otherwise) than other classes in school. In prisons, around 30 per cent of inmates are dyslexic. The path from dyslexia to disaffection to deviance is one well trodden, with its roots in disaffection and reduced self-esteem. However, there are also many luminaries who have dyslexia. Whether they have achieved through adversity, rising to the challenge to be better than those around them in spite of their learning difficulties, or just coincidence is a matter for conjecture.

- Muhammad Ali
- Richard Branson
- Cher
- Leonardo da Vinci
- Roald Dahl
- Winston Churchill
- Albert Einstein.

If left undiagnosed or not dealt with effectively in the classroom, dyslexia will seriously hinder a child's progress throughout their school life and possibly into their adult working life. If planned for in class and treated with sensitivity, a child with dyslexia can achieve at the highest level.

Further reading

www.bdadyslexia.org.uk

www.channel4.com

www.educational-psychologist.co.uk

Bennett, J. and Hailstone, P. (2006) *The Dyslexia Pocketbook*, Teachers' Pocketbooks.

Reid, G. and Wearmouth, J. (2002) *Dyslexia and Literacy*, John Wiley & Sons.

Chapter
24

Dyspraxia

Case study

Marcus's story

'I am a bit awkward. Some of the kids say I walk funny and talk like a numpty. I am always tripping up in class or knocking things off the desk. Some laugh at me, some get angry and thump me, especially if I touch their bags. One teacher thought I did it on purpose and shouted at me. At primary school my parents were called in to see the teacher because I couldn't fasten my shoe laces, tie my tie or even fasten the buttons on my shirt, it was embarrassing. I find the work in class easy but they have put me in bottom sets because I can't keep up with the work and my writing's really scruffy. The others pick on me and call me stupid, it makes me so annoyed. I try to hit them but I am too slow, so I throw their books off the desk instead. I'm always getting into trouble. I want to do well in school but nobody cares so I think, why bother.

I'm always the last to be picked in PE. Nobody wants me on their team, they complain to the teacher when they have to have me. They stick me in nets and laugh as I dive about. Some get angry and shout at me for being crap. I try to forget my kit or lose it so that I don't have to do sport.'

Background

When somebody throws a ball for a person to catch, the receiver goes through a sequence of stages as directed by their central nervous system.

1. The ball being thrown is the stimulus.
2. The eye is the sense organ that detects the ball's motion, speed and direction.
3. This information is sent via sensory neurones to the brain.
4. The brain processes this data and sends impulses, via motor neurones, to the arms and hands.
5. The arms are stretched out in front of the body and the fingers extended in anticipation of catching the ball.
6. They are placed far enough apart to allow the ball to enter yet not so far apart that the ball cannot be gripped before it passes.
7. As the ball enters the space between the hands, the eye detects its position and sends a signal to the fingers to grip the ball.

What is amazing is that most of us can do this automatically. Consider, however, the ball coming in at speed from a short distance. The reaction time needed to carry out the sequence is much faster and will be beyond some people, for example the elderly and the very young, especially as their motor coordination is far slower than, say, that of a teenager. The very young and the elderly will see the ball just as quickly, but the processing skills that convert sensory stimuli to motor movement are not as fast and so they fail to catch the ball.

Children with dyspraxia are very similar in their actions and reactions to stimuli. They may know what it is they want to do, but their execution of the action is much slower than the norm. Or it may be the actual sequence of movements that they have trouble with, placing them in the wrong order or missing one of them out. What would happen if a person catching the ball missed out item 2 or item 6 from the sequence above? At best their attempt to catch the ball would appear clumsy.

Dyspraxia is an impairment of movement. That movement might be the physical coordination of limbs or the mechanics of speech. The outcome is a laboured action that appears slow and deliberate, almost in 'slow motion', giving rise to a perception that the child is lacking cognitively. However, although the child may not be adept at carrying out certain motor skills, dyspraxia does not directly affect their intellect or intelligence.

(!)

Do you know which actions involve motor skills (e.g. running)?

Do you know which muscles are used for speech? (Try saying some words out loud.)

(Answer: motor skills involve the reflex arc actions. Following a stimulus, a message is sent to the brain via sensory neurones. The brain assesses these messages and sends a response via motor neurones, which activate muscle movement.)

Catching a ball is a difficult skill

Source: © Jeff Morgan OY/Alamy

Possible signs of dyspraxia

Children with dyspraxia have problems in five key areas:

- **Gross motor control**. This involves whole body movement (walking, riding a bike, skipping). Dyspraxic children are able to walk, but their movement may be awkward, their balance poor and their timing out of kilter. Their spatial awareness and judgement of distance may be inferior. They are likely to show cross-laterality (using their left or right hand without preference – this is not the same as being ambidextrous). Their muscles will lack definition, making them weak and unable to hold items for long periods (e.g. copying out lots of text). They may exhibit poor posture as a result.

- **Fine motor control**. These are simple actions where movement is voluntary but slight and gentle. Children with dyspraxia have trouble with motor control at this level of sensitivity (e.g. holding a pen, writing, opening a sweet packet, fastening buttons).

● **Speech**. Children with dyspraxia have trouble controlling speech – either the sounds within a word or forming sentences. They also have problems managing their breathing. Their language development may be impaired as a result of these and other issues related to poor short-term memory.

Task

● Consider the fine motor skills needed to say words with more than one syllable (for example, spe/ci/fic or ar/gu/ment).

● Read a paragraph out loud and observe your breathing as you talk.

● **Memory**. Children with dyspraxia generally have a poor working memory (short-term memory). They may forget instructions or miss out items in a sequence. Their organisational skills will be lacking and they may misplace items and miss deadlines. They may even forget tasks learned the previous day. They may have problems answering questions even though they actually know the answer as their processing skills act so slowly.

● **Sensitivity to stimuli**. Many children with dyspraxia are sensitive to certain stimuli. This can manifest itself as over-sensitivity or undersensitivity. They may find it difficult to work in a noisy room or have to wear sunglasses if it is too bright. They may react adversely to certain textures, including food, and may flinch at any sign of physical contact. Being undersensitive can pose a significant problem in that they may put themselves in a position of danger without being aware or concerned (insensitive to pain). Some children with dyspraxia have problems sifting through incoming stimuli and become overburdened, leading to panic attacks.

A common issue that occurs as a result of the above is that children with dyspraxia suffer from fatigue as they struggle to cope with having to manage their daily lives – keeping up with tasks, both physically and mentally, is a strain.

The causes of dyspraxia are not known but there is evidence of a genetic link. It occurs in around 10 per cent of the population to some extent or another, but severe cases occur only in about 2 per cent. It is more prevalent in boys than girls (4:1).

Useful strategies for dealing with dyspraxia in the classroom

While dyspraxia may not affect a child's cognitive ability directly, its impact is likely to be felt indirectly if the teacher does not take the condition into account when planning for inclusion.

Gross motor control is perhaps not something that will be obvious in a classroom setting, however it could be an issue in a sports or playground environment. A child with dyspraxia is not likely to be chosen to be in a team where manual dexterity and speed of thought and action are essential. This can lead to isolation and self-esteem issues. Taking this into account, they can be encouraged to get involved if the activity is a fun activity and not competitive; alternatively, games that do not require a high level of motor control can be used to build empathy between children in the class (board games, heads down thumbs up, etc.). These will allow the dyspraxic child to become included.

TOP TIP!

Working with a dyspraxic child in PE

The main issue is one of coordination and speed of process. The child is unlikely to be able to compete but will want to be included.

The emphasis should be on fun and personal development rather than competition.

- Work on teaching (all the) children correct posture and positioning.
- Use marking spots (cones, lines, etc.) to show children where to move to.
- Get children to describe the sequence of movements needed.
- Allow the dyspraxic child to practise on their own rather than in a team situation.

For older children the emphasis can be on:

- individual physical development (e.g. the use of a multi-gym, rowing machine, etc.)
- alternative sports (golf, swimming, martial arts).

Issues occurring as a result of fine motor control revolve around work presentation and completion. It would be pertinent for a teacher to encourage good working practice, but in the case of the dyspraxic child an insistence on repeating written work until it is of a required standard is likely to prove counterproductive as the child will become disheartened at suffering a continuous sense of failure. If a teacher is looking to encourage better presentation it is best approached by agreeing a target at a point during the term and looking for the child to make progress over a time period of a few weeks. They may even score the work themselves, comparing what the work looked like at the start and how it has improved since (scaling). Getting a dyspraxic child to write out copious notes is not helpful as it is not only a mind-numbing exercise, it also puts their muscles under extra stress. This is not just a case of children complaining because they have to write too much – dyspraxic children have poor muscle tone and prolonged exercise is beyond their capabilities.

In respect of memory issues, a teacher can use a range of strategies to aid the dyspraxic child. This could be as simple as writing the instructions on the board and referring to them when the child wanders off task or loses concentration. Keeping instructions specific yet brief is the aim.

Task

The instructions below appear concise but do not give enough information to a child if they do not know how to carry out the task. Convert these exercises into a series of instructions that is clear and concise:

a) Boil an egg.

b) Take notes from a textbook.

c) Hit a shuttlecock with a badminton racket.

(Answer: a) Half fill a pan with water. Place the egg in the water. Put the pan on the cooker hob. Switch on the hob. Once water boils, allow it to boil for three minutes. Switch off the hob. Remove the boiled egg from the water using a spoon. Notice the detail that has to be given in order to carry out the action. It is tempting to assume knowledge and miss out stages.)

TOP TIP!

When working with dyspraxic children:

- repeat
- refocus
- refresh instructions.

Breaking tasks into manageable chunks (possibly with the set of scaffolding worksheets) will help the child.

A serious concern is the ability of the dyspraxic child to complete the work set. As with dyslexia, if the child is penalised, inadvertently, for not keeping up (punishment in reverse) they may become disheartened. Differentiation by outcome is not a method that would help a child with dyspraxia progress, nor would it be useful as an assessment tool. If a true assessment of their ability is needed, they must be given the time in class to show their true capabilities. This requires careful management. On the one hand, the teacher wants to be fair to all the children, but on the other hand they will work at different speeds. If work is graded from easy to difficult, the class might operate on a cyclical basis. There would be no extra marks for repeated success as the children travelled around the cycle, but such a strategy would allow the teacher to gauge capability at all levels, assuming that enough time is given for the dyspraxic child to complete at least one tour of the cycle.

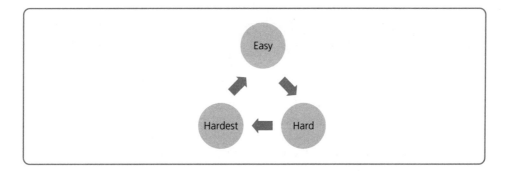

From toddler to teenager, a child with dyspraxia may well experience difficulty in establishing effective relationships with peers. As a result they are likely to be viewed with caution or possibly even disdain, which can lead to bullying issues. Taking part in team games – either sporty or just playing – requires a degree of manual and mental dexterity that dyspraxic children lack and this will almost certainly place the child at the periphery of social groups. If their speech is laboured, further isolation may occur as children target them for being 'odd' or 'strange'. The dyspraxic child may consciously seek to avoid social groups as their self-esteem plummets or they may choose to play with children younger than their chronological age in an attempt to hide their condition, seeking to be among those of similar capabilities. At infant level this differential may not be such as issue, but as the child moves into primary and then secondary school their choice of friendship groups will become increasingly problematic. Within a classroom setting the creation of a buddying system may help reduce the problems of social inclusion.

The issues above may well result in a child with dyspraxia suffering considerably from poor self-esteem. Their awkward nature, both physical and cognitive, can result in bullying that, if not dealt with, can create a spiral of low esteem and underachievement that sees them falling into lower ability groups or results in a lowering of academic expectations as they progress through full-time education. It could be that they become school refusers. The vigilance of the teacher in the classroom is paramount in this situation, not only in nipping any bullying in the bud but also in maintaining high expectations of the dyspraxic child.

In conclusion

Many children with dyspraxia may feel the odds are stacked against them in respect of being successful at school or even being accepted by their peers. Not only do they find it difficult to match effort to their academic ability, they (often) have to work in an atmosphere that is antagonistic, suffering continuous low-level bullying such as jibes and name calling. If they are in lower sets and marginalised, they are unlikely to have a sense of belonging within the classroom. This environment has to have an effect on their self-esteem which, if damaged, is difficult to repair.

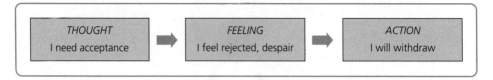

'I feel alone and isolated within my class, nobody understands me. They just laugh when I drop things like my pen or when I trip.'

As we have highlighted throughout this book, poor self-esteem prevents a child from realising their full potential.

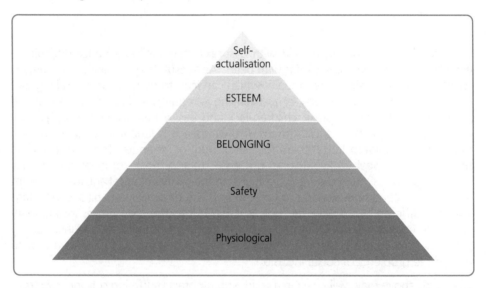

In a busy classroom it can be difficult to distinguish between a child with dyspraxia and a child of lower ability, particularly at an early age. The key to recognising the difference is to listen to and observe the quality of their answers rather than how they are presented. If a child with dyspraxia is not accommodated, their school career is likely to be blighted.

Further reading

www.dyspraxiafoundation.org.uk

Jones, N. (2005) *Developing School Provision for Children with Dyspraxia*, Sage Publications.

McIntyre, C. (2000) *Dyspraxia in the Early Years*, Routledge.

McIntyre, C. (2001) *Dyspraxia 5–11*, David Fulton Publishers.

Whole-school management issues that affect the effectiveness of inclusion

A whole-school approach to behaviour management

Why not try involving students in school policy?

(!)

Before you skip past this chapter and think that it doesn't apply to you, please pause for a moment. This chapter is about how whole-school policies shape what goes on in the classroom in respect of behaviour management and how their presence (or absence) affects each and every classroom teacher. As such, the chapter is essential reading and will open your eyes (if they have been glazed over by management sleight of hand) as to how management attitudes in school influence what you can (and should) achieve.

Case study

'My last school had a policy of inclusion but all that really amounted to was that the teacher in the classroom had to contain the children. There was no indication of how individuals might be dealt with. If you did send a child out into the corridor they would rip up the wall displays or run in and out of another lesson, so you just shut the door and got on as best as you could. The kids told you to f**k off on a regular basis and you just became desensitised to it all. If a child became dangerous you could call senior management and they would come and take them away and maybe exclude them for a day or two. The local authority did not expel children, they just moved them from one school to another. They would arrive at the school, behave for a day or two and then start to be a problem.

The experience made me realise that we are not really in control of the children, all we can do is influence them. The only thing we can control in the classroom is ourselves. I tried everything, from rewards and sanctions to shouting and yelling, but nothing worked. I learned to create a sense of calm and always be polite. It gave me great power as they tried to intimidate me but failed and made themselves look foolish.

My present school is so much better, the backing here is fantastic. At first when support arrived in the class I felt like a complete failure, as if everything was my fault and that I couldn't handle the class, but now I realise that if a child disrupts they are not having an argument with me, they are taking on the school. It's much easier to deflect issues instead of being told blankly 'no' by the children and looking like an idiot. I can just say "Well if that's your choice then I am going to have to take it further" and then they just back down and get on with the work. I have noticed that my stress level to issues like swearing in class has got a lot lower.'

'Great schools are more than the sum of their parts.'

(Ofsted, 12 Outstanding Secondary Schools)

An inclusive school does not occur by chance, it has to be engineered and carefully managed in order to attend to the diversity of needs demanded by its clientele. By their very definition 'exclusive' schools exclude all but the type of child they seek to attract, and many such establishments are surrounded by a snobbery that suggests that the quality of education they provide is somehow superior. In fact, it is the school that is inclusive that in truth provides a superior education, both in academic terms and in a broader educational sense. Inclusive schools provide the foundations for social tolerance, altruism and egalitarianism, but only if they are exclusive in the quality of provision for the children. To be 'blindly' inclusive as an ideology without establishing an ethos and the necessary resources as support is likely to do more harm than good. Teachers working in isolation behind closed doors without the broader support of a continued whole-school commitment are likely to do more harm than good, especially to the children.

Clear and dynamic leadership

Inclusive schools are demanding places in which to teach. They ask much more of their teachers, their management and the local authority, but if successful the rewards are much greater.

'A challenging school can't survive OK leadership.'

(Headteacher, Bartley Green School, Birmingham)

It is essential, therefore, to have a clear and dynamic leadership that sets the benchmark for success in all aspects of school life, including the behaviour of children and providing an understanding of the reasons why children behave as they do. Although realistic and pragmatic in its decision making, a dynamic leadership should seek to improve standards and not allow complacency to set in. If challenging behaviour is to be kept under control, the leadership of a school needs to remain committed to dealing with the problem. If there are weaknesses at the top this will permeate all the way through the school's support systems and behaviour will be compromised.

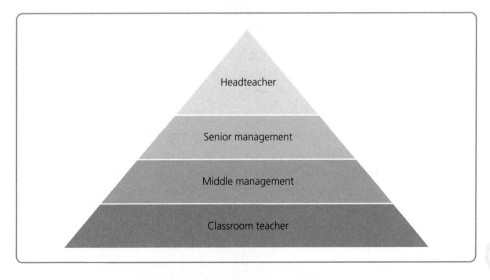

Headteacher

Senior management

Middle management

Classroom teacher

With the wide and varied demands made on the leadership of a school it is easy to take one's eye off the ball when faced with conflicting priorities. Behaviour is something that deteriorates slowly with time and if not kept as a top priority is likely to become endemic and subsequently a lot more difficult to control. The leadership of a school should provide the direction in which a school travels and this is indicated by a school's **ethos**, which should underpin all decisions taken.

Task

Rate the behaviour of the students in your school on a scale of 1 to 10, with 1 being the worst it can be.

Again on a scale of 1 to 10, with 1 being the worst, rate the performance of the leadership in the school in respect of seeking to:

a) maintain and improve standards of children's behaviour

b) provide the necessary resources to support inclusion in the classroom.

Compare your answer with that of other people in your school.

(These tasks should help you put in perspective the degree of the problem in your school.)

Developing an ethos

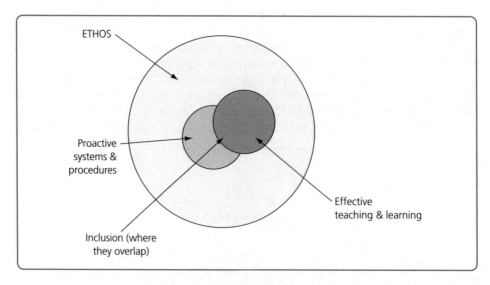

A school's ethos determines the overall culture within a school. Ultimately the behavioural expectation of every student is measured against a school's ethos. While all members of a school's community should contribute to the maintenance of the ethos, it is a school's leadership that is the flag bearer, leading as they should from the front.

In order to help all children (including those with special educational needs) to feel a part of a school community it is important to involve them in the decision-making processes that affect them, and this includes the establishment of an ethos. This empowers the students and will pay dividends when working with difficult individuals. A school's ethos is usually summarised in a mission statement, logo or motto. Getting a whole school to work on a project such as this is not difficult. Once constructed it is essential that a school's ethos is kept active. Laminating key words and leaving them on a classroom wall to gather dust will quickly undermine a school's ethos and leave it hanging as empty rhetoric, sending a significant signal to staff and children alike.

Constructing a mission statement

Mission statements can often be long-winded and are usually written by teachers. If a mission statement is to be understood it needs to be written with the target audience in mind (namely the children). If a mission statement is directed at children it needs to be understood by *all*.

'Not for nothing are the student code of conduct, mission statement and school aims displayed in every classroom in the school. Tutors are asked to go through them with their tutor groups.'

(Headteacher, Greenwood Dale School, Nottingham, 12 Outstanding Secondary Schools, *Ofsted*)

(!)

a) **What is the ethos of your school?**
b) **Does your school have a mission statement, motto, logo?**
c) **Without cheating, write it (draw it) from memory.**
d) **What is the target audience for your mission statement in school?**
e) **Is the mission statement easily understood by students?**
f) **Where is the statement displayed?**

School rules

Once an ethos has been created this can then be the basis for establishing a **code of conduct** which everybody on site is encouraged to follow. This should influence how staff and children interact and help to reduce the frequency of conflicts. It should also **encourage people to take responsibility** for their own actions. Added to these two key points is the need for **health and safety**.

Conflicts can often begin over breaches of school rules (no tie, wearing trainers, being out of bounds, etc.), so it is important that students are made aware of why such rules are in place. If possible, it is helpful to avoid couching rules in draconian terms, but it is equally important to keep them **precise and clear** so that they are easily understood.

TOP TIP!

If a rule is unenforceable it should not be there.

Look out for a rule that is broken with alarming frequency by a cross-section of children in the school.

This will help in making children more aware of the need for the rules. If school rules are reasonable in their request and promote health and safety, etc. they are very difficult to argue against. The fewer rules there are, the easier they are to remember.

Task

Picture yourself as a child (teacher) in school. Make a list of how you would like to be treated.

1) Would your staff accept a code of conduct that is similar to that expected of the students?

2) Try to make a list of expectations that might form the basis of a code of conduct.

3) Make a list of your school rules.

   a) Can they be streamlined? b) Are they user friendly? c) What is the purpose of each of them?

4) Which of your school's present rules:

   a) apply to health and safety, b) reflect the school's ethos, c) promote learning, d) encourage personal responsibility, e) support inclusion?

Another issue relating to school rules is that of consistency. If a school is to have rules then those rules need to serve a purpose, principally to keep order and protect the children (and staff). In this respect all teachers need to be consistent in applying the rules. A teacher who does not adhere to the rules ultimately undermines them and this can (and does) have a knock-on effect, causing conflict in another teacher's classroom. If a teacher has a laissez-faire approach to behaviour, uniform or equipment, children will be quick to use this to manipulate other staff: 'Mr Smith lets us . . .'

'We are looking for consistency, not uniformity. We want staff to work together without losing the natural flair and creativity of teachers.' Headteacher

(Sir Alan Steer, 'Learning behaviour, lessons learned', Institute of Education, University of London, 2009)

It is often how the rules are applied that determines whether a situation ends in conflict. Consider these three requests:

'You were told about jewellery in assembly. Take off your jewellery, now, it is being confiscated.'

'Please take off your jewellery.' (pleading)

'Please take off your jewellery and put it in your bag. Jewellery like that is a health and safety issue.'

> **(!)**
>
> **Do you know what your approach would be?**

Proactive planning and organisation

In many schools, action taken to stop challenging behaviour is primarily reactive and is, by necessity, classroom-based. However, much can be done to help reduce challenging behaviour before the children enter the classroom. A school's ethos is the first step, but there are other, more direct methods of facilitating for better behaviour.

The underlying principles of proactive planning are to:

a) identify children who are likely to exhibit challenging behaviour (**targeting**)

b) seek to keep them all apart (**divide and rule**) as far possible.

This can be aided by:

- the school day
- creative timetabling
- organising class groups
- targeting the challenging students.

When working in concert, these procedures play a significant role in reducing challenging behaviour in the classroom and allow the teacher to focus better on the job at hand. Lack of creative management can sometimes end up with all the most challenging children, irrespective of educational need, in the same class. The mentality of this way of thinking is that by containing them in one group their needs can be addressed collectively while the rest of the school can function 'as normal'. In reality, this does not happen because the children feel isolated and begin to rebel, plus their needs are likely to be so diverse that to attend to all of them in one place at the same time is an impossible task.

The school day

The school day often remains unchanged in a school for many years. The reasons for its timings may be a result of now defunct needs or as a consequence of other extraneous factors. There are few jobs that demand the level of concentration for sustained periods as those found in schools. In other careers, adults can work to a pace and to a timetable that suits them. Teachers, however, are subject to prolonged and persistent pressure to work to the best of their ability hour upon hour, sometimes without a break.

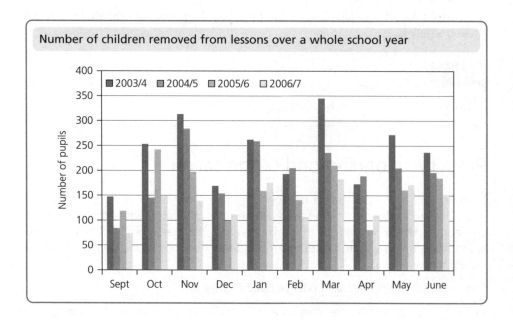

Number of children removed from lessons over a whole school year

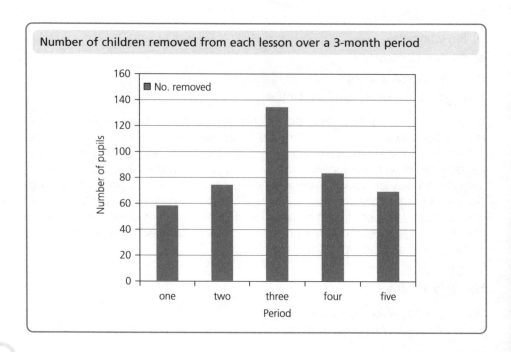

Number of children removed from each lesson over a 3-month period

> **Task**
>
> Study the two charts. The first shows the frequency of children withdrawn from class each month over a four-year period. The second shows the frequency of children withdrawn over a three-month period across the school day.
>
> - What patterns can you see in each?
> - Could you account for these patterns? (What variables might affect the data?)
> - How might each of the schools adjust to take account of this data?
> - Does your school have such evidence to work with?
>
> (Comment: There are rises and falls in each. There appear to be more exits as each term gets towards its climax and with the school day the fluctuation is across the day. The reasons are many, but it is fair to say that teacher and pupil tiredness accounts for some of the rises. As teachers and pupils tire, concentration levels fall and tolerance levels slip, which leads to conflicts and arguments. The skill is trying to keep the work and the teachers/pupils fresh. Why force a boring diatribe on a class when their concentration levels are low? This means not only thinking about what a teacher teaches but when!)

Research shows that:

- we concentrate better in the morning (or at least is this the accepted view of many in education, although there is evidence to the contrary – see Folkard, S., Monk, T. and Bradbury, R. (1977) *British Journal of Psychology*; Jones, P.R. (1992) *The Timing of the School Day, Educational Psychology in Practice*, Routledge)
- the optimum time for concentrating is 30 minutes
- without regular hydration and fresh air our ability to concentrate wanes
- Maslow's hierarchy applies to both staff and children.

If these are the facts then why is it:

- students still find themselves being taught Mathematics last lesson on a Friday?
- many lessons in school are one hour in length, sometimes longer?
- we allow students to sit in stuffy classrooms for long periods of time?

Clearly, how the school day is organised and where and when certain lessons are taught plays a major part in the ability of students to stay focused and as a result affects their behaviour.

> **(!)**
>
> Analyse your school day.
>
> What time do the students start school?
>
> What time do lessons start?
>
> How long are the lessons?
>
> How long do they get between breaks?
>
> How long are the breaks?
>
> Try designing a school day in order to get the 'best' out of the day.

Creative timetabling

Timetabling is subject to many pressures, but if behaviour is to be a priority the timetable and the school day must play their part in creating an environment where challenging behaviour is kept to a minimum. In the primary sector a class teacher can decide within certain restrictions what to teach and when. In the secondary sector teachers are hidebound by a whole-school timetable to which they must adhere. If a whole year group can be blocked within a subject at any one time it gives the head of department the opportunity to arrange the members of each class as they see fit. The more classes that are available, the greater the possibilities for keeping challenging students apart.

> **(!)**
>
> Take a look at your class/school timetable. Find out if there is a balance between practical and passive subjects in respect of the school day.
>
> Try rearranging the timetable in order to:
>
> ● place more practical subjects in the afternoon
> ● alternate passive and practical subjects.
>
> Can you find a way to block timetable all the subjects across all the years?
>
> What are the limitations of doing this?

Lesson length

The ability to concentrate diminishes proportionately with decreasing age and ability, although there are exceptions to this rule as it is also dependent on the task involved and other extraneous factors.

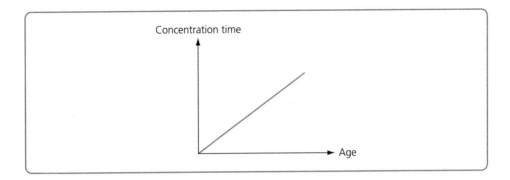

If a teacher is asking a class to sit and listen or study intensively for an hour (or more) the chances of them maintaining a high level of performance (and therefore behaving) become increasingly unlikely as time ticks by. The school may decide to reduce lesson lengths to a more manageable time (30/45 minutes), but the creative teacher can break up the lesson itself into a variety of different (but related) activities. The use of mini-breaks to refresh is another way of breaking up the lesson.

Ofsted advises **starter/main/plenary**, but there are other alternatives.

(!)

> Choose a lesson that might last one hour and is normally 'chalk and talk'. Devise a minimum of three different activities that together deliver a related topic and break up the lesson.

TOP TIP!

> Use VAK as a guide to vary the stimulus.
>
> Have 5-minute mini-breaks in the lesson to refresh.
>
> Break up the lesson into more than three parts.

Departmental/class management

The influence of the peer group should not be underestimated. At primary level it may be a little more manageable, but having more than two challenging children in a class is going to make heavy demands on a teacher's expertise. As the number rises, so each child is likely to draw others to their way of thinking. Pre-planning in respect of studying class dynamics before children are assigned to a class can influence greatly how the class functions.

Managing behaviour within a class or department is based on two basic concepts. The first is that the class teacher/department is proactive when organising class groups in an effort to alleviate possible behavioural problems before they materialise. The second is a cornerstone of the first and its aim is to 'divide and rule', keeping behaviourally challenging children apart from each other as far as possible.

In primary school there may be only one class per year and so the possibility of operating a divide-and-rule methodology is limited. The school may think about vertical grouping as a whole-school policy or even for one or two lessons in the week. This may help to break up awkward friendship groups that are causing a problem.

Things to consider when trying to organise children in respect of behaviour include the following:

- Ensure children are placed in a group commensurate with their ability (irrespective of behaviour, attendance, special needs).
- Where possible, avoid pairing very challenging groups of children (divide and rule).
- Do not be hidebound by strict benchmarks when allocating children to class groups (flexibility is the key).
- Avoid the creation of sink groups (although the temptation to do so may be great).
- If a child has to be removed because of poor behaviour, think about moving them up a set rather than down – a favourable audience is less likely to occur and the likelihood of disaffection as a result of falling self-esteem is lessened.
- If a challenging group cannot be avoided, choose a teacher with the necessary skills to deal with such a group (i.e. not an NQT, supply or teacher new to the school).
- Once groups are settled, avoid major changes during the academic year. Continuity promotes good behaviour via the development of good teacher/children relationships.

Referral systems

In mainstream schools the principal focus is on the education of the children. When children disrupt they have to be dealt with and may therefore be 'referred' to the pastoral team. The reasons for disruption are many and varied, therefore the role of the referral system is to:

a) deal with the immediate consequences following the disruption

b) effect behaviour modification to try to prevent it reoccurring.

The pressure on the pastoral team to 'sort things out' means that the two do not always sit easily together. This is very much the case when remedial action might not have an effect for 12 months. Therefore any referral system must have within its structure a wide variety of skills. These should include:

- pastoral expertise to deal with day-to-day issues
- extra behaviour/learning support for long-term issues

- counsellor to deal with emotional issues as they occur
- attendance officer
- ENCO to deal with specific learning difficulties
- E2L (in a multi-racial school)
- links to outside services (social services, police, probation, psychologist, etc.).

(!)

Which of these does your school have access to on:

a) an immediate/daily basis?

b) a weekly basis?

c) has no point of contact?

In many primary schools the responsibility for all these areas of expertise may rest on one teacher's shoulders. That is not a problem so long as the teacher is well trained and has the time and commitment to carry out their duties in respect of the volume of cases they are asked to deal with. The more support that is available, the more able a school will be to deal with issues that arise from the understanding of challenging behaviour and hence the better at being inclusive it will become.

'Effective early intervention is particularly important in preventing behavioural problems.

- Early years setting and primary schools should ensure staff have the appropriate skills and time to identify Special Educational Needs and behaviour needs and to intervene at an early point;
- Schools need to ensure that sufficient resources are provided for intervention strategies.'

(Sir Alan Steer, 'Learning behaviour, lessons learned')

While it is possible (and likely) that a school will make allowances for a child exhibiting challenging behaviour by providing a safe environment for that student (e.g. learning support unit), the school must also recognise the disruption that a child is causing in class and not be tolerant to the extent where other children's learning is permanently affected. We must recognise the fact that they are disruptive but at the same time be sensitive to their needs, some of which we may not be aware of. It is a delicate balance that we do not always get right. It is common to begin with a sanction-based approach, but it is likely to become apparent early on whether this is effective or not.

If it is not effective, there are likely to be other, outstanding issues that need to be identified and addressed before the student is ready to return to full-time lessons. It is essential therefore that a school does not just stumble on from one crisis to another but sets in motion a series of diagnostic tests in order to identify underlying issues. These should include:

a) academic analysis (cognitive assessment tests or their equivalent)
b) tests to identify any specific learning difficulties (dyslexia, etc.)
c) tests for any cognitive impairment (autism, etc.)
d) tests for emotional literacy (school counsellor, educational psychologist, etc.).

While this diagnosis is taking place, any access to mainstream education should be highly structured and monitored closely, using whatever respite is available that is non-punitive. Once a diagnosis is complete, an Individual Learning Plan can be devised and put in place in order to help the children and the teachers deal with any issues arising. It is the professional duty of teachers to know the needs and requirements of all the students in their class and to act accordingly.

There is rarely a quick fix when it comes to working with challenging children – any progress in respect of behaviour is likely to take months rather than weeks, as years of 'learned' behaviours are replaced by new ones that result in behaviour modification. The more entrenched the behaviour, the longer it is likely to take to change it. In many difficult cases events take over and no positive outcome is effected, but that should not deter a school from trying.

Making a referral

Knowing when to refer and to whom is important if the referral system is to run efficiently. The guidelines below give some indication, but this is dependent on frequency of incidents. If strategies are put in place and a child exhibits persistent behaviours at one level, it is reasonable to refer them to the next stage. It is this frequency and persistence of challenging behaviour that the class teacher should be aware of and that is the point at which thoughts about making a referral should begin. The teacher could also think about taking the child to one side and asking them this question:

'Why did you (hit that child, shout out like that, disrupt the lesson)?'

If the child refuses to give an answer or has difficulty articulating the reason(s) for their actions, there is likely to be an underlying issue. Likewise, if the child resorts to critical judgement of others (transferring the blame), they made be in need of expert help. Giving the child a voice can often release pent-up tensions and anxieties.

If children are referred too quickly, without early intervention on the part of the class teacher, parts of the system can become overloaded and do not work as effectively as they might, resulting in the child not getting the quality attention they need.

Effecting a solution may take time, therefore contingency plans may need to be put in place in order to prevent further disruption while remedial action is undertaken.

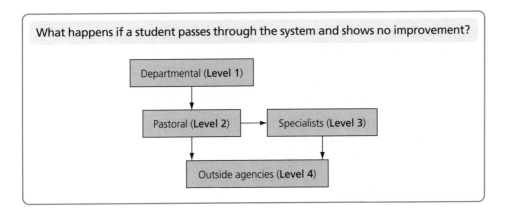

In conclusion

There is much a teacher can achieve working in isolation with challenging children in their classroom. However, their ability to function effectively is heavily dependent on whole-school management policies that should be there to support them. From the headteacher through senior management and down to departmental level, all play their part in facilitating good practice in the classroom via robust policies and procedures. Yet structures alone will not produce an inclusive environment. Ultimately, behaviour management is about people and their relationships and therefore it is the ethos of a school that determines how successful it will be. A key part of that ethos has got to be a good understanding as to why children behave as they do.

'Relationships are crucial; it's not about structures, it's about making it work out there for the children.'

'Every child should be listened to, no matter how difficult they are to talk to.'

(15-year-old girl. Sir Alan Steer, 'Learning behaviour, lessons learned')

Information

The outstanding schools in the sample succeed for the following reasons:

- They excel at what they do, not just occasionally but for a high proportion of the time.
- They prove constantly that disadvantage need not be a barrier to achievement, that speaking English as an additional language can support academic success and that schools can really be learning communities.
- They put students first, invest in their staff and nurture communities.
- They have strong values and high expectations that are applied consistently and never relaxed.
- They fulfil individual potential through providing outstanding teaching, rich opportunities for learning and encouragement and support for each student.

- They are highly inclusive, having complete regard for the educational progress, personal development and wellbeing of every student.
- Their achievements do not happen by chance but by highly reflective, carefully planned and implemented strategies which serve these schools well in meeting any challenges which obstruct the path to success.
- They operate with a very high degree of consistency.
- They are constantly looking for ways to improve further.
- They have outstanding and well-distributed leadership.

(Ofsted, *12 Outstanding Secondary Schools*)

Information

The following characteristics revealed themselves during visits to the schools:

- They provide affection, stability and a purposeful and structured experience.
- They build – and often rebuild – children's self-belief.
- They teach children the things they really need to know and show them how to learn for themselves and with others.
- They give them opportunities, responsibility and trust in an environment which is both stimulating and humanising.
- They listen to their pupils, value their views and reflect and act on what they say.
- They build bridges with parents, families and communities, working in partnership with other professionals.
- They ensure their pupils progress as fast as possible and achieve as much as possible (outperforming both similar schools and many with fewer challenges).
- In short, they put the child at the centre of everything they do, and high aspirations, expectations and achievement underpin the schools' work.

(Ofsted, *20 Outstanding Primary Schools*)

(!)

Do you know how your school matches up?

Further reading

www.ofsted.gov.uk

Rogers, B. (2007) *A Whole School Approach to Behaviour Management*, Sage Publications.

Index